T0293072

TREND
FOLLOWING
Masters

VOLUME TWO

Also by Michael W. Covel

Trend Following: How to Make a Fortune in Bull, Bear, and Black Swan Markets (5 editions)

The Complete TurtleTrader: How 23 Novice Investors Became Overnight Millionaires (2 editions)

The Little Book of Trading: Trend Following Strategy for Big Winnings

Trend Commandments: Trading for Exceptional Returns

Trend Following Analytics: Performance Proof for the World's Most Controversial & Successful Black Swan Trading Strategy

Trend Following Mindset: The Genius of Legendary Trader Tom Basso

Trend Following Masters: Trading Conversations—Volume One

Broke: The New American Dream (Documentary)

Trend Following Radio Podcast

TREND FOLLOWING
Masters

VOLUME TWO

Trading Psychology
Conversations

MICHAEL W. COVEL

Harriman
House

HARRIMAN HOUSE LTD
3 Viceroy Court
Bedford Road
Petersfield
Hampshire
GU32 3LJ
GREAT BRITAIN
Tel: +44 (0)1730 233870
Email: enquiries@harriman-house.com
Website: harriman.house

First published in 2023.
Copyright © Michael W. Covel

The right of Michael W. Covel to be identified as the Author has been asserted in accordance with the Copyright, Design and Patents Act 1988.

Hardback ISBN: 978-0-85719-999-7
eBook ISBN: 978-1-80409-006-0

British Library Cataloguing in Publication Data
A CIP catalogue record for this book can be obtained from the British Library.

*To those convinced they cannot
do it, they are right.*

Every owner of a physical copy of this edition of

can download the eBook for free direct from us at Harriman House, in a DRM-free format that can be read on any eReader, tablet or smartphone.

Simply head to:

ebooks.harriman-house/trendfollowingmasters2

to get your copy now.

CONTENTS

INTRODUCTION

I N *Trend Following Masters Volume One* I wrote:

I'm lucky. I get to talk to people. All kinds of interesting, bright, accomplished, and successful people.

Sometimes in person, sometimes on Zoom, sometimes on the phone. It's become my passion, my obsession.

How did this start?

After my first book *Trend Following* (2004), I picked up the phone one day in early 2005 and contacted 15 traders managing collectively around $15 billion. Most agreed to meet with me. On my dime I started flying around the world to talk with trading legends like David Harding, Toby Crabel, and Larry Hite. Lots of interviews.

Then my second book, *The Complete TurtleTrader* started. That required getting the secretive Turtle traders to open up and talk. More interviews. Then I started a documentary film project that spanned three years around the world and 100 filmed interviews.

Then I started a podcast on a lark in 2012. That podcast is now over 1,000 episodes with hundreds of interviews and millions of listens, covering topics from trading to psychology, economics to health, and even the CEO of Dunkin' Donuts (one of my favorite interviews). I'm proud to say that I have interviewed so far seven Nobel Prize winners.

Volume One featured interviews centered around a style of trading known as trend following. Volume Two is something different. It features interviews that center around the psychological side of trading. That means topics like:

- Mindset
- Prospect Theory
- Deliberate Practice
- Heuristics
- Forecasting
- Bayesian Thinking
- Poker Parallels
- Motivation
- Strength and Fitness
- Modeling
- Neuroeconomics
- Performance Coaching
- Self-Sabotage + more

Some of the interviews included herein are with traders or trading experts who exist primarily in the investing realm, but others included have no direct connection to investing. That said, their wisdom is central to good investing, and thus it was an easy decision to include them.

I guarantee the pros I feature will have you reassessing how you think and act across all aspects of your life.

I hope you enjoy these conversations.

Michael Covel
September 2023

Note: If you would like to reach me directly, I can be found here:

www.trendfollowing.com/contact

To receive my free interactive trend following presentation, send a picture of your receipt for this book to **receipt@trendfollowing.com**.

CHAPTER 1

DANIEL KAHNEMAN

Studying Human Complexity

DANIEL KAHNEMAN is Professor of Psychology and Public Affairs Emeritus at the Princeton School of Public and International Affairs, the Eugene Higgins Professor of Psychology Emeritus at Princeton University, and a fellow of the Center for Rationality at the Hebrew University in Jerusalem.

He has been the recipient of many awards, among them the Distinguished Scientific Contribution Award of the American Psychological Association (1982) and the Grawemeyer Prize (2002), both jointly with Amos Tversky, the Warren Medal of the Society of Experimental Psychologists (1995), the Hilgard Award for Career Contributions to General Psychology (1995), the Nobel Prize in Economic Sciences (2002), the Lifetime Contribution Award of the American Psychological Association (2007), and the Presidential Medal of Freedom (2013).

Michael note

Daniel Kahneman has been called "the most important psychologist alive today." For those of you in the trend following world, for his prospect theory, and his views on behavioral economics and finance, you know.

Michael Covel: At what point in your life did you start to realize that you were comfortable looking at the world, people, behavior from outside the norm?

Daniel Kahneman: Difficult question. In science you publish things because you think they're new; what we didn't see was how far our research would be taken. Amos Tversky and I began our work by studying judgment under uncertainty—a limited set of problems of judgment. We worked on that for five years and we wrote an article at the end of those five years in 1974, which was published in *Science*. That article had a lot more impact and resonance than we had anticipated. It was in seeing that reaction that we realized we had done something unusual. It was somewhere between 1974 and 1980, we became aware that people were taking this as new.

Michael: If people were to say to me, "What's the best way to learn about being successful in the markets?" I would point them towards your work. I don't think you intended to have so many people on Wall Street thinking fondly of your work, but it happened that way.

Daniel: This all came as a surprise; we had not expected it. There was going to be some reaction to the assumption of rationality and to the dominance of the rationality assumption in finance and economics. We provided an instrument that people inside the discipline could use to question the dogma of rationality.

It's an interesting anecdote how this happened and the reason why our work had impact, because it was accidental. It had impact because of the way that we presented our ideas by examples in the text of questions that people tend to get wrong. The leaders who are not psychologists—leaders outside the discipline—read this and they saw that these demonstrations worked on them. When something works on you, you're inclined to change your views about human nature. Merely getting data about undergraduates with some other people responding to questions does little to people.

Michael: Reading about others is one thing, but when you see the change internally in your own self, that's when the magic can happen.

Daniel: When you see yourself tempted to make mistakes, the idea that people who are as smart as you make mistakes is a discovery. It makes it harder for people to distance themselves from the findings. It's this accidental format that caused our work to have the impact it did.

Michael: I want to shift away from your early work to something else that's been near and dear to you, and that's the subject of happiness—the idea of the remembering self and the experiencing self.

Daniel: There are two types of questions that you can ask people about how happy they are. We can ask them, "How do you feel right now? What is your mood right now?" And the self that answers this question, I call the experiencing self, because it talks about what's happening right now. But when you ask people, "How was your vacation? How happy were you during your vacation?" Or, "How happy have you been over the last year?" Or, "How satisfied are you with your life?" you're asking something entirely different. You're asking, "How do you feel about your life? Now that you're thinking about your life, how does that make you feel?"

Crowd behavior is biological.

How you feel as you are living and how you feel when you're thinking about your life are two very different questions. You can measure subjective well-being in both ways: by asking people to report on their experiences, or by asking people to think about their life and evaluate it—and different factors turn out to be important for experience and for life evaluation.

Michael: There's confusion between the two. For example, you have shared a story about taking photographs on a vacation.

Daniel: In many cases we plan our vacations as constructing memories for use in later consumptions, and photographs are symbolic of that. My argument is that if you look at it in terms of how much time people spend consuming their memories, it's negligible compared to the amount of time they spend having experiences. And yet we put a disproportionate amount of weight on the consumption of memories.

Michael: You watch young people today, everyone's got a smartphone

When something works on you, you're inclined to change your views about human nature.

and they're constantly taking pictures of themselves. Instead of living and experiencing the moment, everyone is trying to capture an artificial moment and capture a memory.

Daniel: The ability to record so many things as they are happening to you must be changing the experience of life, because you are evaluating your experiences as future memories. In a way, when you're taking pictures of what you see, you're adopting a different stance on the experience itself. Certainly this is having an effect—what effect I don't know. I haven't analyzed it.

Michael: A quote of yours that I've seen goes: "A person who has not made peace with his losses is likely to accept gambles that would be unacceptable to him otherwise." Now, that can have meaning for different fields, but in the world of trading, not making peace with a loss is the downfall of so many investors.

Daniel: We weren't thinking specifically of investors, but it turns out there is research that demonstrate this. We know about traders that if they've been losing in the course of the day, they take more risks later in the afternoon. That seems to be the idea of you haven't made peace with your losses and you're trying to make up those losses, which tends to make you risk-seeking. It probably is costly to traders. In extreme cases, some of them get caught up in cycles of fraud and they become rogue traders, but those are the exceptions.

Michael: Let me shift gears slightly and talk about bubbles and crowd behavior.

Daniel: Crowd behavior is biological. When we see a lot of people running in one direction, we are by and large wired to run in the same direction. A few clever people will run in another direction, but the majority of us, we see the herd moving one way, we move with it. That has large consequences for market behavior. By and large, it causes people individually to do far less well than the market says they should because they tend to come in too late when the market is rising. People's timing is way off as a result of trying to follow the herd, and they do much less well than they would if they were adopting a policy and sticking to it.

Michael: Is there anything else you'd rather be doing in your life than this?

Daniel: I've retired from my academic career and I now do consulting, which I enjoy as much as I enjoyed science. When I started out on this line of research 45 years ago with Amos Tversky, it was sheer fun because he was a funny person with a marvelous sense of humor, and we were laughing all the time. We laughed for about 12 years doing our research. What made it funny was that we were studying our own biases and our own mistakes. Our point was not that people are stupid—because we never thought that people are stupid and we never thought that we were stupid—but it's our own mistaken intuitions we were studying. That must have been the best fun I've had in my life, those years of working on that topic.

> There is increasing recognition of the role of well-being in government policy.

Michael: I assume the two of you were off on your own island and doing your thing, engaged 100% in your endeavors. That feeling must have been great.

Daniel: Yes, it was. We were friends and for more than 10 years, I think, we spent about half the day together talking, which is unusual in scientific collaborations, so we were extremely fortunate. We liked each other's company and our topic was one that could be studied while having a fun conversation—that is, you examine your own intuitions, you raise puzzles, you see how the other responds, you develop theories and puzzles and intuitions of the same kind. It was great to do.

Michael: We're looking at the example of you and your partner at that time being happy to go through this learning process and you're finding all these new things out. But it seems like when it comes to public policy, you don't ever hear any of today's leaders talk about happiness. It's left out of the equation.

Daniel: That's not quite right, actually. The study of happiness has been an official task within the UK government. The Conservative/Liberal Democrat coalition government of 2010–15 put in subjective well-being as one of the objectives of policy. Trying to keep a happy population is rapidly becoming an accepted objective of policy.

There've been major international commissions. A formal measurement of happiness is now routine. In the UK, Canada, many European countries, and Australia, things are beginning to move in this direction. And even in the United States, there is serious talk of implementing measurements of well-being. There are questions about how this is to be done and whether we are ready for it, and whether the measurement and our understanding of happiness is mature enough to base policy on. There's room for debate about that, but that there is increasing recognition of the role of well-being in policy, I think, is beyond doubt.

Michael: Emotion in individuals is driven by possibility and not probability. That's probably intuitive, but it's not necessarily good when it comes to decision-making, is it?

Daniel: I suppose what you're talking about is hope and fear. Entrepreneurial activity, we have argued, is largely driven by optimism, so that when people take risks, much of the time it's because they don't know the odds that they're facing—they're deluding themselves. My view of risk takers is on the one hand they're loss averse, they hate to lose, but on the other hand they're optimistic, quite often to a delusional degree, so that they don't know the true probability that they face of losing. That's the combination that produces risk taking, but it's mainly driven by optimism.

You can see that in entrepreneurs, you can see that in people with discoveries they are trying to bring to market, you can see that in people who start small businesses. The average small business in the United States has a 35% chance of survival after five years, as I recall, but most people who start a new business assign themselves a probability of 80% or higher of success. It's that delusion that keeps them going. I've called optimism the engine of capitalism, because it is in that sense beneficial to society, but many people would not be taking the risk if they knew the risk they are taking.

Michael: How much of a dent do you think prospect theory has made? It's made a dent, but in terms of acceptance? For example, we have all observed over the last 15 years some quite fantastic bubbles and some quite fantastic busts in the US equity market.

Daniel: I'm not an expert in behavioral economics and behavioral finance. My impression is that bright people are trying to develop theory, but it's early days.

When you ask has it made a dent, the answer is clearly yes, because some major economics departments and finance departments have behavioral economics and behavioral finance as a central part of their curriculum. The Harvard Economics Department, one of the best in the US, has some of the major stars of behavioral economics and many of the best students are going there. In the near future, there's going to be a lot of behavioral economics because many bright scholars are going into the field.

Michael: I guess I was thinking more about the more established field of economics, the more rational side of the coin, where you're coming at it from a different perspective, and there's always going to be that conflict between the two.

Daniel: Oh, there is. The 2013 Nobel Prize in Economics was given to two people, both of them students of finance, with radically different ideas. You have Eugene Fama, who is a traditionalist and believes quite passionately in the rationality of markets. And on the other hand, you've got Bob Shiller, who speaks about irrational exuberance and doesn't believe in the rationality of markets. Both of these currents are alive and well within finance. My impression is that a lot of the younger people may be drifting in the direction of behavioral finance, but I'm not sure.

Michael: It's difficult for some people to relate to somebody that has received a Nobel Prize, but they can relate to that person as a young man. I'm wondering if you might talk about your early experiences. There was one experience, I believe in France with a German soldier, and you walked away changed.

Daniel: It was during the war, I was seven years old—1941 in occupied

France, occupied by the Germans. They were beginning the measures against Jews; it wasn't extermination yet, but they were getting ready. Jews were supposed to wear a yellow Star of David and there was a curfew. I was playing with a friend and I went past the curfew, so I put my sweater inside out and walked home. Near home, in a place I still remember—this was in Paris—there was a German soldier facing me and walking towards me. He was wearing a black uniform, which I knew was bad, although I was only seven years old, because it meant he belonged to the SS. He approached me and I must have been shaking, I don't remember every detail, but what I do remember is he picked me up and hugged me. I remember being terrified that he would see the yellow star inside my sweater as he was hugging me. Then he put me down and opened his wallet and took out a picture of a little boy and showed it to me, and then he gave me some money and I went home. It was the complexity of that experience—that he was a man who was clearly quite ready and perhaps eager to kill people like me, but he has a son, he loved his son, and I reminded him of his son. This experience of the complexity of human beings has guided me and inspired a lot of my work. I've been curious about people all my life.

I've been curious about people all my life.

Michael: I highly recommend people your book, *Thinking, Fast and Slow*.

Daniel: That's the book in which I told the whole story of my research and related research of other people. It's not an autobiographical book. It's about thinking and decision-making.

CHAPTER 2

K. ANDERS ERICSSON

Deliberate Practice

K. ANDERS ERICSSON was an internationally renowned psychologist who studied expert performance in domains such as music, chess, medicine, and sports, and how expert performers attain their superior performance by acquiring complex cognitive mechanisms through extended deliberate practice. He was the author of nearly 300 publications and the author or editor of several books, including the 2016 book *Peak: Secrets from the New Science of Expertise*, which he co-wrote with Robert Pool.

Michael note

K. Anders Ericsson was one of my top five favorite interviews, and I have conducted 500+ interviews! If you have infinite excuses about why you can't do this or that, then you won't like Anders's research and wisdom.

Michael Covel: Stephen Curry is probably the best basketball player in the NBA today. He's not a big guy, no huge physical attributes, but he has hit three-pointers like they're going out of style. I posted on Facebook, "This is all a result of deliberate practice." Immediately, somebody jumped in and said, "Oh, no. He was born with it. His father played in the NBA. It's the genes." I thought to myself, "I wonder what the professor would say?"

K. Anders Ericsson: We know of a number of fathers and sons who were successful in sports. It raises the issue, "Why does that happen?" There are two extreme accounts. One would be that you're born with the genes that allow you to do it. The other one is that you're born to a father who early on helps you guide your practice in such a way that once you reach adolescence and adulthood, you've had this practice history that can explain your superior performance.

Michael: How did this become your passion? What were the triggering moments early in your life when you realized, "I want to go down this deliberate practice route?"

Anders: That would go back almost to high school. A lot of people are interested in trying to understand how they can get better. I was interested in reading biographies of people whom I admired. As I started my doctoral work, I wanted to find a method of tapping into what the experts were thinking when they were exhibiting this superior behavior. That was the key step here, because at that time, there wasn't all that much work on the subject. People were skeptical as to whether experts could report anything relevant that could explain their superior performance.

> **One of the keys to purposeful practice is that you get immediate feedback on your performance.**

When I started to ask, people were reporting information that helped me understand how they were able to achieve a higher than average performance. The next step was when I was invited to go and work with Herb Simon, who later got the Nobel Prize when I was a postdoc in his lab. The reason why I came to him was to come up with a theoretical framework for the ways people express their thinking when they're engaging in activities. That framework would help us to relate that information to models that could regenerate superior performance on various tasks, ranging from chess to mental multiplication and other kinds of activities.

Then I started working with one of the senior professors at Carnegie Mellon University, where Herb Simon was at the time. We were interested in whether it is possible for people to change their capacity. At that time, people thought that short-term memory—how much you could think about at a given time—was capacity that couldn't be changed. One way to study individual differences in that capacity is to read people some numbers and see how many they would be able to repeat back perfectly. If you put somebody in a lab situation and read them a series of digits, they were able to get seven numbers 50% of the time. They would be even better if you only read them six digits. They would be virtually perfect if you only read them five. But the number of digits that a person could hold on to and report back exactly in order was on average seven—something between five and nine captured what average people could do.

We then started to ask the question: "If you give people practice on that particular task, can they improve performance?" We found a volunteer who, after about 40 hours, was able to do over 20 digits. By collecting all the reports on what changes in his thinking processes were developing along with his increased ability to do this task, we got a better understanding of how people could improve their memory in this particular task. With even more training, he could recall sequences up to 80 digits. We trained a friend of his who was able to get over 100. We studied some people in China who at the time had the world record. They were able to do over 300 digits.

Michael: The insights on to how to break through those thresholds were starting to piece together for you and your team.

Anders: That came a couple of years later, when people were starting to ask me, "Who cares if you can remember digits? Okay, you've shown that this performance, which seems incredible, was trainable." Because obviously, when you train an individual, the person's genes and DNA don't change through the training. I started thinking that if you can train that particular performance in that particular task, could you use training to improve performance generally, or improve it in other particular tasks like planning chess moves, or making medical diagnoses? The key insight was that you could train one specific task. This was consistent with what we found in the digits case, because if we tested the guy who could do 80 numbers, he could only do about six consonants. It was a domain-specific skill. He was able to improve his performance and his memory capacity, but it was limited to a particular type of material and a little bit to the characteristics of the task more generally.

Michael: If we stay with the numbers memorization example, to use some of your terminology, this was not naive practice, this was purposeful practice. What is purposeful practice compared to what many of us might think of as practice?

Anders: One of the keys to purposeful practice is that you get immediate feedback on your performance. Especially in a professional context, you often have to wait to know whether you were right. Doctors diagnosing a patient will obviously try to do the best they can, but they don't get feedback on whether they were accurate or not until much later, and sometimes never.

In our digital memory task, we could tell the subject immediately whether he made any mistakes. That gave him a feedback loop so he could think about what he was generating. He formed meaningful associations primarily with running times to group them into three digits that would be a mile time. Four minutes and 32 seconds would be a good model time for an amateur athlete. He was then able to realize when he made mistakes and he could experiment with new ways of encoding the digits to allow him to progress and remember longer and longer sequences.

Michael: To jump to another example, which I find fascinating, taxi drivers in London are a special breed. They go through intense training. They have to learn London streets inside and out, and this changes their brains physically.

Anders: The taxi driver story is particularly interesting because we're talking about people who aren't special in any way. In fact, they've tested their cognitive abilities and found that they're pretty much normal people.

But in order to pass the test that allows them to be cab drivers, they are given arbitrary starting points and end points, and from memory they have to report what would be the most efficient route to take a passenger between those destinations. This is something that they've done well before we had GPS and all this electronic help. It took many years of training to pass this qualifying test, which required them to learn over 10,000 streets and all the interconnections.

When Maguire and colleagues in England scanned the brains of individuals who had mastered the map, they found that they had changed. Their study showed how increased memory can influence the basic structure of the brain. There are now plenty of other examples. But Maguire's study was interesting because she analyzed and compared cab drivers to bus drivers, who are driving as much and have the same level of experience, but the bus drivers did not exhibit these brain changes associated with mastering the map of London streets.

Michael: The learning of the streets by London taxi drivers is all about deliberate practice. But if one stops being a taxi driver, if one ceases to perform this particular skill, will you see a regression in the brain changes? Will the brain changes revert to the mean, so to speak?

Anders: We see in a number of domains that maintaining the practice is key for maintaining high levels of performance. A lot of people will recognize that when they stop exercising, their performance after a couple of years reverts back to the normal level. That seems to be a key in all the skills that we've looked at. Without practice, you revert back to where you started if you wait long enough.

Michael: For many skeptics out there, they might look at some of these child prodigies and draw inferences and conclusions. I can think of two in particular that you discuss in *Peak*. Wolfgang Amadeus Mozart—a fantastic example. Everyone has some general understanding of the brilliance of this child from a young age. Also, the first female chess grandmaster, Zsuzsa Polgár.

Elaborate for anyone that says, "Mozart, he was a child prodigy. He was born with it. Zsuzsa Polgár, all of her sisters, they're all brilliant at chess. What does practice have to do with this?"

Anders: Let's take Mozart, because he is the one most people are familiar with. What we're saying is you need to look at Mozart's upbringing. One of the things people don't recognize is that Mozart's father was a famous musician. When Wolfgang came along, I guess his father had some ideas about the possibility of training young children. He's actually the first person to write music training for younger children. He invested pretty much his whole life training Mozart and his older sister.

Recent research has shown that some of the characteristics Mozart exhibited—for example, his remarkable ability to listen to a tone and be able to say which key on the piano produced that particular tone—are abilities that virtually any child seems to be able to attain if you give them the training, but it has to be quite early. Similar to Mozart starting to play when he was three or four years old, you have to start the music training that early, when the brain seems to be receptive to learning those kinds of distinctions. You can then preserve those abilities as an adult, but it's difficult or almost impossible if you start practicing at an older age.

Michael: People might be thinking, "I don't want my child to have such intense deliberate practice at a young age." You're not making a value judgment here. You're saying the data shows there is something to be said for this early start in childhood.

Anders: I would like to clarify that it's important if you want to produce a healthy, happy adult, you make sure the training is consistent with what the child wants to do. You're simply providing the child with opportunities for training. I've had some contact with László Polgár, the father of the three Polgár daughters who were so successful in chess. A key idea of his is that you have to put the child in charge. You're helping them to master whatever the activity is that they select in a motivating, supportive environment.

Michael: Break open the idea that nurture can win out—that it's not necessarily what you're born with. We get caught up in the idea that we're fixed, but in terms of being able to change, even if we go beyond the discussion of elite performers, average people who might want to master something later in life are not etched in stone, are they?

Anders: One key that I found helpful when I talk to adults who want to acquire skills is to realize that younger prodigies might spend half an hour or so where you're training them with an explicit goal, so they have to be 100% concentrated. But if you push children to do a lot more than that until they're ready to increase their time of training, they are going to feel averse and not be willing to do it. When it comes to adults who want to run a marathon, I've heard of people who go out the first time and run for maybe 45 minutes and then they're so sore they never do it again.

> Maintaining the practice is key for maintaining high levels of performance.

If you're going to change the body, it's got to be gradual. You need to stimulate and push for change, but you can't go so far that you're harming the body and stretching your motivation to a point where you no longer want to pursue it.

Michael: In terms of making these achievements, we are constantly up against homeostasis. But breaking through boundaries is part of deliberate practice.

Anders: I would say that if you're not trying to change something, you're probably not doing deliberate practice. The key idea of deliberate practice is that you're trying to do something that you can't do well. By figuring out ways to do it better, you will raise your performance to a level that you didn't have before.

Michael: Chess is a fantastic example. The best chess players are not looking at all the individual pieces on the board, they're thinking in patterns. They've developed their ability to analyze based on pattern recognition. Explain the notion of chunking, or mental representation, using chess as an example.

Anders: If you take a paragraph written in English, English speakers will read it and it will make sense. If it describes some physical situation or interaction, people will form an image in their head of that interaction. I would argue that the chessboard is a little bit the same for a skilled chess player. They can see the structure, what are the weak spots, and where likely attacks would be successful. By having chess masters think out loud when they're seeing a position and trying to pick the best move, we can learn what features they notice. The way they probe the position is to make a move in their mind and then think of what the opponent's move would be. They keep doing that maybe four or five times, or even more, in order to diagnose what would happen if they make a particular starting move.

Understanding what's going on in the chess player's head raises the question, how did they get to be able to do this type of thinking? That gets to the core of what we've been studying here. How do you build up these mental representations that allow you to think through issues in your head and then decide on the best action in a given situation?

Michael: We sometimes hear examples of a chess player playing against 25 people at the same time, or maybe even blindfolded. It sounds so impressive, but what's interesting is that once you get to that level where you have put in the time to develop those mental representations, it's not necessarily difficult for those particular players to play 25 people at the same time blindfolded—it's a parallel skill that comes with having already reached grandmaster level.

Anders: What most people find difficult to understand is how you can play blindfolded. You have to make the chess position in your head and think about it. You can't look at any kind of perceptual configuration. That seems to be a skill that people don't practice; it comes about once you learn to plan the moves in your head. Eventually you acquire the skills that allow you to do it without the chessboard—you can do it completely mentally.

When you want to play several games, you're doing that same thing. I've heard that players try to pick different kinds of games, so as not to confuse one game with another. There's a lot of minor skills that people acquire in order to be able to play multiple games. The amazing thing is this building up of that mental representation that allows you to do things in your own mind that other people need to do perceptually by seeing the chess pieces on the board.

Michael: I want to go back to the NBA basketball player, Stephen Curry.

When you get to this high level of achievement, it doesn't stop, it allows you to get to the next level. You can't skip steps.

Anders: We don't have evidence that there's any sort of magic goal improvements. But if you monitor what the individual has been doing up to a given point, you can see the improvements in the things that they're working on. The hallmark of an expert is being able to identify things they can do differently or better. Once you've reached that high level, you're able to work on things that other people wouldn't even notice in order to increase your performance beyond your already exceptional level.

Michael: Across your many years of studying expert performers, do they ever come out and say that their improvement was easy?

Anders: I have had a chance of being on a couple of panels with Olympic medal winners, musicians, and chess players. I'm yet to find anybody who wouldn't recognize this process of incremental improvement—this kind of continuous commitment that once you practice, you're going to do it with full concentration, because otherwise you're wasting your time. During 30 years of research, I've probably encountered some 50 cases where people initially claim this was an exception. But by looking more closely at the evidence, I've been able to construct what I think is a plausible explanation that's based more on this continuous practice, even though the practice may not have been observed by people who thought the improvement occurred spontaneously.

Michael: There have been many authors of popular books who have been inspired or influenced by your work—among them would be Malcolm Gladwell. There's a couple of issues in his work that I would love you to address. One that has become ingrained into society is that you can become an expert in 10,000 hours. And explain the example of how The Beatles got to be The Beatles.

Anders: The research that we did with violinists in a music academy in Berlin showed that the most talented, or the ones that the music teacher viewed as having the highest probability of succeeding as musicians, were also those that reported spending more time practicing by themselves.

We argue that this is effective when you have a teacher telling you exactly what you need to do and then you go ahead and do it. The more you do, it's likely that you will get better. We reported that those academy students, when they were 20 years old, had practiced on average for 10,000 hours, which is a pretty amazing number.

I guess Gladwell was struck by this. He came up with a rule that was a little oversimplified. He said that in order to achieve an international level of performance, you need to have spent 10,000 hours. He pointed to the Beatles as a group that played a lot of music in Hamburg, Germany before they became famous. The issue I have with his statement is that there's nothing I know of that makes it a magical 10,000 hours. The estimates that I've seen for piano competitions would require these individuals to spend more like 25,000 hours to win. There are other skills where it seems you can be world-class with less than 1,000 hours of deliberate practice.

We checked some of the biographies of the Beatles and they didn't play more than maybe 1,500 hours in Hamburg in total, although they were playing pretty much 10 or 12 hours a day. I would argue that playing in front of an audience only improved their ability to play as a band. The Beatles were mostly famous for their ability to compose music and then perform it. To explain how they got to be better composers would make me look for activities that were more directly related to improving their composing ability.

Again, you need a lot of practice—we totally agree with Gladwell about that. But there's no magical boundaries. It doesn't make someone an expert when they've done 10,000 hours of an activity. The key is to spend a lot of time trying to improve specific aspects. If you can sustain that amount of training for thousands of hours, evidence shows that you are likely to be exceptional. If you keep pushing, you may end up being world-class.

Michael: Malcolm Gladwell brought up another issue that I thought was interesting, which has to do with birth dates.

Anders: If a sports coach is trying to find the most talented kids, it would make sense to pick out the ones who are performing a little bit better. It's been found that people who are successful and reaching the highest levels are much more likely to be the oldest in their age cohort who

I wanted to find a method of tapping into what the experts were thinking when they were exhibiting this superior behavior.

were practicing together as children and adolescents. Now, it's also been pointed out that these effects are not incredible except for certain types of extreme situations—for example, the best 13-year-old soccer players in England were the oldest among their cohort rather than those born in the latter half of the year.

Michael: One of the things that's fascinating about your work is the motivational aspect. You look at the examples and you say to yourself, "I can do anything if I want to!" But motivation's a tricky thing. For example, the movie *Whiplash* is about a young jazz drummer and a demanding teacher who pushes him. The young guy cracks at several points but, at the end of the movie, he accepts the instruction. He has the push—it's unclear where it comes from exactly, maybe it was the teacher—and something finally clicks. Why don't you speak about social motivation—whether we're talking about extraordinary performers or the corporate world, because your work translates to the corporate world as well. The "I can't" attitude is, as you describe, a real red flag, isn't it?

Anders: I was struck by the convenience of claiming that you can't do something, or that you lack the talent. Take learning a foreign language—I've encountered a lot of people who say they can't do that. Essentially, what that means is they're not going to put in any energy if they're only going to waste it. A colleague of mine fell in love with a woman who only spoke Spanish. He had always had difficulty learning languages, but he successfully mastered Spanish because he had a concrete reason. Also, when you're interacting with another individual, it's a pretty good learning environment because you get immediate feedback about whether they understand you or not.

> If you're not trying to change something, you're not doing deliberate practice.

It's interesting when it comes to music teachers. It's convenient to tell some students that they lack talent because they're not willing or able to make progress. It almost takes away the responsibility of the teacher to help the student find the motivation they need in order to progress. Once we identify motivation as something that teachers—especially good ones—are able to instill in their students, then it changes how we view education. Similarly, if we can convince students to find the right kind of training that will help them improve, this will give them the motivation and confidence to succeed.

It is a paradox that if you don't believe you're going to get any better, it's difficult to motivate yourself to put in the practice. That belief needs to be changed before it makes sense for the teacher and the student to invest in this gradual progress. I also think that having good metrics is key, so the student can see how they're improving. By not getting the immediate feedback that is an essential component of deliberate practice, you don't have a sense that you're getting better. That may confirm your sense that it's a waste of time.

Michael: I'm thinking of comedians—guys like Jerry Seinfeld, Jay Leno, Garry Shandling—who put in immense hours on stage and in small comedy clubs in their early 20s, then 30 years later they've become some of the biggest celebrities out there. What's interesting about comedians is they are always willing and able to talk about who came before them. In a different domain, chess grandmasters will study the games of their predecessors. Many people like to imagine, "I must invent it out of whole cloth. I must come up with it on my own." But you've seen in your work that expert performers look at the experts before them, don't they?

Anders: That gets to this effect of learning. We see it in all sorts of domains. For example, in the 14th century it would take a lifetime to understand advanced math because students had to discover it for themselves. Today, you can get that same level of information from math teachers and the curriculum. The same thing with music—the level that people are playing at today is vastly superior to what they were doing in the 19th century.

These historical changes are the direct result of young individuals finding teachers to fast-track them to learn things in the correct way. They can then go beyond what previous practitioners have done in order to create a unique contribution. This applies to virtually all the major creative individuals. For example, Mozart's father had him copy pieces by other composers as a way of learning the structure of musical composition. Picasso excelled in the traditional skills of drawing natural scenes, thereby acquiring the techniques that allowed him to do things that hadn't been done before, and to make what he was seeing in his mind's eye.

People are afraid that they're somehow going to erase their unique contribution, whereas it's more a case of needing the tools to realize whatever contribution you are going to make. I don't find good evidence that learning these tools will somehow remove any originality.

Michael: As a guy that used to play baseball as a right-handed hitter, I know that I have a big difference between my right and my left hip. One of the most fantastic examples to give people a flavor for deliberate practice and what can happen physically is that of a great tennis player like Roger Federer. So much practice at such a young age. It's not just the muscles in the racket arm that are changing, it's the actual bones, isn't it?

Anders: The kind of changes you can observe are far-reaching. Talking about bones, we know that height can't be changed by training, but it influences the thickness of the bones. It's clear what the mechanism is. Hitting the tennis ball creates vibrations in the arm, which releases chemicals that stimulate bone growth. If you take x-rays of tennis players, the arm they use to hold the racket has much thicker bones than the other arm. If you study endurance athletes, the muscles of the heart are restructured to maximize the pumping capacity. Even the arteries grow to allow more blood to circulate. We also see more capillaries surrounding those muscles that need a lot of oxygen to be able to sustain running, swimming, or whatever the endurance activity is.

Michael: Amazing that not only can deliberate practice develop a skill, but it can also change the structure of the brain or the body. You've dedicated your life to studying this. It's going to be up to other people to come along and say, "Anders got all this wrong." That's going to be a tough challenge.

Anders: I'm doing my best to keep up with developments in genetics and other domains to monitor any relevant evidence. Interestingly, in genetics, people believed that once we were able to describe DNA we would find differences in genes between elite athletes and other people who didn't have any obvious genetic problems. But that research has not uncovered any individual genes that would explain why some people perform so much better than others.

Personally, I see interesting evidence that training history provides a much better explanation for individual differences. If we take something like the outstanding performance of Kenyan runners, the kind of training history they have and the benefits of training at a high altitude as young children would seem to contribute to differences in performance.

Michael: Many have talked about barefoot running playing a role as well.

Anders: Exactly. Once you start looking at what sets apart the best runners from the less successful ones, it is the efficiency of their running— their ability to run without using up more energy and oxygen. They have been able to come up with training that allows them to maximize the effectiveness of the whole bodily system as opposed to some kind of specific thing that would be more a plausible target for a single gene.

Michael: I had a chance to interview Vernon Smith, who shared the Nobel Prize with Daniel Kahneman for their behavioral work. For those of you that might not know, Vernon Smith has Asperger's. I went to interview him in his college office and we were setting up cameras, lights, and everything. I said, "Dr. Smith, we're going to bug you here. We're going to be making a lot of noise setting everything up." He looked at me and he said, "I will never hear you." It was such an interesting comment.

Six months later, I was at the offices of one of the most successful hedge fund managers in the world. I mentioned to him that I had seen Vernon Smith and we started talking about Asperger's. He said, "Oh, yeah, we've got a ton of guys working at our firm who have Asperger's because these guys can focus like no tomorrow." Why don't you address the issue that these people might have a perceived advantage by being on the autistic spectrum?

Anders: I have not personally done any research on the issue of Asperger's and these kinds of syndromes. But I've been working with numerous expert performers, and when you put them in the lab, one of the things I've noticed is how they start out being relaxed, then as we get closer to the actual test they become completely focused and are able to sustain it. I think it would be interesting to research whether there are individual differences in how able people are to reach that state of full concentration.

But to me, one of the prerequisites for being able to stretch yourself is that you focus all your attentional resources on improving whatever aspect you've chosen. When I talk to these individuals, they tell me how important it is for them to get enough sleep. In order to be able to exhibit full concentration for maybe three or four hours a day, you need to have a lot of time for relaxation and recuperation. Five hours seems to be the upper limit for full concentration. The best data we have is on authors with no other responsibilities, who write for about four or five hours starting in the morning and use the rest of the day to recuperate, so they wake up refreshed for another four or five hours of productive writing. I've talked to surgeons and other individuals who are aware of balancing that level of full concentration with recuperation. If you want to maximize how much you're putting in and getting out, you'd like to keep on a pretty stable daily schedule.

Michael: Having written books myself, the interesting aspect for me is when those moments of intense focus happen inside—when you enter that flow state—time can stand still. Maybe you don't achieve a huge volume of work, but the quality and the precision that you can find in a flow state is addictive.

Anders: A lot of people refer to flow as highly enjoyable. But several people have pointed out that if you reflect on being in a flow state, you're no longer in it. It's almost like you can only recognize it afterwards. Some people have compared the flow state to being totally relaxed, where you're not trying to impose any constraints on what you're doing. I would argue that the flow state you were referring to is more like being so focused that you're no longer aware of the time that you're investing. Those are two different states: the playful enjoyment of skiing downhill and having a sense of effortlessness is a different kind of phenomenon than the one where you have that sustained focus and where time disappears.

Michael: Deliberate practice takes hard work and effort, but it's not something you can do with a team, is it?

Anders: Given that you're trying to improve some aspects of your own performance, to optimize the benefits of deliberate practice you have to be in control of your own training. I often mention the example of playing doubles in tennis. You miss a backhand volley, then the game continues and you get another opportunity maybe 30 minutes later. You're not going to do that any better. Compare that to a training situation where you have full concentration and the resources of a coach. The coach will give you a backhand volley that's easy and you're standing up by the net. Then as you perfect your control over this, the coach starts to place increasingly more difficult volleys. Eventually, you have to move away from the net. The endpoint is that you're rallying and he includes a backhand volley within the rally. One or two hours of working like that with a coach is going to improve your backhand volley so much more than maybe a year or two of playing games with your friends.

Michael: You've spent a lifetime studying expert performers, but your own career has also been about deliberate practice. Anyone that has a focused direction in life has a lot of experience of deliberate practice. What are some of the changes you think you've seen in yourself over your career?

Anders: I would point to a couple of important events. When I started my career, like most people, I spent as much time as I could on all the various activities, ranging from teaching to doing research and all sorts of things. Then I got the opportunity to go to the Max Planck Institute. This is where we did the research on the violinists at the music academy. That position was a little bit different from my previous job at the University of Colorado.

> The hallmark of an expert is being able to identify things they can do differently or better.

I didn't have any teaching and I had a lot of free time. That was the first time I realized that I could put in more hours working hard than I could get benefit from—the sense that there was a maximum. Setting aside three or four hours to write and then doing other less demanding activities made me feel much better than trying to fill every minute with various things. You need to take control over your time and also maybe even say no to activities. You can ensure your schedule is aligned with your priorities in terms of what you want to put in your best hours on. A lot of people I've talked to since then have found that to be a useful idea.

When it comes to issues related to doing science, I would argue that deliberate practice—at least in a generalized way—corresponds to seeking out people who disagree with you. I've found that some people in research don't like to be criticized. They get annoyed. I've tried to establish dialogues with people who have different views. I've found that instead of doing things I've always done and talking to people who agree with me, trying to convince people who don't agree with me often generates a lot of references to new stuff that I didn't know about. By understanding their views, I can do a better job of describing what I think is compelling evidence.

When you submit a manuscript, you get reviews, and it got to the point that I could anticipate what the reviewers were going to say. It gave me a sense of self-confidence to feel as if I knew what they were going to be concerned about. Sometimes, you can disagree about how compelling certain evidence is, but at least if you understand where other people are coming from, you're more likely to be successful than if you don't understand what makes them upset.

Michael: You talk about JaMarcus Russell, who was a phenomenal quarterback at Louisiana State University. He left college as a junior. He was the first pick in the draft, but he flamed out and didn't make it. Then you look at a guy like Tom Brady with the New England Patriots— he was pick 199. Professional sports is big business, but it seems some teams have not yet figured out how to project who is going to put in the deliberate practice.

Anders: My view is that the best football players are also the ones that have a deeper understanding of the game. I had a chance to talk to several of the Eagles players and coaches, and they recommended some players that they felt were standing out. I was compelled by hearing their history of how, from early on, they were able to figure out what other people on their team and the opposing team were doing. They started out having a refined grasp of what was going on in the game. That gave them the ability to assess what they needed to do to be able to behave in the most effective way. It's so commercialized in the NFL that it's hard for a coach with responsibility for a whole team to find the time and the resources to help individual players.

> If you don't believe you're going to get better, it's difficult to motivate yourself to put in the practice.

Some people might say, "By the time you get to NFL, you should've learned these things already." Maybe college or high school might be a better place to introduce these ideas. Maybe you would find people who are even more motivated to develop more effectively.

Michael: I would have loved for someone to have told me these insights when I was a serious baseball player at the age of 15. Because you get caught up in other things. You practice hard and you get to a certain level, but then you plateau. You don't necessarily know you're plateauing, but if you had the insight of deliberate practice and the motivation, you could see that plateau more clearly and then perhaps push through it. It's a fantastic way to think for young athletes, in particular.

Anders: The part I like is that as you get better in your understanding of yourself and the game environment, every game becomes more interesting, because you have a more refined way of analyzing it. Then once you have the experience, you can go back and identify things you can improve. It's almost like you're reaching over a peak and you can see beyond to things that you weren't able to conceive of previously.

That psychological richness comes closely with this idea of representations and your ability to evaluate your own performance. Then you can use that to direct your own training and see how you're getting better. When I talk to some athletes, they're just doing what they're doing—they're not able to appreciate what's possible. That appreciation might make it much more interesting for them, and thereby enhance all sorts of things related to the activity they're involved in.

Michael: Clearly, the work that you've put together is not age dependent. But with the youngsters you've studied, when do they start to have this self-appreciation versus being involved in deliberate practice but not necessarily seeing the bigger picture?

Anders: A finding that is interesting with respect to child prodigies is that a number of music prodigies don't have successful adult careers. Some people have argued that if the parent has taken control of the early training, when the child reaches late adolescence and early adulthood they have to take control themselves and go beyond what the teacher or the parent was helping them do. The idea of allowing the child to be, as László Polgár said, a co-author in the process of developing their own performance is critical. The more you can listen to the child and make sure they are understanding and always building up these representations that allow them to take over more and more—that generates self-confidence. But it's also critical that to keep moving ahead, you need to have mastered and internalized all the things that you're required to do.

Michael: Even if it's later in life, you can drastically improve yourself at almost any stage of the game. You've pointed out that people might decide they want to run a marathon at 80 years of age. That's motivating.

Anders: Once you start looking at the experience of making improvements, you get that same excitement that some people get from climbing mountains. It's something that you can do even if you live in the middle of the city, because most of the improvements are happening in your own mind. If I could contribute to providing people with an opportunity to enrich their lives, that would make me happy.

CHAPTER 3

GERD GIGERENZER

PART 1
Simple Heuristics

GERD GIGERENZER is a German psychologist who has studied the use of bounded rationality and heuristics in decision-making. He is director emeritus of the Center for Adaptive Behavior and Cognition (ABC) at the Max Planck Institute for Human Development, and director of the Harding Center for Risk Literacy. His books include *Cognition as Intuitive Statistics* with David Murray, *The Empire of Chance: How Probability Changed Science and Everyday Life*, *Simple Heuristics That Make Us Smart*, *Reckoning with Risk: Learning to Live with Uncertainty*, *Gut Feelings: The Intelligence of the Unconscious Rationality for Mortals*, *Risk Savvy: How to Make Good Decisions*, and *Simply Rational: Decision Making in the Real World*.

Michael note

Gerd Gigerenzer is an expert in heuristics. If you trade or invest, which means you must navigate risk and uncertainty in your life his topics are paramount for superior decision-making.

Michael Covel: I would describe your work as the philosophical foundation of trend following success, even if you did not set out for that to be the case. For example, the big question of how we all make inferences about the world that we live in with limited time and knowledge—that gets right at where you start with your work, doesn't it?

Gerd Gigerenzer: Yes, totally right. But it's not what most economists are talking about. Uncertainty is confused with known risks, where one tries to model people's behavior as if they could calculate all the risks. What I'm doing is to try to develop an alternative, to find tools that can deal with uncertainty, and heuristics are some of these tools.

Michael: One of the heuristics that I know you've used is the gaze heuristic—specifically I've heard you use the baseball example.

Gerd: The question is, how does an outfielder catch a ball? If you look into explanations of that, you will find that many people think if the problem is complex, we need a complex solution. What would it be? Not, obviously, that the outfielder somehow calculates the trajectory of the ball and runs to the point where it's coming down.

You can find people like Richard Dawkins in *The Selfish Gene* writing exactly that. He suggests people behave as if able to compute and know everything, and is uninterested in how actual people make decisions— here outfielders. A number of experiments show that they don't compute trajectories and don't run to the point that has been computed, but they rely on a simple heuristic that can do the job in the limited time and also in a situation where one has insufficient information to estimate all the parameters you would need to determine the right trajectory, such as the initial distance, wind direction, spin speed, and so on.

One of the simplest heuristics among a number that outfielders use is the gaze heuristic. It works if the ball is already high up in the air and it's simple. It consists of three building blocks. First, fixate your eye on the ball; second, start running; and third, adjust your running speed so that the angle of gaze remains constant. And then you will end up at a point where the ball ends up.

Here is a different philosophy. There is a complex problem and what's needed is a simple solution. When we look hard enough, we often can find it.

Michael: In my world, one of the problems is how to make a good investing decision. There's so much information out there, there's so many different variables, and many traders have figured out why don't they focus on one piece of information—for example, the price itself. If the price is going up, I want to be long with that investment; if the price is going down, I want to be short. The simple heuristic of using price action as a decision-making cue has worked extremely well.

Gerd: In trading we have the same two philosophies. It's a complex and difficult problem and many are looking for complex solutions, ranging from the traditional finance model from Markowitz's optimizing, to all kinds of computer-based and highly sophisticated calculation procedures. The alternative is to realize this is not a problem of known risk. Trading is an uncertain world and optimization models will not necessarily work. So, we need something that's robust, something simpler. And the heuristic you described is a member of a class of heuristics that I call one-reason decision-making. You try to figure out what's the single most important reason and then you ignore all the rest.

Many studies in social psychology and behavioral economics have concluded that this is irrational, but these studies overlook the important distinction between of a world of risk and a world of uncertainty. In a world of risk, ignoring relevant information is irrational, or at least it's a sign that it's not so important as a problem. But not in a world of uncertainty. Here, I want to show this mathematically—a good decision requires ignoring part of the information. If you try to make a complete pro/contra list, then you will likely fail.

> Many people think a complex problem needs a complex solution.

Michael: Why is the miracle on the Hudson River such a great example?

Gerd: These heuristics are often used unconsciously, like the gaze heuristic. If you interview a baseball outfielder, you'll find most of them cannot say

Good decision-making in an uncertain world needs to find a balance between ignoring and knowing something.

how they do what they do so well. There's more in our mind than we can describe. The same heuristics can be used deliberately.

The miracle on the Hudson River is a case in point. As you will recall, the plane took off from LaGuardia airport and within a few minutes something totally unexpected happened. A flock of Canadian geese collided with the plane. Modern engines are built in a way to be able to digest birds, but not Canadian geese. They are too fat. The unlikely event happened that they flew into both engines and it got very quiet in the plane. The pilots turned around and had to make an important decision: Will we make it to LaGuardia Airport or will we hit the ground before it? That's a decision about life and death. How did they do this? They might conclude it's a complex problem, so we need to compute the trajectory of this plane, but they didn't.

They used the same heuristic as the baseball outfielder uses—the gaze heuristic—in a different situation. You look through the windshield in the cockpit and fixate on the control tower—if the tower goes up in your windshield, you will not make it. You will hit the ground before you get there.

Here's an example of the same heuristic that many people use unconsciously, now being used consciously, and it is more accurate than calculations and, in any case, much faster, so the pilot has the time to do other important things. It's also a lesson that one can use this study of the heuristics people intuitively use in order to inform experts how to make better decisions. And it's also an illustration that the common opposition between heuristics and conscious reasoning is wrong. Every heuristic we've studied is used both unconsciously and consciously.

Michael: You've come at risk and uncertainty in a way the establishment doesn't like. Many careers have been built off a different direction.

Gerd: My work has caused many controversies but that's nothing bad. Science is there to discuss, to debate, to change, to improve. And the distinction between risk and uncertainty that is fundamental to my research is not one that I came up with. You can find it in the work of the economist Frank Knight in the 1920s, you can find it later, but it has not been taken seriously. Moreover, most of that intellectual effort has been put into building methods that reduce uncertainty to known risks and then applying probability methods.

Probability is a wonderful instrument, and I rely on it, but it has its place. It's not the only tool in our toolbox. Thinking that probability theory or Bayesian theory or any other instrument is the only tool that can solve all problems would be like mistaking a hammer for an entire toolbox and then thinking that everything in the world is a nail. The entire idea of an adaptive toolbox of different strategies is something that not many people are comfortable with, but it's the same way our body is built. It has not one super organ but many—and there's a reason for that: because they work better.

Michael: How do you answer when someone says, "Gerd, are you an intuitive man or a rational man?"

Gerd: It's not an "or." That's a big error. It's not an opposition—we need both. We need our brains, and we need our guts. More precisely, we need deliberate thinking, but also sometimes we need to trust our intuition. The only question is when? The point is not whether intuition is superior to deliberate thinking or deliberate thinking is superior to intuition. You can show that good expertise is almost impossible without good intuition.

> Trading is an uncertain world and optimization models will not necessarily work.

A composer needs intuition to compose—they cannot calculate the piece. A chicken sexer needs intuition. Chicken sexing is the art of finding out whether a one-day-old chicken is male or female, and if you ask a chicken sexer how they do this, they can't tell you. It's intuitive. Then there are other problems where it's better to calculate—to do explicit pro and con lists. The attitude in much of social sciences is to put the one quality against the other, and look down on one.

Intuition is often based, according to my own research, on simple heuristics. Why? Because intuition mostly has to deal with real-world problems that are characterized by uncertainty, not by known risk. If you play roulette, you can calculate how much you will lose in the long run. You don't need any intuition. But if you want to find out whom to trust, whom to marry, what job to take, what to do with stresses in life, you can't calculate that. Only parts can be calculated. There is the rest. This is what we usually call an experience. But it's an experience that's not in language, that we cannot express. This is why many people are suspicious of it.

Michael: The element of surprise is hard for people. And you can't prepare for a surprise.

Gerd: The moment one tries to review all forms of uncertainty to known risks, surprise is out of the equation because nothing new can happen. For instance, the financial crisis of 2007–08 shows why using standard models for estimating risk has overlooked every crisis and prevented none. We were surprised by things that should not have easily happened. So, dealing with uncertainty and devising and testing tools for uncertainty is also dealing with surprise. We need flexible methods and flexible heuristics in order to adapt to new situations that are quite unexpected.

Michael: One of the great lines that I've seen in your work is the idea of knowing what one doesn't have to know, that less is more. It's simple, it's intuitive, it's common sense. As a society, we've got to this point where complexity and data has become overwhelming. We all have cell phones, we all have computers, the information overload never stops. A large section of the population thinks that all this extra information is helping. But if you pause for a second, you ask yourself if it's distracting.

Gerd: This is part of the belief that I've always talked about—complex problems need complex solutions. It's also a vision of big data to hope that you can find your needle in the haystack not by knowing anything but by having more computation. In an uncertain world, this is not correct, because you need to have sufficiently simple solutions in order to make better decisions.

Here is a simple illustration of this "less is more" effect, which describes a situation where if you know more than a certain amount, your performance deteriorates, at least to a certain point. Stephen Gould and I have studied how people answer simple trivia questions, such as: Which city has more inhabitants, Milwaukee or Detroit? About 60% of Americans that we tested got the right answer: Detroit. Then we asked the same question to Germans and 90% got the answer right—not because they knew more, but because they knew less. Most of the Germans had not even heard of Milwaukee, only of Detroit, so they relied on a simple heuristic that we call the recognition heuristic—you've heard of Detroit but not of Milwaukee, so it's probably Detroit. The Americans could not rely on this heuristic as they had heard of both, so they needed to rely on facts or recall. Here's a situation where less is more, where we can show and prove that a sufficient degree of ignorance can actually help. The art of knowing what you don't need to know can be a conscious version of these types of heuristics that are usually used unconsciously; realizing that in an uncertain world the attempt to calculate everything is an illusion of certainty, and it will probably lead to failure.

Good decision-making in an uncertain world needs to find that balance between ignoring and knowing something. This balance can be mathematically described by the so-called bias/variance dilemma, which shows us that when we need to make estimations, we should not try to fit every data point, but we have to ignore something and try to be a little bit biased in order to make better decisions. So, in our work, bias has a positive meaning and not the meaning that it has in much of work in social psychology, where every deviation from a so-called normative model is called bias and people are blamed for it.

Michael: I'm interested in this idea of recognition and an experiment that you did about people selecting stocks for investing purposes.

Gerd: That's a study I did with some colleagues a long time ago. We wanted to test a simple heuristic for picking stocks. In order to use this recognition heuristic you need people who are semi-ignorant of the stock market, so we went to downtown Chicago and asked pedestrians which of a long list of stocks they recognized by name, nothing more. Then we did the same thing in downtown Munich. Then we asked a number of business students. We built portfolios of, say, the 10 most recognized stocks and as a control portfolio, the 10 least recognized. Then we waited a half a year and looked at how much money randomly picked stocks made compared to a certain number of well-known blue-chip firms, and some stocks picked by experts, and all kinds of criteria.

The study showed that the recognition heuristic portfolios, based on the semi-ignorant pedestrians, made most money. We replicated the study a few times in contexts that have been redefined by stock journals and others, and found similar results. This will not always replicate. But I would bet that a simple heuristic does at least as good as professional stock pickers. This is an illustration that in a highly complex and uncertain world, you can actually do quite well by simple heuristics—in this case, interestingly, heuristics that need semi-ignorant people. There's usually a time where some knowledge helps, but then there will be a tipping point where too much knowledge will lead you astray.

Michael: A few years ago I had a chance to spend the afternoon with Harry Markowitz, whose name will be familiar to most people in the finance world. Why don't you briefly describe Markowitz's findings and then maybe add some critique on ways that he might have got it wrong?

Gerd: First, Markowitz didn't get it wrong. He developed an optimization model called the Mean Variance Portfolio that works if the assumptions of his model are in place. But the claim that the Markowitz model would work in the real world of finance is a different one. If someone makes this claim, then it's likely that the person gets it wrong. Interestingly, when Harry Markowitz made his own investments for his retirement, did he use this Nobel Prize-winning optimization method? No, he did not. He relied on a simple heuristic: divide your money equally. So, if you have two options, 50:50. If you have three, a third, a third and a third. 1/n. The question now is, how good is 1/n—a simple heuristic, no complication, no free parameters—relative to the Markowitz optimization model?

What most of the studies show is that in the real world of investment, 1/n typically leads to better returns than Markowitz optimization. The real question is, can we identify the situations where the simple heuristic does better and the situations where the Markowitz model would do better? To the best of knowledge today, these situations are that the higher the uncertainty, the better for the heuristic. Second, the larger the number of n—so, assets that you have—the better for the heuristic. If a small number, that is where the Markowitz model is profiting because it doesn't have to estimate so many parameters. And finally, third, the larger the sample size, the better for the Markowitz model. So, given the uncertainty of the stock market, if you have n=50 assets, for instance, how many years of stock data would you need to argue that the Markowitz model finally does better? From the simulations that have tried to answer this question, the answer is roughly 500 years. So, that means, in the year 2500 we can start to distrust our intuition and do the computations—provided the same stocks are still around in the market in the first place.

Michael: Once you got into this subject area—looking at risk, looking at uncertainty, doing the experiments, doing the research—this became a lifelong project for you. You are 100% passionate. You love this.

Gerd: I do. I learn so much about the role. For instance, this basic research about how to deal with uncertainty is relevant for so many different fields that not only includes finance, but also management. It also includes the law: I have taught about 50 U.S. federal judges in decision-making. It includes healthcare: I have personally taught about a thousand German doctors to understand risk.

I probably learn as much as these experts learn from my own work about how the world is functioning. And there are situations where you need to teach people how to understand known risks or risk communication, which doctors still don't learn in their medical education. Then in other situations we need to teach them how to use heuristics, and also the difference between risk and uncertainty.

> In a world of uncertainty, a good decision requires ignoring part of the information.

At the end, we have to teach them there is not only one method out there for how we have to deal with the world. We need a toolbox, which we call the adaptive toolbox, in order to make better decisions. It's true, it's always been a fun part of my life. And I continue to learn new things about different areas in my environment, including the psychological factors of decision makers such as defensive decision-making.

So, if you go to your doctor and you believe that they give you the best advice, you may be the lucky outlier. But most doctors in the United States practice defensive decision-making—that is, they suggest something that's the second or third best option for you, but which protects themselves from being sued by you. You treat your clients differently from, say, your relatives. In one study, 93% of U.S. doctors admitted they did defensive decision-making. You cannot blame your doctor for doing it, because you are the one who is suing.

You have to understand the system and there are some simple heuristics that may help you. For instance, my mother went blind in one eye and there was an experimental therapy. I called up the person who has done most of these experimental therapies, explained to him the case and asked him, "What would you recommend for my mother?" And he said, "Okay, try the therapy." Then I realized I asked the wrong question, because he will be in a defensive position. I could sue him. So, I said, "Look, if it was your mother, what would you do?" He said, "I wouldn't do anything." His mother wouldn't sue him, so he's cautious.

Michael: There's a classic chapter in Stephen Jay Gould's book, *Full House*, where he talks about surviving cancer and how he put aside his doctor's advice and looked at his own situation. That's what you're saying here: Take the power into your hands and don't simply trust.

Gerd: There are a number of psychological factors that also are important in order to understand decision-making as a risk.

Michael: I hear there is an interesting video of you on YouTube somewhere and I believe it's a commercial and I believe music is involved?

Gerd: Yes. This is from an earlier career. My life has not only been about studying risk and uncertainty. I was a musician in the entertainment business, and the video you're referring to was the first TV spot for the VW Rabbit, which was called Golf then. I had a band at this time and we won the contest for the TV spot and I'm on the steering wheel, in case you don't recognize me. That's a long time ago!

Michael: I'm going to go find it!

Gerd: I hope to make the theme of decision-making and risk less abstract and less remote from what real experts and people in daily life do, which is about calculating probabilities and utilities. In most cases we cannot calculate the probabilities, nor do we know the utilities, so we need something else. And I hope that is a viable alternative that brings academic science into more contact with the professions that have to deal with uncertainty.

PART 2
Making Informed Decisions

Michael Covel: I know you have a good-natured, collegial debate with Daniel Kahneman, but I wonder if you could outline your perspective, and perhaps the difference in how you both see the big picture?

Gerd Gigerenzer: Let's start with the commonalities. We both believe that people use heuristics—that is, simple rules to make decisions, at least in many situations. The disagreement starts because Danny Kahneman and many of his followers believe that heuristics are always second best and that statistics would always give you the right answer, and this is an error.

In a world of uncertainty, where you cannot calculate all the risks, statistics and optimization doesn't help. It brings you to some point, but you never know the best solution, and in that kind of situation heuristics can do well, as we have shown. Not only do people use heuristics, but heuristics can often be better than so-called optimal.

That leads to a new perspective about heuristics: not only can they describe how people make decisions, but also prescribe. That is a normative perspective of heuristics that poses the question: can we describe the environment in which a simple heuristic such as "divide your money equally over the N assets" can outperform so-called optimization models? This is the study of ecological rationality.

Michael: One of the best examples are medical checkups—perfectly healthy 30-somethings going to get full body scans, looking for every possible thing that can go wrong, or men of a certain age pondering the idea of a PSA test.

Gerd: This is about situations where you can calculate the risks clearly, and cancer screening is a good example.

A PSA test is about early detection of prostate cancer. In that situation, many Americans don't think about whether they should participate in PSA testing or not, but rather follow the trusty doctor heuristic: if you see a white coat, then do whatever the wearer is telling you. That's a valid heuristic when doctors know the medical evidence, don't have conflicts of interest, and don't practice defensive decision-making to protect themselves against their patient as a potential plaintiff. But none of these three conditions holds in the US, or in many other Western countries, which means the trusty doctor heuristic is not ecologically rational, and here you need to think for yourself.

It's a well-known trick to use relative numbers when absolute numbers would give you a very different picture.

The evidence for a PSA test is quite clear: we do not have evidence that lives are saved. There's a little controversy on whether PSA testing reduces mortality from prostate cancer, maybe a few in 1,000, but in total cancer mortality there is no evidence that there is any difference. But the consequence of this test can be terrible for many men. For instance, if you're lucky to live a long life, say 80% of 80-year-olds almost certainly have some form of prostate cancer, but only 3% die from it. So, if everyone has screening and the condition is detected, most of these cancers are not technically relevant to life expectancy, but then there is treatment and maybe half or so of men being treated end up incontinent for the rest of their lives. This is why the US Preventive Services Task Force recommends against routine prostate cancer screening.

Nevertheless, many doctors and clinics recommend prostate cancer screening, for one of three reasons. First, many doctors we have studied don't know the medical evidence. Second, they have conflicts of interest. Clinics earn money from doing the tests and more money from the surgery, which is often unnecessary. And third, there is defensive decision-making. So, maybe doctors who themselves would never take a PSA test recommend it to their patients, because they don't want to deal with the situation that most men in old age get some kind of prostate cancer and they might sue the doctor for not having done the PSA test.

We developed so-called fact boxes that were originally developed by Lisa Schwartz and Steve Woloshin in Dartmouth College and made their way into the Obama Health Catalog, but they've never been published. This is one of the major tools in healthcare to help doctors and patients understand medical evidence. Using icons like smiling faces and sad faces, the fact box shows you what happens to 100 men who participate in PSA tests, and 100 who don't, 10 years later. This shows the mortality rate: no life is saved, but about 20 of every 100 men suffer from taking the tests, either by having false positives and unnecessary biopsies, or by having a non-progressive version of prostate cancer and being treated unnecessarily.

Michael: The heart of this revolves around when you're going to take risks, do you follow your own instincts or expert advice?

Gerd: With expert advice, you need to be careful, because you need to analyze whether these conditions that I mentioned hold. Whether the expert knows the evidence, whether there is conflict of interest—the expert may make a choice between giving you the best advice and losing money—and defensive decision-making.

The man who invented the PSA test, Richard Ablin, said that no man should routinely take the test: "I never dreamed that my discovery four decades ago would lead to such a profit-driven public health disaster." This is about how to learn to make informed decisions, and also to relax with your anxieties and take back control of your emotions.

Michael: There was a debate online between groups of frequent travelers over traffic fatalities in the United States versus Thailand, and it was 38 deaths per 100,000 in Thailand and 11 per 100,000 in the United States. Some people immediately read that and said, "Oh my gosh, it's four times more dangerous to drive in Thailand!" I said, "But hold on, the absolute numbers are pretty close, 38 to 11 out of 100,000 people." It seemed to me a classic example of looking at the relative comparison, and not thinking about the absolute risk.

From studying risk taking in the real world, I have learned to make decisions faster and more relaxed.

Gerd: It's a well-known trick to use relative numbers when absolute numbers would give you a different picture. The same trick is used in cancer screening, where—to take another example, mammography screening—out of 1,000 women aged 50 who don't participate in screening, 10 years later about five of them die from breast cancer, and out of 1,000 women who participate in screening, the number is four. So, the reduction is from five to four—or in other words, one out of 1,000. But that's usually not told to women, rather that breast cancer screening reduces mortality by 20%, often rounded up to 30% or 35%. I've

> Statistics only works in situations where you can be sure that you can predict the world very well.

analyzed the brochures, and the latter is typical in the UK. In the US, most brochures don't even give numbers, because the assumption is that women are frightened of numbers. So American women, most of the time, get no numbers at all about the benefit of medication; instead they get other numbers that are irrelevant. This is a case where relative numbers are used to mislead people.

Another example is the Lipitor advertisement, which claims that if you take Lipitor or another cholesterol-reducing drug, you reduce your risk of a stroke by 50%. Studies show that out of 100 persons who are already at high risk, two who don't take the drug suffer a stroke and the figure reduces by one among those who take the drug. So, that's the effect: 50% is the same as one percentage point.

These are simple tools that everyone could learn. Always ask, what's the absolute risk? And don't be impressed by relative numbers.

Michael: Benjamin Franklin built a ledger. Explain Franklin's thinking in his ledger.

Gerd: Benjamin Franklin devised a recipe for how to make rational decisions. It's a pro and con list, which later became what every business school or economics school teaches—the maximum utilization and expected utility. In a famous letter to his nephew, Franklin explains how, if in doubt, he should set down all the reasons pro and con, and weigh them. He ends, "By the way, if you do not learn it, apprehend you will never be married." I have nothing against pro and con lists, but they work in a world where you can predict the future well, in a world of known risk, but not so much in the world of unknown risk, and in relationships all kinds of things happen that you never foresaw.

I have asked many of my friends who are economists, mostly men, how they made their own decision about whom to marry. The universal answer was no, we didn't follow our own theory. I found only one economist who said, of course I followed my own theory. He told me that he listed all the alternatives and all the consequences, such as will she let me work in peace, will she take care of the children, and then he estimated the probabilities for each of the women that this would actually happen, multiplied it by the utilities and made the calculation, and proposed to the woman who had the highest expected utility. She accepted. He never told her how he did it. Now they are divorced, but that happens to many people.

Some people may laugh about that, but think for a moment. The problem is that expected utility theory maximization is proposed as the recipe for every decision, based on statistics—as if statistics are the answer to everything! Statistics is an enormously important tool, but it only works in situations where you can be sure that you can predict the world well.

Modern dating sites use this kind of algorithm for matching partners and weighing hundreds of personality characteristics for the perfect date. And I bet these sites have no more success than the classic way with someone experienced who knows you well making the decision for you, as is still the case in many Asian countries. There is certainly no evidence that these dating site algorithms lead to romantic relationships that are superior to traditional ways of finding partners.

Michael: People believe in it.

Gerd: There is a big movement towards replacing good judgment with algorithms, and mistrusting intuition and gut feelings. You find the statement that human intuition is sometimes good, but sometimes bad. Which is true, of course, but statistical optimization models are also sometimes good and sometimes bad, and the 2007–08 financial crisis made that clear. The algorithms of the rating agencies and value-added risk computations that the banks use created illusions of certainty and prevented no single crisis, and predicted nothing.

We need to think more about a toolbox—not one tool that's always right and human intuition is always wrong. That's a big error.

Michael: You suggest that if an experienced person with a good track record has a strong hunch about a decision, we should listen to them, and not just demand facts.

Gerd: I've worked with many large companies and asked the managers through the entire hierarchy up to the executive committee, how often is an important professional decision in which you're participating a gut decision? In confidential interviews, you get the answer that roughly every other decision is, ultimately, a gut decision. A gut decision is not caprice, not a sixth sense, but it's a form of unconscious intelligence. These managers have long experience, yet usually they are buried under a mountain of data, partially contradictory, and there is no algorithm to decide whether or not the company should establish a branch in Saigon. But if they have a feeling based on their experience where to go, it's intuition that counts in the end. The decision makers can't explain it, but they would never admit to this in public, because if you have made a gut decision, you take the responsibility.

I have observed that in large companies, the way to deal with that anxiety is to find reasons after the fact. Either an employee is tasked to find reasons in a short space of time, and then the decision is presented as fact-based. Or the more expensive version is to hire a consulting firm that finds reasons and presents a 200-page document with PowerPoint. This is all a waste of time, intelligence, and money, because people are scared to make good intuitive decisions. One of the reasons is the literature in behavioral economics in other fields, where people learn that intuitive decisions are suspect. We are told to mistrust intuitive decisions and to blindly trust logic and probability theory.

Michael: Another great example you use concerns the best way to order food in an upscale restaurant.

Gerd: I have learned myself, from studying risk taking in the real world, to make decisions faster and more relaxed. When I'm in an upscale restaurant, I don't even open the menu, but I ask the waiter what they would eat that evening there. In a good restaurant, the waiter knows what's happening in the kitchen and what's best that day, so I've never regretted this decision—and it leaves you time for conversation. While many of my dear friends, they can't not open the menu and they try to maximize every piece of information, every word, and they'll often end up with something which is second best. It illustrates there are many of these simple heuristics where you're usually better off than trying to maximize.

Michael: You make a case that there are ways to use smart gut judgments to navigate decisions much more effectively.

Gerd: I take issue with the view that we are hopeless in taking risks and need to be nudged by governments or other authorities into better behavior. This is not my view of a democracy or the 21st century. It's old-fashioned paternalism.

We have shown that in order to be risk savvy, you need two tools. In a situation where one can calculate the risk, you need statistical thinking; in a situation where one cannot calculate the risk, you need good heuristics. That doesn't mean that one always makes the best decision, simply because in a world of uncertainty, nobody can predict what the best outcome will be.

But in general, we should invest more in people, rather than blaming them and trying to find ways to nudge them. For instance, many of my colleagues think it's impossible to educate people out of their so-called cognitive illusions. But think ahead—a few centuries ago, few people would have believed that we could ever succeed in teaching everyone to read and write. In the same way, I would bet that if we only try, we can teach everyone to become risk savvy. There's nothing inborn or misfired in our brain. We have problems, but often can find good representations to understand risks better.

> If we only try, I bet we can teach everyone to become risk savvy.

CHAPTER 4

SPYROS MAKRIDAKIS

The Illusion of Control

S PYROS MAKRIDAKIS is the rector of the Neapolis University of Pafos NUP and an Emeritus Professor of Decision Sciences at INSEAD, as well as at the University of Piraeus, and one of the world's leading experts on forecasting, having written many journal articles and books on the subject. He is famous as the organizer of the Makridakis Competitions, known in the forecasting literature as the M-Competitions. Spyros' current interest centers on the uses and limitations of forecasting and what we can do with the resulting uncertainty and risk given our inability to accurately predict a wide range of future events (e.g., the 2000 burst of the internet bubble or the 2007–2009 major financial crisis).

Michael note

Spyros Makridakis's calling is to poke holes in the notion that we can forecast with accuracy, which dovetails with the idea that simple is better. His classic paper from 1979 showed that moving averages are a far better predictor of tomorrow than the most complex econometric models.

Michael Covel: As I was preparing for our conversation, I came across that famous passage from the former US defense secretary Donald Rumsfeld about known knowns, known unknowns, and unknown unknowns.

Spyros Makridakis: He's right. There's another part, the unknown knowns, which he didn't mention, which is also important. For instance, there are a lot of things that we know, but we don't want to believe—what we call the illusion of control. Right now, as a matter fact, I'm doing a paper about a survey of forecasting and uncertainty. We conclude that what we can forecast is very, very little, and we're not willing to accept the uncertainty.

To give you an example, which is how well doctors can predict what's going to happen to us—the fact is they cannot predict at all, it's an illusion. For instance, they did a study of 160 cases of diseases that had been diagnosed and asked physicians to make a diagnosis. In the difficult cases, only 7% of the diagnoses were correct.

Michael: It's worse than flipping a coin.

Spyros: It's much, much worse than flipping a coin, because with a diagnosis there are many different possibilities. The worst thing is that when they asked the doctors how certain they were about the diagnosis, only 7% admitted they were not certain.

We have a lot of problems with realizing the uncertainty in our forecasting. The fact is we're not willing to accept it and this has serious implications.

Michael: Lead me through the two main types of uncertainty.

Spyros: There are some uncertainties that we can quantify and there are a lot that we cannot quantify, and that's what Nassim Taleb calls black swans. For instance, the tsunami that hit in 2004—the previous one was several centuries before and it was not as big, but it can happen. This is the uncertainty. The 2008 financial crisis from the subprime situation was something that nobody could have predicted, but it happened, and it almost destroyed the global financial system. These are the unknown unknowns of Rumsfeld, the uncertainties that we cannot predict, and they hit us.

Another type of uncertainty—for instance, how much electricity we're going to consume during the next day—is something that we can predict pretty accurately, unless there's a blackout, which is also a possibility. But there are many other types of uncertainties we cannot predict and we're so afraid that we pretend they don't exist.

What we did in our research was to ask, what are the most important aspects of our life? The first thing people say is health. The second is wealth. And the third thing they say is happiness. How well can we predict each one of these three? The answer is zero. The paper that I'm doing right now shows that in medicine, in which our ability to forecast is probably the most critical factor, it is absolutely zero.

There are so many examples of what doctors say today is the correct thing, and then a month or a year later, new research shows that it's not correct. There are a lot of standards that show the great majority of medical research is wrong, but this is what doctors base their diagnoses and recommended treatments on. And then later, they find out that the new research changes the old research.

Michael: Look at cholesterol-reducing drugs, for example.

Spyros: There is a lot of talk that the whole thing is a myth. Many doctors don't believe anymore in cholesterol, and others say the drugs cause negative side effects. It's not only cholesterol, there's so many things. For instance, for so long, doctors were saying, "Take an aspirin a day." Now, they found out that it causes bleeding in the stomach if you take one every day, so they recommend not to take aspirin. The latest thing is not to do any preventive tests for breast cancer in women or prostate cancer in men. New evidence shows it does more harm than good.

Michael: You have pointed towards a lack of good forecasting models. You make the point that simple moving averages work best—versus the massive econometric models that people spend decades of their lives creating.

We're not
willing to accept
uncertainty in
our forecasting
and this
has serious
implications.

Spyros: When I first did this work back in the late '70s, there was so much resistance to this research finding, and now it has been proven beyond the slightest doubt that sophisticated models don't work. The simpler the model, the better it is.

Michael: There are many successful traders who trade quantitative methods. They talk about advanced understanding, but when you get behind the scenes, they're often using something like a simple moving average to trade.

Spyros: Consistency is probably the most important aspect of trading. If you have a rule, a lot of people are not consistent on what they get. Good news is over-discounted and bad news is under-discounted. That's what creates the problem. It's been also proven constantly that simple decision rules outweigh expert judgment.

Michael: Many in business and academia don't like what you and your co-authors have to say.

Spyros: Of course they don't like it! The worst bunch are the doctors, who don't like all this new evidence. In the United States, for instance, we spend 17% of gross national product on medicine—that's a huge amount. What's important is that patients who spend much more on their treatment don't necessarily live longer than those who spend less. This is what doctors call the wallet test. You go to hospital, they see how much money you have, and then they decide what treatment to give you to maximize their revenues.

Another point which is clear relates to caesarian sections. The World Health Organization published a study that says caesarians should be between 10% and 15% of births. In some countries, it's more than 70%. It's harmful for the mother, it's harmful for the child, yet doctors still do them because it increases their revenues and it's much more convenient. Instead of being called at three o'clock in the morning, they program it at three o'clock in the afternoon on the days they are available.

Michael: You looked at what happened to the 11 companies identified by author Jim Collins as having made the leap from good to great, and it turns out none of them have appeared in the *Fortune* Top 10 of most admired companies between 2001 and 2015. Yet Collins's book *Good to Great* is still on sale everywhere. What do you think is driving us to keep giving people research that is no longer valid?

Spyros: We like hero stories, right? And Jim Collins is a hero. We like to listen to things we think are going to help us. But just as most hero stories are wrong, the same is true that a lot of books about management are wrong, but still people like to read them. Maybe they apply some ideas and maybe there will be some improvement, but this is not based on past research, it's based on a kind of a placebo effect. It makes us feel better.

Michael: You mention the hero issue—so many people want that person to appear on TV and say, "I know what will happen tomorrow." There's no evidence that this sort of prediction works, but everyone still clamors for it.

Spyros: This is the illusion of control. We prefer to have the illusion that we can control the future rather than the reality that actually we cannot control it. That's the reason we take out fire insurance for our house, because we accept we cannot predict when there will be a fire, so let's try to do something to anticipate it.

Michael: What are some of the best ways to begin operating in an uncertain world?

Spyros: It's difficult to accept the uncertainty, because psychologically we're not willing to live in a world that we cannot predict, where anything can happen, which is the reality. I mean, cancer can hit us in any place at any time, right? Now, what can we do about this? The problem is we can do nothing. Going for a prostate cancer test, for instance, doesn't help—as a matter of fact, it makes things worse. When I give talks about why men should not take the prostate cancer test or woman the mammogram, I ask them, "Do you accept evidence?" And they say yes. And then I ask them, "Are you going to continue doing this test?" And they say yes. They feel that by doing the test, somehow they protect themselves, and that's the illusion of control—but it's exactly the opposite. That's the way people think. How are you going to change it? You need a massive educational campaign that nobody is willing to do.

Michael: There's this small army of people, like yourself, your co-authors, guys like Daniel Kahneman, Gerd Gigerenzer, Nassim Taleb—all of whom I'm sure you respect—and you're all working to open the curtain, so to speak. I wonder how much of a dent you think you and your peers are making in getting something like the illusion of control better understood?

Spyros: Very little. We have to be honest, because the illusion of control is deep inside us and it forces us to go into a certain direction. So, somebody comes along and says, "Look, I have five easy steps to tell you how to become a millionaire or how to live longer." And then I come along and say, "Look, all of this is nonsense." People don't want to believe it's nonsense, because deep down we feel it would be nice to have some certainty because our world is really, really uncertain.

For instance, to return to the example of prostate cancer and breast cancer, there are so many who suffered

> **It has been proven beyond the slightest doubt that sophisticated models don't work.**

tremendously because of the test and yet people are not willing to accept it. They think it's better to believe in the illusion of control rather than the reality of what is happening. In the example of the doctors, there is a group of doctors now who believe that things need to change, but nothing happens. There is a quote from Bertrand Russell. He said that to teach how to live with uncertainty yet without being paralyzed by education is perhaps the chief purpose of philosophy. I believe that's at the center of what is happening.

Michael: What drove you into this passion? Who were your mentors, your influencers? When did you decide, "I want to go this way"?

Spyros: I did the first study that proved that sophisticated models were less accurate than simple models and it was published in 1979 in the *Journal of the Royal Statistical Society*. What surprised me was the reaction of statisticians. There were comments attacking me saying the reason I found the result was because I didn't know how to apply these sophisticated methods.

I then organized another competition where the forecast was done by experts and we found exactly the same results, that simple models were much more accurate than sophisticated ones, and that's what drove me to this. It made me realize that what the majority of experts believe is not necessarily true. Forecasting, as a matter of fact, provides little value and usually only for the short term. It's like weather forecasting—it's accurate for the next three days, but after that, it becomes chaos theory.

Michael: As a young man, even before you did the research and you could prove things, were you trusting the system? You don't seem like that type of person.

Spyros: When you go to school, when you get the PhD, they teach you to trust the research. But they don't tell you that research is done for many, many reasons and people publish because they want some benefits. Somehow you believe that the conventional wisdom is correct. But in my case, I realized that the conventional wisdom was not correct. My field was forecasting, so my interest was to prove that sophisticated models were better. As a matter of fact, I was teaching the sophisticated model and I was doing consulting and I was making money out of it. And then suddenly, I realized it's not worth it. Could I continue fooling people or did I have to say, "That's the truth"?

> We prefer
> to have the
> illusion that
> we can control
> the future.

Michael: That's a big career change.

Spyros: Yes, it is. But I believe truth is the driving force of everything. In my conscience, I had to come out and say these things. The fact that I would lose some consulting jobs didn't matter.

Michael: Here you are with a PhD. You're going down the direction of forecasting and trying to show how these complicated predictive models work. But was there a trigger moment when you decided, "I can't do this anymore. The simple method is the way to go."

Spyros: Yeah. But I didn't realize the reaction. I thought that once you prove something scientifically, the others will come and say, "Oh, you're right. Let's change the way we think and let's try to find ways to deal with the problem," but it didn't happen like this. The reaction was absolutely devastating, for me, at that time. I was a young researcher saying, "Look, you don't know what you're doing. Because you are in a business school, you don't do statistics. You don't know how to apply these models correctly."

Michael: The future is never exactly like the past. We want to imagine that the past is going to show us the way in the future and it doesn't work like that. Once you have that deep in your bones, even if people are throwing slings at you, it's still exciting once you know how it works, even if you can't get everybody else on the same team.

Spyros: It is exciting. We must educate the world—or at least as much of the world as possible. For instance, you say to men, "Don't do the prostate cancer test." Richard Ablin, the guy who discovered the test, wrote a book called *The Great Prostate Hoax*, which says, "Don't do it. It's devastating."

Michael: When dealing with a physician, we can ask the simple question: "What if I do nothing?"

Spyros: The chance of surviving five years after you have chemotherapy for breast cancer is, I think, 1.5%. Yet the studies don't say what will happen if you don't have chemotherapy, how long you're going to survive. But for me as a statistician, 1.5% is not worth doing chemotherapy, yet doctors recommend it because it brings them tremendous revenues.

Michael: It also plays into the fantasy that we're all going to live forever.

Spyros: Another fallacy is it can happen to others, but not to us, right? Again, that's the illusion of control.

Michael: That's an interesting point. Put the doctor on the spot and ask: "How much longer will I live with it or without it?"

Spyros: But they don't know and they don't want to tell you. Then they start... saying, "Oh, there is hope."

CHAPTER 5

ALISON GOPNIK

Bayesian Babies

A LISON GOPNIK is a Professor of Psychology and Affiliate Professor of Philosophy at U.C. Berkeley, where she also heads the Cognitive Development and Learning Lab. She's written more than 100 journal articles and several books, including *The Scientist in the Crib*, *The Philosophical Baby*, and, most recently, *The Gardener and the Carpenter*.

Alison understands babies and children as the R&D division of humanity. From her cognitive science lab at Berkeley, she investigates the "evolutionary paradox" of the long human childhood. When she first trained in philosophy and developmental psychology, the minds of children were treated as blank slates. But she's led on the frontier, helping us see how even the most mundane acts of a three-year-old, nine-year-old, or teenager, from extravagant pretend play to risky rebelliousness, tell us what it means to be human. Alison's work shows how the creativity of the young human brain literally helps us all stay creative—and growing—as a species.

Michael note

Alison Gopnik's concept of Bayesian babies is literally how trend following works. I never expected her work to dovetail into my trend following work. We live in an endlessly fascinating world!

Michael Covel: How did insatiable curiosity begin for you?

Alison Gopnik: I had an interesting childhood, but a big feature of it was that I'm the oldest of six children. I was involved and engaged with children for as long as I can remember. My parents were graduate students and then young faculty, but they were crazy bohemians.

We had an amazingly wonderful, rich, slightly crazy life. I was a child actor, for example, for five years when I was a kid. And we drove from Philadelphia to New York to see the opening of the Guggenheim when I was four and my brother was three. That was the sort of thing my parents thought made a lot of sense to do.

Also being the oldest of six meant that I was conscious of what the younger children were like and how interesting they were and, in some sense, how much people outside didn't appreciate how smart and fascinating they were.

Michael: Is there a particular moment in time you can think back to—something that struck you early on?

Alison: The moment I can remember most vividly was when I was about 10 or 11, I read Plato's *Phaedo*, which is one of the dialogues where he talks about the fact that people would have to exist in another world, another platonic universe, before and after this life, because it doesn't make any sense to think that we have this limited existence in the world and nothing comes before and nothing comes after. What struck me was that it seemed obvious that the way you continued in the world was through your children—that each generation of children was going on in the world.

Later, when I was studying for my first degree in philosophy, it was amazing to me that for these incredibly smart philosophers whom I tremendously admired, like Socrates, the possibility of even thinking about children didn't show up in the dialogue. I can remember being struck by the fact that they weren't going to the obvious answer, which was thinking about the way that children make you immortal and extend you into the future and the past. That reaction has shaped the whole of my career. Here's this deep, important, interesting question. It's obvious that children are going to be able to tell you something about it. And yet the attitude towards children for all those years, even when people were sort of abstractly interested, was that they were part of the world of women and domestic life and weren't part of the serious, intellectual, philosophical universe.

Michael: I love the way you've described babies as the R&D operation of the human species.

Alison: Exactly. Another vivid moment that I remember was when I was in my first year of graduate school. Andrew Meltzoff, who became a famous developmental psychologist, was a young fellow graduate student. We were sitting in a field looking at a bunch of babies who were crawling around on picnic blankets, the way babies do, and we counted up how many experiments a baby does in the course of five minutes. It's a fascinating exercise.

Take anybody under the age of three and watch them for five minutes, and count how many things they find out about, how many things they think about, how many things they try, in that brief period of time. Compare that to how many new ideas or new discoveries you have in the course of maybe five years. It's clear that babies are finding out more about the world in five minutes than most of us do in five years. That's an important biological fact about who we are as humans.

One of the things I've been working on is the idea that there's this kind of basic tension between exploration and exploitation. You see it in neuroscience, computer science, and technology. You're trying to solve a problem. One way is to try to explore as many different possible solutions as you can. Another way is to narrow in on one or two solutions and make them happen. It's important that you need to do both. We would not want a world where everyone was like a four-year-old. There's something to be said for the adult skills of focus, narrow attention, executive function, and planning. But all of that wouldn't have nearly as much potency if we didn't also have individual people, or times in our lives, or developmental periods, when instead we could be exploring and finding out new things for the hell of it.

At Berkeley, there's a lovely study my colleagues in AI did where they took a powerful machine learning algorithm and gave it curiosity. They added a bit that said, "When you're trying to solve these problems, go out and try to get more information for the sake of more information."

It looks as if that would be counterproductive, right? You're supposed to be solving a problem, you're not supposed to be going around and trying to find out more about the world. But it turns out that kind of system is more effective than a system that's narrowly focused on accomplishing particular goals.

That's the function that preschoolers play for us. If you sit down next to a preschooler and watch them for a while, one of the great pleasures of developmental psychology is you can actually see that happening. You can see it unfold before your eyes.

Michael: Why don't you explain life history from your perspective, and perhaps contrast with that of other animals? Us humans are different.

Alison: If you talk to evolutionary biologists, one thing they come back to again and again is the idea of life history. Life history is the way an organism develops over its entire lifespan. Not only what it's like at its peak, as it were, but how long a period of childhood does it have? How long does it live? When does it reproduce? When does it become senescent? When does it die? That trajectory is an important factor in lots of arguments in evolutionary biology.

If you can imagine a biologist from Alpha Centauri coming to Earth 150,000 years ago and looking at these new creatures that had evolved, these funny little primates scurrying around on the vale, and trying to figure out, "What's special about these creatures? What makes them distinctive?" the thing that would leap out at her is, "My goodness, these creatures have a bizarre life history." Because what she would have noticed is that human beings have twice as long a childhood, twice as long a period of immaturity, as any of our closest relatives.

> It's clear that babies are finding out more about the world in five minutes than most of us do in five years.

Chimpanzees are producing as much food as they're consuming by the time they're seven. Even in hunter-gatherer cultures, we aren't doing that till we're 15. My son is 30, and we're still writing tuition checks and rent checks! That seems paradoxical. Why would you set up a species so that there's this long period when they're not producing anything, and, worse than that, they're actually requiring all these resources simply to keep them alive? It's a distinctive, striking thing about humans. If you compare us to, say, chimpanzees, our closest primate relatives, we seem to have a lot of other adaptations designed to deal with that long period of immaturity.

We have pair bonding. We have males and females who are close and who take care of children together. Only 5% of all mammals have pair bonding. We have what anthropologists call alloparenting, which means that we have non-biological kin who are helping to take care of babies. And we have my own personal favorite, namely grandmothers. Another distinctive thing about our life history is that we have females who are living past menopause. In general, we live to our seventies, as opposed to chimps, who live to their fifties.

Not only do we have this long, extra period early in life, we have this long, extra period later in life. It's striking because when you look at lots of other animals—not just primates, not even just mammals but, say, birds and even insects—you see this relationship between how long a childhood a species has, and how smart, flexible, and good at learning they are as adults. There seems to be some connection between this life history, this long childhood, and the distinctive capacities that we have as adults for flexibility and learning.

Michael: Perhaps adult society is thinking, "Those babies are just there. They're not doing much." On the contrary, they are doing quite a lot. Explain your expression, "Bayesian babies."

Alison: One of the things that psychologists have said for a while is that people are bad at doing probability and statistics. It's true that adults are bad if you give them actual statistical problems. But it turns out that even eight-month-olds are extremely good at doing probability and statistics, and they can do pretty sophisticated kinds of Bayesian inference, but they do it unconsciously.

What we've been doing in my lab over the last 15 years or so is giving children problems to solve that from the child's perspective are just a problem, such as, "Look, here's this machine, and I'm putting blocks on it. Tell me how the machine works. Sometimes the machine lights up, sometimes it doesn't. What's happening? How can you make the machine work?" That's a simple, practical thing that babies and children are excited about doing. With that simple setup, you can show that children are doing sophisticated analyses of the data and ways of combining them.

In interesting experiments that we've recently done, the preschoolers are in some ways better than adults, in the sense that they take the data more into consideration. The adults seem to be designed to rely more heavily on what they already know. It takes a lot of new data to change an adult's mind. Whereas, for the children, who know less to begin with, they seem to be designed to pay attention to the data that's around them. That's the thing that's most important for them. The children seem to be able to do things like use conditional probabilities to infer causal structure from the time they're two or three years old, which is only one of the amazing things that have come out of work in developmental psychology over the last 30 years or so.

Michael: Some might be thinking, "Gosh, that's not the case for all kids." Children with less privileged upbringings don't have all the advantages. It's the nature/nurture issue.

Alison: One of the things we know—and again, this goes with the whole life history perspective—is that you can only have that period of exploration if you also have a protected, nurturing environment. There's at least some evidence with non-human animals that animals that are stressed early in life, for example, seem to mature more quickly. They are forced into that adult state more quickly than animals that are nurtured. It's important to say that nurturance means having people around you who love you and care for you. It doesn't mean having people who are putting you in mini-Harvard preschool, or going out and giving you flashcards.

In fact, there's some interesting recent studies that suggest that when children are in a pedagogical situation where they feel as if they're being taught, it narrows the range of options they can consider. It makes them explore less. We were curious about this, so we carried out a study on children in Head Start programs in Oakland and children growing up in low-income suburbs of Lima, Peru. We thought maybe these children would have more trouble with the causal inference tasks than the children in the middle-class preschools. What we discovered was, if anything, the opposite. Especially the children in Peru were doing incredibly well on the causal tests. With the children in Head Start, even though they did worse in formal IQ tests, for example, we were surprised by how good they were at solving these kinds of spontaneous learning tests—as good as or better than the middle-class kids.

Remember, from the kids' perspective, this isn't learning, it's not school, it's, "Here's a cool toy to play with," and they're trying to figure out how it works. But it's important to state that although the kids were low-income, they had parents who cared enough about them to make sure they got into Head Start programs or into schools in Peru. Kids need this kind of nurturant, supportive extended family environment; they are not going to do well in situations of stress, violence, isolation—situations in which many children in the United States, by the way, are growing up. But it isn't as if they need middle-class parents hovering over them and making sure they do their worksheets.

Michael: Why are you so passionate?

Alison: There are some professions where you do something because you think it's important abstractly, but you don't have an immediate sense of it being important every day. One of the nice things about working with kids is that it hits you over the head every time you see a three-year-old how smart, interesting, and open to the world they are.

One of the questions that people often ask is, "As an adult, how can you keep this open sense of exploration and possibility that children have?" Hanging out with children is an important part of that. Even though we give lip service to the idea that children are our future and children are important, if you're giving a talk to a room full of people and you say that you study children, you can see the eyes glazing over. That's not quite so true anymore, because people are starting to realize how important this early period is. But it's ironic that the way they realized it was because economists started telling them there were going to be good returns on investment. Whereas it was obvious to me from sitting in the room with three-year-olds.

One of the exciting things that's happening in the AI community is that people are starting to make systems that can learn. The real advances have all been in machine learning, but the people who are doing that work are starting to realize they're bumping up against the limits of the kinds of learning that machines have done so far. They're realizing that even a wonderful deep learning algorithm with enormous amounts of data can't do things that every three- or four-year-old can do. So, they're getting excited about talking to cognitive development people.

I'm teaching a course at Berkeley called Cognitive Development for Computer Scientists. The students—and, indeed, a lot of the faculty—are computer scientists who want to know how babies and young children are the best learners we know of in the world. If learning is going to turn out to be the key thing in AI, we should be looking at these kids. Again, there's this nice thing about having all these nerdy electrical engineering and computer sciences guys suddenly saying, "Gee, babies and children— they're cool and interesting!"

Michael: One great thing about play is you feel good. What are some of the benefits of childhood play?

Alison: Play is another one of those evolutionary paradoxical phenomena, because all animals play, not only humans—and it's a characteristic of young animals rather than older ones. Of course, the definition of play is that it's doing a bunch of things that don't have immediate benefits. Why is it that so many species spend so much time doing things just for fun? The thought is that the "fun" is a reward for this wide-ranging exploration.

The paradox, which I think people are familiar with, is sometimes if you're trying too hard to do something, it keeps you from doing it. Pulling back, exploring, and having fun makes you more effective in the long run, and play seems to serve that function in the animal kingdom. The kinds of play that we do reflect the functions we need as adults. For example, baby rats wrestle and fight. You can do an experiment with rats where you see the difference between ones that get to play when they're young and ones that don't. It isn't any one specific thing they do, it's how flexible and resilient they are, how good they are at changing, doing something different quickly in a new context. That seems to be the general story.

If you want to do one specific thing and do it well, the best thing is to train a system to do that one specific thing well. But if you want to be resilient, to be able to face a new problem that you've never seen before and do something intelligent about it, playing helps. There's some wonderful work by a roboticist called Hod Lipson. He was designing a robot that had a period to begin with when it messed around. It did silly

There is a connection between humans' long childhood and the distinctive capacities of human adults for flexibility and learning.

dances. It played with its own body. It turned out that the advantage of that period of play was that if you cut off the robot's leg, it could figure out how to walk even without the leg. A robot that was trained to walk could be good at walking, but if you changed the situation, if you cut off a leg or you put it in a new room, it would fall apart. Whereas this robot which had gotten the chance to play could adjust to a new situation. And of course, that's what we human beings are better at doing than anything else. That's our great evolutionary niche. We're the ones who are highly adapted or aware, because sometimes we live in the unknown unknowns. That's the environment that we do best in. And there have been more and more unknown unknowns as we've gone on in history.

Michael: Back to the Bayesian babies: Test, adjust, test, adjust. The younger we are, generally, that's easier. When we get older we don't test, adjust, test, adjust anymore. We come up with an idea and we stick with it. We don't adjust to new information.

Alison: As you can probably tell, I'm pro four-year-olds. I love that wild, unspoiled creative side. But the truth is that there's a genuine trade-off between that and the ability to make things happen. To some extent, if you want to make things happen, you have to ignore a lot of distractions. You can't readjust your strategy every time there's something new. The great challenge is how do you go back and forth between exploring, taking new information into account, and being focused enough to be able to do the thing that you want to do? From the perspective of neuroscience, there is a part of your brain that is designed to hold lots of different possibilities. But the trouble is, when you act, you don't get to do 30% of one possibility and 70% of another. You have to choose one and follow through.

The way that people solve this sometimes in computer science, the way evolutionary biology seems to have solved it, is by having alternating periods: a period of play and exploration, being protected from the immediate environment, and then a period of taking the things that you've learned in that play and exploration and putting them to use. Or sometimes a division of labor between different people with different personalities and different strengths and weaknesses—so, people who are good at general exploration and people who are good at making things happen.

Michael: The last time I was around a four-year-old a lot, it was my nephew. We used to go together to watch his older brother's T-ball games and I would say to him, "Hey, I'll give you a dollar if you run around the field." It was maybe three-quarters of a mile. This four-year-old boy would run around the field perhaps eight to ten times during the game to collect a dollar from me. Now he's a teen and an exceptional athlete, and we adults say, "It's natural." But I look back to the four-year-old, and I say, "You know what? That kid had a plan. Maybe he couldn't describe it. Maybe he didn't know exactly what it was, but that kid had a plan."

Alison: One of the things that's interesting is you can see all of these individual differences in what kinds of things different children think are fascinating, exciting, and worth exploring. You mentioned your nephew being a teenager; we've started working on the idea that adolescence may be a revived period of plasticity when this kind of possibility and exploration happens. The traditional picture of adolescence has been a negative one: how can we keep them from getting into terrible trouble all the time? But increasingly, there's more evidence that adolescents are actually exploring more.

I mentioned that we did these studies that showed that preschoolers were more exploratory than adults. Now, that was a physical problem about how to put blocks on a machine to make it go. But we also did it with a social problem: why is this person acting in the way they are? We discovered that the adolescents were actually the most flexible. The preschoolers were flexible, but got less flexible in school age. The adults weren't flexible in the way they thought about why someone could do what they did, but the adolescents were. The adolescents were paying most attention to the data rather than the priors, to put it in a Bayesian way, when the problem was about human action and social relationships. It seems as if that might be an extra burst of exploration that happens with teenagers.

Michael: When James Damore at Google was let go, he had a certain view about Google's diversity policies that he wrote down in a memo. Could you explain his perspective and your own perspective?

Alison: One of the fundamental questions that you come up against as a developmental psychologist is how much of anything we do is the result of nature or nurture, how much is the result of genes, and how much is the result of environment? A natural way of thinking about it is, okay, there's one set of forces—nature, genes, biology—and then there's this other set of forces—nurture, parents, environment, teaching, culture— and you could treat them as if they're a vector, and figure out how much of one force or another is shaping the way that people turn out. And then you could say, "35% of this is nature and 65% is nurture," or however the numbers would work out.

That's such a natural way of thinking about it. It's seductive. There are smart, popular psychologists who talk that way, but it's totally wrong from a scientific perspective. It's not even the wrong answer—it's the whole wrong way of asking the question. That's certainly true for nature and nurture, and especially for things like the sex differences that Damore was focusing on. It's the wrong categories.

There are lots of examples of this. If you look at actual development, what you see is that from the moment there's a fertilized egg, nature and nurture are interacting. Not only interacting, but interacting in complex, nonlinear, feedback-driven kinds of ways. It's not a good question to ask, "Are women naturally less suited to tech than men?" "Naturally" doesn't mean anything from a developmental perspective. Larry Summers famously got into trouble for making these kinds of arguments as an economist, and I always feel it's as if I went to him and said, "Larry, look, here's my idea about economics. We need to find the right price for things. And if we find the right price and we make sure that everyone is selling everything at the natural price for that particular commodity, then the economy will work well."

Now that's not even wrong. It's not even getting the most basic things about how economics works. Even though for many thousands of years, that was the natural way that people thought about economics and money. And it's kind of like that with the "Is gender nature or nurture?" kinds of disputes. It's not even the right category for thinking about the problem.

Michael: You're saying take a step back and think about this as a scientist, and then you're not left with such black-and-white answers.

Alison: It's not even a case of not black and white. Let me give you an example of one of the studies that I talked about in my column in *The Wall Street Journal* after the Damore thing came out. This is a neuroscience study, so one of the things that people talk about is, "Male brains and female brains are different." In fact, there are various kinds of brain measures and on average, you'll see a difference between men and women on particular measures, which led people to think, "There's a naturally male brain and a naturally female brain." But it turns out that if you look at the correlation among those features, there isn't any. Most people will score high in the male direction on some brain parts and high in the female direction on other brain parts.

Sometimes if you're trying too hard to do something, it keeps you from doing it.

The term that neuroscientists use is a "mosaic." Even though when you average together large numbers of people it might look as if there's a correlation, each individual person is going to produce a complicated mosaic of different kinds of features in different brain areas. The same thing's true about people's psychological capacities.

The other thing is that there's much more within-group variance than between-group variance. So even if there's a little bit of difference in the overlaps, there's much more difference among different women and different men than there is between men as a group and women as a group.

Even the physical fact of being biologically male or biologically female, you might say, "That's determined by your genes," but actually, there's a long, complicated bidirectional set of occurrences from the moment you have a particular set of chromosomes to the moment you end up with female or male genitalia, let alone a brain that has particular characteristics. It's taking something complicated and making it simple in a way that speaks to social categories rather than biology—in particular, it speaks to development.

Another important point to make is that people act as though if something's in your brain, it must be there innately and it must be genetic. That's not true either. Even if I took a whole bunch of adult men and women and discovered that their brains were different, that's what I'd expect given that their behaviors are different, given that their social status is different—of course their brains are going to be different. The question is, what happened from the time that they were a zygote that led to those differences later on?

Michael: Your perspective is a stark contrast to modern life where we take things and put them into partisan silos immediately. In reality, it's all so damn complicated.

Alison: There's a tension for scientists when we go out into the world at large; we can't tell the whole story in all its detail and complexity in 700 words in *The Wall Street Journal* or even an hour-long podcast. Are we oversimplifying? Can we represent the science in a good way? We don't have a choice. People are going to have beliefs and make decisions based on what they think the science is, whether the scientists are conveying it properly or not. So if we don't do it, somebody else will. In my field of developmental psychology, that's vivid. There's no foundation degree on parenting. Anybody who wants can write a book and say, "Look, if you do this to your children, then they're going to come out great and go to Harvard." There's nobody to stop that, except real developmental psychologists trying to say something about what the science says.

Michael: Have you done work on what we are starting to see with early tech in the hands of children? What are we learning, for good and bad?

Alison: This is one of the examples where everybody thinks they know the answer, apparently, including some of the big funders for Apple. Everyone is convinced that this is terrible and that screens are going to destroy children's minds and that we need to keep them away, and so on and so forth. It's amazing how deep the conviction is, given how completely lacking the data is. It takes scientists 15 years to do any kind of study, let alone try to figure out the long-term consequences of something like the iPhone that only launched 10 or so years ago, but it's starting to happen.

My take is, if you look at the big picture, adolescents and children have always been the ones who do the technological innovation. Whether that's putting a new design on a pot, or figuring out a new way to throw a spear, or having a train, or having a telegraph, they're always at the cutting edge of that kind of technological change.

Now, this time may be different from all the others, but it seems like every time change happens, the previous generation is convinced that the world is going to hell in a hand basket. For Socrates, for example, it was reading. He thought reading was a terrible idea. It was going to mean that nobody remembered anything anymore and people would think anything written in a book was true. He was right! People don't remember all of Homer anymore. People do tend to think that things that are written down are true. But on balance, we feel the advantages of writing and reading outweigh the disadvantages.

My guess is that's what's going to happen with the new technologies as well. We'll figure out how to deal with both the positive and the negative sides. The experience for the next generation, the children who have been doing this from the time they were two years old, is going to be different from the kind of disruptive, distracting experience that it is for us adults.

It might be that 20 years from now we're going to discover that this is finally the technology that's destroyed us all.

Michael: We can all call out disadvantages of new technology. But from the research standpoint and the ability to connect with people, and wanting to find any piece of information, especially for those people that have a curiosity, the tech gives you a head start. I don't know how any of us can say that's bad.

Alison: It's interesting if you look at any kind of technological innovation. Printing is an interesting one. There's a wonderful book about the French Revolution and the Ancien Régime, which points out that when printing first became widespread and cheap, the first thing that happened was the world was full of terrible scandal, libel, polemics, pornography, and all the kind of rubbish that you see on the internet now. That was what a lot of the first printed pamphlets were like. It took a while for things to sort themselves out and to figure out a way for people to handle this amazing new source of information. I don't think anyone would look back and say, "Oh, printing. That was a terrible idea. Being able to have books that were easy and cheap to produce, that was awful and led to the end of civilization as we know it."

My own personal examples are the telegraph and the train. The truth is that nothing technological that we've done in the last 100 years has had the same kind of impact that the telegraph and the train did. For thousands of years, the fastest you could go was the speed of a fast horse. Then suddenly, literally, information could travel at the speed of light. That was a gigantic transformation, and it had good effects and bad effects.

Now we look back and we think, "Isn't that quaint and sweet? How lovely to be riding on a train." People at the time were convinced that trains were going to completely destroy the world. In a way, they did—they destroyed the world of the 18th century. The new tech, in some ways, is going to destroy the world of the 20th century. It's going to be up to the next generation to build the world of the 21st century. One way I put it is the day before you were born is always Eden, and the day after your children are born is Mad Max. That seems to have been true for all of history.

Michael: A great line of yours that you've used many times, which I love, is, "What's it like to be a baby? Being in love in Paris for the first time after you've had three double espressos." Explain how that one came to be and what you mean.

Alison: One of the big philosophical questions that we can ask about babies—and I talk about this a lot in my second book, *The Philosophical Baby*—is what's it like to be a baby? What's consciousness like in babies? Philosophers, who didn't think much of babies for all those years, often said, "Babies don't have much consciousness." In fact, they used to do operations on young babies without anesthesia because they thought they didn't have feeling, or consciousness.

> The day before you were born is always Eden, and the day after your children are born is Mad Max.

It's a hard question to answer. How do you know that anybody has consciousness, let alone a baby? But when you look at the neuroscience and the cognitive science, it suggests that we may have a different kind of consciousness when we're babies. The way I like to put this is it's the difference between the kind of spotlight of consciousness we have as adults, where we pay attention to one thing and it's vivid and everything else around you goes dark, and thinking about the child's consciousness as being more like a lantern. It's more like something that's illuminating the whole world.

We know that chemicals in things like nicotine and caffeine have the effect of broader plasticity, leading to a brain that changes more easily. And we know that putting yourself in the position of a baby, like going to a new place, has the same kind of effect. Consciousness gets to be much more vivid and intense, even if your practical ability to get through the world is damaged. If you put all that together and being in a new state, in a new place, and having all these changes to your neurotransmitters that are making them more open and plastic, that sounds a lot like being in Paris for the first time after you've had a bunch of double espressos. As I point out, that is a wonderful way to be, but it does mean that you tend to wake up at three o'clock in the morning crying, which may be how it feels to be a baby.

CHAPTER 6

PHILIP TETLOCK

The Art of the Forecast

PHILIP TETLOCK is a Canadian-American political science writer and is currently the Annenberg University Professor at the University of Pennsylvania, where he is cross-appointed at the Wharton School and the School of Arts and Sciences.

Philip has published over 200 articles in peer-reviewed journals and has edited and written several books, including *Superforecasting: The Art and Science of Prediction*, *Expert Political Judgment: How Good Is It? How Can We Know?*, *Unmaking the West: What–if Scenarios that Rewrite World History*, and *Counterfactual Thought Experiments in World Politics*.

Michael note

Philip Tetlock is at the intersection of psychology, political science and organizational behavior. His book *Superforecasting: The Art and Science of Prediction* provides sound insight into probabilistic thinking—a must-have perspective in the modern world.

Michael Covel: I was thinking back to my days in grad school, and specifically the fall of 1992 and the rise of Bill Clinton. It was interesting that none of the main players would run against then President Bush, because his approval rating was so high. Into that vacuum walked an unknown governor from Arkansas, who was trying to boost his political resumé and had no thought of winning necessarily. But then a funny thing happened. How in the world could that have been predicted—could it have?

Philip Tetlock: Absolutely. It's so difficult to reconstruct our past days of ignorance. In *Superforecasting*, we talk about that *Saturday Night Live* episode in which the leading lights of the Democratic Party in 1991 bend over backwards to avoid the risk of being nominated to run against the invincible president, George Herbert Walker Bush.

Michael: You look back over time and it seems like this was all expected to happen, but it could have unfolded in a completely different manner. It's something that most people accept, but there's usually not much follow-up. We don't ever check to see what's happening. There are all these highly paid experts, but you have figured out through a lot of research that regular folks can beat the experts at their own game.

Philip: Essentially, that's right. The best forecasters are talented people, I don't want to downplay their credentials, but it is remarkable that the group of citizens we were able to recruit for the forecasting tournament sponsored by the U.S. intelligence community were able to beat U.S. intelligence analysts at their own game.

Michael: Why don't you start from the beginning of your process, and how you were able to get to the point where regular people could compete with or defeat people with unlimited funding?

Philip: This is a research project that never should have occurred if the most basic laws of bureaucracy had held. Bureaucracy 101 tells aspiring bureaucrats, never sponsor something that has the potential to be embarrassing and come back and bite you in the butt. The Intelligence Advanced Research Projects Activity (IARPA)—the research and development branch of the Office of Director of National Intelligence, which presides over that $50bn dollar bureaucracy—had the temerity to do that. It was as if Goliath took David aside and said, "Here's some money. Try to develop a good slingshot."

Michael: Was there a side of you that already knew your work was going to present results they might not like?

Philip: It was a formal competition. IARPA launched it in 2010. A lot of universities and consulting firms competed for the money. My wife and collaborator Barb Mellers and I were still at Berkeley at the time. We put together a proposal that was a joint Berkeley–Penn proposal, because we moved to the University of Pennsylvania at the end of 2010. We were in competition with major research universities and consulting operations. For various reasons, the coalition of researchers we put together, which we

It's so difficult to reconstruct our past days of ignorance.

called the Good Judgment Project, was successful in recruiting good forecasters, was successful in developing methods of training them and teaming them, was successful in developing algorithms that distilled wisdom from the crowd—and the net result was that the Good Judgment Project prevailed in the competition. It won so decisively in the first two years that essentially IARPA terminated the other teams, let us poach the best talent, and put us in direct competition with a prediction market and internal benchmarks they had.

Michael: In the long run, your type of work is going to challenge many people who are used to making predictions with no one checking them.

Philip: It's going to be a long-term change. We're talking about changing some basic practices in the political world. We're going to see more and more quantification of uncertainty in advanced tech companies and advanced sectors in the most sophisticated government agencies. It's even going to extend beyond domains where we already do it with big data into domains that were previously thought to be the exclusive preserve of soft, subjective human judgment, which will increasingly be pressured to be more explicit and to demonstrate that it is value added. It's not enough to say you're a pundit. Someday, it will be the case that if you talk about things being a distinct possibility or this could happen or might happen or may happen, people will say, "You're essentially saying nothing."

Michael: Let me go to an example that a lot of people can relate to. The Iraq War in 2003, the weapons of mass destruction (WMD) issue—usually it's a highly partisan thing, but what's interesting is that George Bush and Hillary Clinton were on the same side of the fence, which tells me that behind the scenes, the intelligence agencies were delivering something that let two partisan groups believe the same result. Both sides of the fence, except for people like perhaps Barack Obama and Bernie Sanders, believed WMDs were there.

Philip: The Iraq WMD case is an important one because I don't think the research project, or even the tournaments, would've happened had the intelligence community not made so massive an error. When the director of the Central Intelligence Agency tells the president of the United States and other principals that he thinks it's a slam dunk there are WMDs—when the most senior officials in the intelligence community use terminology like that in a situation where there is at least some degree of ambiguity—that's telling. When you look back at the information available to key policy makers and intelligence agencies around the world, the preponderance of opinion was that Saddam was up to something—that he was violating UN sanctions. There was no smoking gun, but there was a lot of circumstantial evidence. Saddam encouraged the impression that he had something, perhaps because he didn't want to appear to be weak, so he was actually making it easier for the hard-liners who ultimately destroyed him, which is another ironic subtext to all this.

It's not enough to say you're a pundit.

What probability would a perfect information processor have assigned to Saddam having WMDs in Iraq before the invasion? We know it's not 1.0, but we also know it's not zero. If you were to construct some kind of weighted average of all the sophisticated observers and their perspectives on Iraqi WMD, you would find that the probability of Iraq having something, given the information they had then, would've been higher than 50% and certainly less than 100%. So, it's somewhere in between. Let's say it was 75%. Would the US Congress have voted to approve the use of force if they had thought the probability was as low as 75% as opposed to a slam dunk? It's a good possibility they would not have, and I think world history would've unfolded quite differently.

Michael: How did the experts get into a position to make such a statement? Is that where the politics took over, that instead of coming out with the probabilistic estimate they came out with the political slam dunk?

Philip: It's difficult to reconstruct. Robert Jervis at Columbia University has written an interesting postmortem of the WMD intelligence analysis. Part of the problem was that this was happening in the aftermath of 9/11, and nobody wanted to make a false negative mistake. Within two years of having failed to warn adequately against the risk of Al-Qaeda's attacks, two big false negative errors in a row would be politically damaging. If you're going to make an error in the blame game culture of Washington DC, make sure it's not the same type of error you made last time.

Michael: The talking heads are smart people. They present themselves well, but they don't put these probabilistic weights on their predictions. And even if they did admit they had a chance of only being 60% right, it means they could be 40% wrong. If we start to get closer to this probabilistic way of thinking in public discourse, where does that leave us? As a society, dealing with uncertainty becomes a real educational process.

Philip: That's absolutely right. The accuracy of probability estimates of single events is inherently indeterminate, as long as the forecaster is not so foolish as to say zero and the event happens, or 1.0 and the event does not happen. Otherwise, the forecaster can always argue that something unlikely happened when they appear to be on the wrong side of maybe. This means we're going to have to start thinking about forecasting and judgment the way we think about sports. We have to be at least as sophisticated about this as we are in thinking about, say, the batting averages of players in major league baseball, or the free throw percentages of basketball players, and so forth. It's a probabilistic thing.

You don't draw the inference that a forecaster is bad simply because they were on the wrong side of maybe on a particular call. It's tempting to do that. We talk in *Superforecasting* about how one of the most sophisticated journalists in the United States, David Leonhardt, who created "The

You don't draw the inference that a forecaster is bad simply because they were on the wrong side of maybe on a particular call.

Upshot" section of *The New York Times*, wrote after the Supreme Court narrowly upheld Obamacare in 2011 that the prediction markets had been predicting a 75% probability the Supreme Court would overturn the law, and he said quite categorically the prediction markets got it wrong.

Now, when the markets say a 75% chance, that means there's a 25% chance it's not going to happen. How much confidence should you lose in those prediction markets when you learn that they put a 75% chance on something that didn't happen? Should you throw them all together and say, "Huh, these guys are clueless. I'm not going to pay attention to them anymore"? Or should you say, "Well, these prediction markets have made hundreds of predictions on hundreds of topics over several years, and we know that on average when they say 75% likelihood, things do happen about 75% of the time, so this market appears to be pretty well-calibrated"?

Now, is it good news for the credibility of the market that they're on the wrong side of maybe on this call? No. You should lose a little bit of confidence in them, but how much should you lose? Let's say you thought there was a 90% chance that markets were great beforehand, and now you learn that they're on the wrong side of maybe on the Supreme Court call. How much should you move downward from 90%? Maybe 88%, 89%. You surely shouldn't go down to zero.

Michael: You bring up the use of probability statistics in sports. When I think about Wall Street, so many traders are playing a game that never stops. It isn't necessarily about your winning percentage or your losing percentage, it's whether you have a positive mathematical edge that you can bet on. And that takes it a step further than looking at percentage accuracy, which might be great for the weather, but for serious parts of life it opens up the question of betting and finding a positive mathematical expectation.

Philip: For sure. It's easy to convince people in finance that there's an advantage in becoming more accurate in your assessments of uncertainty. We talked with Aaron Brown, the chief risk officer of AQR, the big hedge fund. Aaron also happens to be a serious poker player, and he made the observation that you can tell the difference between a world-class poker player and a talented amateur because the world-class players are better at distinguishing 60/40 bets from 40/60 bets. They know it in their bones that it helps to be granular. In finance it's a pretty easy sell, because there are options and you can back out quite readily—for example, the implied probabilities that oil's going to bill above or below some threshold price—because you're buying an option to purchase things at a designated price.

Michael: You bring up an interesting example in *Superforecasting* of Robert Rubin, who was at Goldman Sachs. He worked under Clinton. A great probabilistic thinker, and many loved him and thought he did a fantastic job during the late 1990s, and then the 2008 crash comes and he's suddenly a terrible, terrible guy.

Philip: Probability guys aren't always right, just as the prediction markets weren't right about Obamacare. But they tend to be pretty well-calibrated, which means that if you knew nothing else, you would be wise to listen quite carefully to what they have to say.

Michael: The 2008 crisis was interesting, because if you look at comments in 2005, 2006, 2007, even early 2008, people did not foresee problems with real estate. But then, a funny thing happened. When the S&P started to tick down over the course of 2008, that price action seemed to be a heuristic for something. One of the things superforecasters are looking for are sources of aggregated data—it might be betting on sports, looking at Las Vegas odds, going to the various sports books, but it's also the price action in markets.

Philip: That's right. Superforecasters recognize that there's valuable information lying around in the world that's been pre-processed for them, so they don't have to reinvent the wheel when they approach many problems. Now, the stock market is far from a reliable indicator of whether there's going to be a major economic recession. Paul Samuelson famously joked that it's predicted nine of the last five recessions, but that doesn't mean the stock market is a zero predictor. Superforecasters are acutely aware of the wisdom of the crowd—they're also aware of the potential madness of the crowd. They approach these things somewhat wearily, but a good wisdom of the crowd indicator is London bookie odds on the latest prediction market results, so if they knew nothing else but that, they would probably want that to be their starting prediction.

Michael: A brief excerpt from your work: "Researchers have found that merely asking people to assume their initial judgment is wrong, to seriously consider why that might be, and then make another judgment, produces a second estimate which, when combined with the first, improves accuracy almost as much as getting a second estimate from another person." This isn't intuitive.

Philip: It's not intuitive, but we talk to ourselves all the time. We know that there are quite often conflicting opinions in our own heads. It's not as strange as it sounds to ask somebody to offer two separate estimates.

Michael: Another aspect that you talk about in your work—and I believe this starts with Daniel Kahneman, who I know you're quite fond of—is the idea of the inside/outside distinction and how that plays into the superforecasting technique and training.

Philip: One of the bigger advantages that superforecasters have over regular forecasters is their tendency to start with the outside view and work into the inside slowly, rather than start with the inside view and rarely consider the outside view. In the forecasting tournament, our forecasters were asked an extraordinarily diverse range of questions about Sino-Japanese clashes in the East China Sea, Greece leaving the eurozone, Ebola, Arctic sea ice—all over the place. No forecaster, super or regular, is going to be an expert on anything more than a tiny fraction of the questions posed, because they're so heterogeneous. This is putting a premium on mental agility.

> Superforecasters recognize there's valuable information lying around in the world that's been pre-processed for them.

Let's say, for the sake of argument, you're in the tournament and someone asks you a question about whether a particular African dictator is likely to remain in power for another year, and you can barely spot the country on a map, still less say anything intelligent about who the dictator is. You know almost nothing as your starting position for the forecasting problem. If you're a superforecaster, you don't know nothing, you know something. They're able to extract information quickly. And there is a kernel to that question, which is that dictators tend to be sticky. Once a dictator has been in power for a certain period, the likelihood of that dictator making it another year is extremely high. That doesn't mean you're going to say, "Oh, there's a 0.95 likelihood of this particular dictator remaining in power," but it does mean that your initial estimate is going to be that there's a high probability of dictator survival. Then you're going to adjust from that in response to new evidence about the particulars, the inside view of that situation; so if you discover that this dictator is 91 years old and has advanced prostate cancer, you're going to say, "Hmm, I'm going to downplay it." And if you discover there's intense fighting in the suburbs of the capital between rival military units, again, you're going to adjust. You're going to start with a reasonable base rate judgment, and then you're going to adjust in response to the particulars. Most people jump into the particulars right away, and that is not a good idea if you want to get a good Brier score, which is the accuracy measure we used.

> Many people who are not currently superforecasters could become superforecasters if they were so inclined.

Michael: So many of us get fixated on the why, but the superforecasters are more about the how. Their approach is data-driven, breaking things up into pieces.

Philip: This distinction between how and why thinking is an important one. We talk about how superforecasters are less likely, for example, to believe in fate than regular forecasters or indeed most citizens. There's an interesting body of psychological work that suggests that when you remind people of all the flukey circumstances that led them to make an important decision in their lives—how they came to be married to a particular person or wind up living in a particular city or doing a particular job—when you highlight all of the no probability events surrounding those outcomes, the effect for most people is to persuade them that the event in question was meant to be. That's even true for lottery winners, for example. When they win, they don't think it was a fluke. They often infuse it with some deeper metaphysical significance.

Superforecasters don't think that way. They think, "Well, things happen." Someone had to win. Improbable things do sometimes happen. It is unlikely that unlikely things will never happen. It would violate the laws of probability. So, superforecasters are that way. It's a rather unromantic worldview. It means that the superforecaster might look at their spouse and say, "Well, I guess I could have wound up with any one of 433,000 other spouses, but we wound up together, and let's make the best of it."

Michael: What's interesting about your work is that you're not attempting to tell people, "Hey, this is about meaning," or, "This is about happiness." You're explaining how you can start to forecast and predict social phenomena with greater accuracy than you might expect and greater accuracy than perhaps extremely well-paid experts. But you're not attempting to tell people this is the way the world is and you should feel this way. You're saying, "Here's the data. Take it or leave it."

Philip: That's exactly right.

Michael: Are there people who you respect, who you've worked with, such as Daniel Kahneman or Nassim Taleb, who might have some criticism of the notion of superforecasting?

Philip: These are matters of degree more than kind. Nassim Taleb puts more emphasis on radical unpredictability of high-impact events like so-called black swans. I think we agree that extremely high-impact, low-probability events can have a huge impact on history—this is manifestly true. We prefer to think of there being a continuum from white swans to light-gray swans to dark-gray swans to black swans. We think it's useful to ask how good can early warning and early opportunity indicators be for swans of varying degrees of grayness. It's not a dichotomy between white and black swans.

So, I think we see greater value in investing energy in improving the accuracy probability judgments, whereas I think Nassim Taleb in his most recent book on anti-fragility sees greater value in investing in contingency plans to cope with black swans. It's a different emphasis. I don't see how you can make contingency plans without also attaching probabilities to scenarios, so I don't think there's any avoiding probabilities. You can try to cover them up, but I don't think it's wise to try to do that. So, there is a difference of opinion there.

The differences with Danny are even slighter. They have to do with the degree to which he is less optimistic than we are about the feasibility of finding better forecasters who will be consistently better, of training them to be consistently better, of teaming them, of finding algorithms that prove to be consistently better. I don't think he denies that there's some potential for improvement. He's probably a little more pessimistic than we are about the magnitude of the potential, but these are subtle differences, and I think each of us is willing to move in response to evidence. Inevitably, we are going to run into low predictability years in which the best forecasters are hard-pressed to do any better than dart-throwing chimpanzees.

Michael: Prediction is not certainty. Forecasting is not certainty. This is getting back to the whole theme of this conversation, which is about developing and maintaining a probabilistic mindset.

Philip: Imagine you're with a superforecaster in a bar and conversation turns to global warming and someone says to the superforecaster, "Hey, do you believe in global warming?" Your typical superforecaster would look at that as a stupid question for two major reasons. First, global warming is ill-defined. Does it mean the temperature of the earth will be 3.6 degrees centigrade warmer in 2100 than it was, say, in the average of the 20th century? What exactly is the threshold for global warming? Is it two degrees centigrade? One degree? Superforecasters don't like vague verbiage when it comes to the outcomes of forecast. They also don't like vague verbiage when it comes to things like using distinct possibility as opposed to numbers. And the second reason is, they don't like saying, "Do you believe?" as though your beliefs are something like a light switch that can go off and on, zero or one, because they distinguish many degrees of uncertainty. The right way to ask the question of a superforecaster would be, "To what degree do you believe that the average surface temperature of the earth in 2100 will fall into the following temperature band differentials?"

That's not exactly casual barroom conversation. It's not exactly a thing that even political ideologues can get all heated up about. It becomes a pretty technical matter of let's sit down at the table, try to calculate and go through the time series, go through the causal models, go through the climate models and look at how accurate they have been, look at what the critiques are, and reach a reasoned judgment about the likelihoods.

Probability estimation of messy, real-world events is a skill that can be cultivated.

Now, you're not going to mobilize the political will to do something about climate change if you are saying, "Well, I think the probability based on the 2015 temperature spike has moved from 0.86 to 0.88 of a temperature in 2100 being 1.3 degrees centigrade or higher." People's eyes start to glaze over. All the fun of politics seems to be drained out, all the opportunities to denounce the other side for being stupid or gullible or rigid—all the fun stuff in political psychology.

Michael: The math can get a little more advanced, but the process in simple form is: try, fail, analyze, adjust, try again. This is how we all learn as kids, but something happens to us when become adults. We forget this whole skepticism in an attempt to have some scientific principles in our lives.

Philip: That's because a lot of these questions, like "Do you believe in climate change?" or "Do you support X or Y or Z?" are not asking you for a considered probabilistic judgment about the consequences of going down one policy path or another. They're asking you, "What political tribe do you belong to? Are you one of us or are you one of them?" And that's a game that superforecasters tend not to play. It is interesting that superforecasters' backgrounds are quite heterogeneous—they're diverse, but there is over-representation among people who are accustomed to thinking about complex problems in ways that decompose them into tractable components, such as software people, financial analysts, and some political risk analysts as well.

Michael: Do you see the superforecasters as different kinds of people, or as people who do different kinds of things, which is ultimately a nature versus nurture question?

Philip: That is one of the key questions. It's both. It's not true that anyone could be a superforecaster—there are certain cognitive and motivational prerequisites. A surprising number of people could improve their probability estimation skills quite a bit if they followed the guidelines in *Superforecasting*, so there is a lot of room for improvement for a lot of people. Certainly, many people who are not currently superforecasters could become superforecasters if they were so inclined.

Here's the core of it. I'm sometimes asked, "How could these amateurs have beaten intelligence analysts?" I don't think it's because the amateurs were more intelligent than intelligence analysts, and I certainly don't think it's because they had more political knowledge. It's because the superforecasters believe that probability estimation of messy, real-world events is a skill that can be cultivated and is worth cultivating, and they took a shot at it. They invested effort. It doesn't matter how high your IQ is or how much political knowledge you have or how exalted a status you have as a political pundit. If you're not going to take seriously the challenges of probability estimation, you're never going to get better at it. You don't learn to distinguish 60/40 bets from 40/60 bets by using vague verbiage forecasting like, "I think there's a distinct possibility of X." The only way is by making your judgments explicit, getting feedback, and learning.

Michael: Probabilistic thinking is not necessarily new, but you are right there at the frontline of getting people to look at it in a different way with some great examples. It's quite fun, isn't it?

Philip: It's fun. I started the work before Gorbachev became general secretary of the Communist Party of the Soviet Union, and the experts then weren't able to predict that, but everybody could explain it after the fact. It doesn't seem to matter how high the stakes are, the thinking is equally sloppy and contentious and self-serving. So, I see this as an important part of human progress, of moving the enlightenment agenda forward. When people look back 400 years from now on how primitively we conducted political debates, they won't judge us any more charitably than we judge the people who ran the Salem witch trials.

CHAPTER 7

ANNIE DUKE

PART 1
Teaching the World to Think Probabilistically

ANNIE DUKE is an author, corporate speaker, and consultant in the decision-making space. As a former professional poker player, Annie won more than $4 million in tournament poker before retiring from the game in 2012. Her books include *Quit: The power of knowing when to walk away*, *How to Decide: Simple tools for making better choices*, *Thinking in Bets: Making smarter decisions when you don't have all the facts*, and four guides to playing poker.

Michael note

Annie Duke and I talk psychology, expected value, loss aversion, and decision-making. We also discuss the parallels between her world of poker and the trading and investing world. The crossover is tight.

Michael Covel: I have to tell a quick story about why we're talking today. Sometime in 2007, I was in Macau, China, on a ferry going back to Hong Kong. I heard a group of people ask a guy what he did for a living. I caught wind that he was involved in ESPN, in poker programming. I tracked him down at customs in Hong Kong. I said, "Listen, I'm doing this film. I'm talking to all these traders, all these investors. They keep talking about these connections to poker in their investing mindset. You've got to help me. I need to land some people in the poker world." And that was how I ended up in the house of a very nice, tall guy in Las Vegas, who gave me some great understandings about psychology and odds—a tall guy who I think you know.

Annie Duke: That sounds like my brother, Howard Lederer.

Michael: Exactly. And the guy that I talked to was Matt Marantz. It was completely random that I found this guy on a ferry coming back from Macau to Hong Kong. That was how I was able, all these years later, to send you a little email and say, "Hey, by the way, I met your brother." It's a small world.

I want to ask you, as someone who's well known for poker but also pursued a PhD in psychology, what started your odds thinking? Was it even before playing poker that you started to think in terms of odds?

Annie: That's interesting, because you're asking me to recall something, and one of the things I think about a lot actually is how bad our memories are. It's difficult once you know something to recall when you didn't know it. I have spent so much of my life thinking about things as probabilistic that now, if you ask me, I'll give you some kind of answer like, "Well, I imagine when I was seven, I didn't think that way." And I know that when I was in my 20s, I was thinking that way. We were playing cards and games all the time, so those concepts of chance and volatility were pretty prominent in our everyday activities. It's hard for me to go back and say, "Well, when exactly did that happen?" As humans, we're incredibly bad at that. Once we have a belief, we sort of think that we believed that way all the time.

Michael: Do you look at things all day and go, "Oh, 18.5%"?

Annie: Yes, pretty much. It's incredibly important to think that way. If you're going to be a good decision maker you have to be thinking probabilistically, because you have lots of alternatives in front of you all the time. One branch of that tree is not 100%, even though it might feel that way, because what people generally mean when they say, "Oh, that's 100%," is that it's highly likely.

Let's say you think something's 80%—the tendency is to round up to 100%, which stops you from looking at the other 20%. So, when you think that something's going to happen the majority of the time, that prevents you from considering other alternatives. When you explore those alternatives, you can come up with some pretty creative solutions, and sometimes you figure out that the thing that you thought was 80% was not actually 80%, because when you go down those other branches of the tree, you realize some new things.

To be a good decision maker, you have to think probabilistically.

The other thing that happens—which in some ways might be worse—is that when it doesn't work out, so by definition it wasn't 100%, you assume you were wrong instead of having explored in advance the possibility that it was 80%, and 20% of the time other stuff was going to happen. So, you're much more likely to change your behavior in a way that's actually not productive.

This is something that I trained my kids in, because I think it's extremely important. When they say things like, "I'm 100% to get the job. I went into the interview and I did so great and I'm 100% to get it," I'll try to get them to think more clearly about what their percentages are. When my son was going in for his driving test, he declared 100% on passing it. And I got him to think a little bit better about, well, what do you think are the chances? He actually didn't pass it on first try.

Michael: I'm thinking back to the first time that I was exposed to the concept of mathematical expectation inside of trading. It was the light bulb moment. From the poker perspective, was that the moment you saw that this was what the top players were doing, and having that edge was so critical?

Annie: I had an advantage coming into poker because my PhD work was in science. We were thinking about expectancy all the time. In that case, you're thinking about p-values, which have to do with confidence intervals. Different sciences have different p-values that they allow. In psychology, generally, a 5% margin of error is okay; in physics, you'd want it to be much less than 1% before you'd have any confidence. That idea of confidence intervals, and different sciences demanding different levels of confidence before you'd accept a result, was already in my thinking.

I went into poker with that mindset, but it is something that absolutely separates out the top thinkers from everybody else—this idea of expectancy and thinking about things in terms of expected value over time.

What's interesting is, what do good luck and bad luck mean? I feel like for traders, good luck and bad luck mean something specific. As an example, if you're laying me 2-to-1 on a coin flip and I lose the first time, I wouldn't call that bad luck, right? I had positive expectancy there, but I haven't run enough iterations to realize the gain yet. But if you're laying me 2-to-1 on a coin flip, and we flip 50 times, and I somehow manage to lose, I would consider that unlucky because now I've gone against expectancy, and I've certainly run enough iterations that are way out at the tails.

> **Thinking about things in terms of expected value over time—expectancy—separates top thinkers from everybody else.**

But colloquially, the way most people use these terms in everyday life is bad luck is a bad thing happened, and good luck is a good thing happened. And even if they get past that, they think about things as 50/50, right? So, if you're above 50% and it doesn't work out, that's bad luck. And if you're below 50% and it does work out, then it's good luck. But most people don't get beyond that step. And so, in terms of luck versus skill, how deep into the thinking about expectancy are you getting?

Michael: That also brings us to process versus outcome. People get this fixation on outcome, whereas they should be turning it on its head and saying, "Hold on, what's our process?"

Annie: That's incredibly important for several reasons. When you focus on outcome instead of process, you actually reduce innovation in your company, and that's because innovation requires failure. Innovation requires a lot of bad outcomes because innovation is high volatility. You know that you're going for a big win, but you're going to have a lot of losses along the way. If you, as a manager of human resources, are outcome-focused, you'll create in the people that are working for you a motivation to achieve a lot of wins, a lot of good outcomes, but that reduces your expectancy. So, you have to tease those two things out. If what you're trying to do is book the biggest number of wins that you can, that does not mean that you're maximizing expectancy, and often, you're actually in some ways minimizing it.

You can think about a poker analogy where what would happen if my goal was simply to win a lot? I would go in and play, and any time that I got to above zero, I would quit the game so that I could mark the win down in my books. If I happened to win the first hand, I would quit because I'm not going to risk losing that win. I'm going to mark it down, and I'm going to leave.

Now you can see right away how that's not a winning strategy. Because what happens when I lose the first hand again? Now, I'm winning, but my losses there are going to be much bigger than my wins because I'm taking a lot of small wins. So, I could actually look over the month and say, "Look, I played 20 days," and I could win 16 of them, and still end up either losing for the month or maybe winning a small amount where I wasn't actually maximizing the amount of time that I was playing at the table in some sort of positive expectancy situation.

You can see that, for example, in sales, where people are closing sales at a much lower number than they could actually be getting, to be able to say, "I closed this many people this month." They would, for example, be sitting in a zone which was incredibly far from ever breaking a deal in order to make sure that they were closing the sales. That's leaving a tremendous amount of money on the table. If you never ever break a deal, you have to know that you're doing something wrong.

You can see how a start-up can come in and beat a large company. How does an Apple come in and completely crush an IBM, when an IBM can afford all of the talent, they have the market, they've got the eyeballs, they've got the consumers, they've got all of that? In a large sense, it comes down to this question of how outcome-focused you are. In a start-up environment, failure is expected because you're trying to do something incredibly high volatility, so you can get incredibly big innovation. In a large company like IBM where people are having to answer usually in some kind of quarterly fashion, you're not going to get a lot of failures.

It's going to be about all of these small wins and you're going to lose the innovative side of the business.

The incredibly important thing about being outcome blind is that it allows people to focus on good process, which actually fosters innovation. The other problem with focusing on outcomes is that you tend to change course too quickly. A bad outcome does not necessarily mean a bad decision process.

Michael: As you brought up tech and you talk about bad outcomes, I thought there was a different way to look at it as well. If I think about all the venture capitalists out on Sand Hill Road in Palo Alto, they're saying, "We know we're going to fund 20 start-ups, but we also know there's going to be a high degree of failure." And so the one big winner will pay for those 19 losers.

Annie: That relates to something that I teach in poker, and then expand out to teaching everywhere else, which is that people think far too hard when they're playing poker about whether they have the best hand. I try to tell them that what you should be thinking about is whether you can win the hand enough of the time. That's an important distinction. I'm not going to think too hard about whether I can get to 100% on whether I have the best hand. What I'm going to think about instead is can I win the hand enough of the time for the return that I'm getting?

For example, there's a form of poker called limit poker where the pricing situation can get very big. By the end of the hand, you can be in these 10-to-1 situations where for every dollar I bet, I'm going to win $10. And I say to people, I don't spend much time thinking hard about whether I have the best hand in that spot, because if I have the best hand 10% of the time, I'm winning a lot of money. And built into that is that I can lose nine times and that's okay, because if I win the hand 10% of the time, over the long run, my bank account's going to grow because I'm getting 10-to-1 on the investment for my dollar. I could sit there and think for a long time, but 90% of the time I'm allowed to be wrong and still make money. Instead, I shift my thinking to, is there a chance that I can win this hand? And if my answer is yes, I don't think past that point, I go ahead and invest it.

That's how venture capitalists are thinking as well, right? I know that when tech companies win, they win because they're like Uber or Angry Birds. I don't have to think too hard about whether this particular company that I'm investing in is going to win. I have to think about how often I need it to win in order for me to be profitable from the kinds of decisions that I'm making. They could make a decision that they think the company's going to succeed 25% of the time, and they're totally fine investing in that. That means 75% of the time that company's going to fail, but that's totally fine with them. They just need to get to 25% and they're okay.

Michael: Many people aren't familiar with this type of thinking. They don't see that your winners are going to be much larger even though the percentage is lower. They get fixated on this percent winning, and the percent winning doesn't tell you anything by itself.

Annie: Exactly. That's outcome dependency. Because obviously, part of the process is thinking about your return on investment. People say to me, "Well, I try to make sure that I win when I'm playing 90% of the time." And I'm like, "I don't even know what that means." I don't understand that thinking.

I've done seminars with people who are firmly intermediate players who have been playing for a long time. They're not necessarily professionals, but they are avid recreational players. They're also willing to spend a lot of money to come to a seminar with me. And we would sit down at tables and there'd be an instructor at each table, and they'd be playing cards, and I'd be deconstructing the hands for them. And I would always start off asking them a question such as, how much money is in that pot, and they'd look at me like, "What?" And then I would tell them, and they'd say, "How do you even know that?" I would say, "Well, there's five people in the pot. I announced that. Everybody got $150 in before the flop, so there's at least $750 in there." And then there's some antes and blinds which you can kind of estimate out or you can come up with the exact number if you want to work that hard. That's fine.

And I'd say, "But how can you possibly determine whether you should bet or call if you're not tracking what's in the pot?" Because in poker, the pot's the market. It's telling you what your return on investment is. If I know there's $750-plus in the pot, and you now bet $300 at me, now I know there's about $1,100 in the pot, and I have to call $300 to win that, so I'm getting a little over 3.5-to-1. That means if I'm winning 25% of the time, I'm definitely in profit.

If you're not doing that stuff, what you're doing is tracking the percentage that you win, but not understanding that actually determines whether you're winning or losing. I try to explain to people that I can set up situations where you're winning 60% of the time and you're losing to it. And I can set up situations where you're winning 10% of the time and you're winning to it, because the percentage of times that you're winning is only relevant in relation to what you're getting in return.

Michael: Daniel Kahneman. Obviously, he's become extremely well known—a Nobel Prize winner. If I look at what he's done, it's helped the trading world to have a behavioral understanding of what people are doing in terms of their betting strategy, their trading strategy, and their investing strategy. It's a dense subject, but there's little things we can break apart, like the disposition effect. People sell their winners and hold on to their losers. But the thing I like that you've taken from poker is the concept of tilt. Could you explain that from your perspective and how you are bringing that out beyond the poker world?

Annie: That's a good question because it's something that is underappreciated. I haven't played poker for over three years now. What I do instead is I go talk to people in all sorts of different areas, a lot of finance, a lot of human resources, and sales groups. I've done a lot of work in the energy sector recently, which tilt applies to right now. In the way that we process information, we come to conclusions in the way we remember things and the way we imagine things. Doesn't matter what industry you're in, the same concepts are going to apply. What I think about is not specific to poker, it's specific to the way that the human brain works.

The reason why poker's a good place to be looking at this stuff is because game theory, which is decision-making under conditions of uncertainty over time, happens to be a good definition of the game of poker. This is not accidental because John von Neumann, the father of game theory, modeled his original thinking on the game of poker. He was an avid gambler, and he understood the difference between a game

When people
are looking for
places to invest,
they tend to look
for consistency,
which is exactly
where they
shouldn't be
looking.

like poker and chess, which is to do with uncertainty, and the uncertainty comes from two places: hidden information and volatility.

The question is, what happens to people when they're making decisions under those conditions? Hidden information and volatility combined create a problem, which is that you don't know what's in your control and what's out of your control because you don't have perfect information. If I lose to you at chess, I know exactly why I lost, right? We can go back and analyze the situation. I can't shift it off to luck. If we come up with a game that has complete information but volatility, like backgammon where you have the dice, people can pawn it off to rolling poorly. Even if they lose over time, they can say, "I rolled below average." Obviously, in poker, you have the deal of the cards.

When you focus on outcome instead of process, you reduce innovation in your company.

Now, what happens to poker players is when they lose a hand where they were sure that there was positive expectancy, or a couple of hands in a row, the ball goes against them—they proceeded, they got unlucky, they will go on tilt. Tilt essentially means I'm so emotionally distressed by something that has happened to me recently, most likely something that I perceived to not have been in my control, that I will now make terrible decisions going forward because I'm in an incredibly hot state, and my limbic system is totally lit up, and my frontal lobe has now completely shut down, and I'm ruminating on how unlucky I am and how I never win at anything, and now I do all sorts of ridiculous things going forward because of that. And we have wrapped that up into a nice little one-word thing called tilt. It's an important concept to poker players.

The reason people don't think about tilt applying out that much is because people only consider one particular type of tilt, which I term extroverted tilt, which means people kind of go crazy. They'll increase the volatility of their game in an attempt to get their money back, so they get into a losing position. When you give people a low volatility choice versus a high volatility choice, on the winning side, they always take the low volatility choice, because if they were to lose to the volatility, they would frame it as a loss. You can take $100, or you can roll the dice and half the time you'll get zero and half the time you'll get $200. Everybody takes the $100 because they would frame the downside as a loss, whereas on the losing side, they seek out volatility. You're going to have to pay $100, say, for a parking ticket, or you can roll the dice, and sometimes you'll pay zero and sometimes you'll pay $200. Obviously, the expected value there is the same either way, but on the winning side, they say, "No, I don't want to roll the dice," and on the losing side, they say, "Yes, I do indeed want to roll the dice," because they've already booked it as a loss, so if they win to the volatility, now they get a chance to book it as a win.

That's exactly what poker players are doing when they get into these losing positions and they seek out volatility. They also say things like, "If you can't beat them, join them." They decide, "Oh, that guy beat me with such a bad hand, I'll start playing bad hands too, and I'll show them." And I think there's a little schadenfreude that gets in there too: "Oh, when I get to turn over the bad hand on them, they'll feel bad too, and then I'll be right with the world."

Michael: What I like about the word tilt is that it brings everything down to this self-awareness. It seems in the poker world a significant number of people understand this emotional out-of-control state can result, whereas I don't see that type of phraseology in investing or trading.

Annie: Part of the reason is that in poker you're making these decisions so quickly that it comes out in a way that you can see it so well. But one thing that people don't think about much in poker—which I think about a lot—is once you get out of the losing position, there's all this work to be done on the pain of paying, which is hard for us. We do a lot to avoid it, but when you have a strong memory of the pain of paying, what will happen is you will get this other kind of tilt that is not a short-term problem—it's long term.

If you could choose between one or the other, you would take the short-term problem where you seek out volatility. It's easy to spot yourself, and there's a lot of physiological cues. Your heart rate goes up. Your palms sweat. Your cheeks flush. You'll feel hot. And when you start feeling those things, you can get up from the table and walk away, or there's a lot of strategies you can do in order to overcome them. You can start focusing. You can start engaging your frontal lobe by analyzing the hand that you lost, as opposed to ruminating on your bad luck—so, making it a useful experience. And once you engage your frontal lobe, it will shut down your limbic system, because those two things stand in opposition to each other. That kind of tilt is relatively easy to deal with.

The long-term problem is that you become volatility avoidant. Once we've experienced the pain of paying too intensely and too many times, we start behaving in a way that avoids the pain, which means that we make conservative choices. I've already described to you how that happens at the poker table. The minute we feel like we're winning, we are likely to find excuses to quit the game, so we can book the win and feel the happiness that we get from winning and avoid the pain of paying, which is losing. And now, we play in a way that avoids that. There are lots of examples that we can see of that. We all know people who have gotten out of a bad relationship and then stop asking people out because they don't want to feel the pain of being rejected again. That's a simple example of how people go on tilt.

You can set up structures in your company that will encourage both kinds of tilt. Let's say someone's in the bottom 25% in terms of performance for that year. They're not thinking about process, they're only thinking about outcome here, and they know they're coming up to the end of the year. You're going to tend to see them making much higher-volatility choices than someone's who's in the top 25%, who probably is making choices that are too low-volatility in order to maintain that position, because they think the bonusing is dependent on outcome and not on process—which,

Being outcome blind allows people to focus on good process. of course, it shouldn't be. If someone's on the gold desk and someone else is on the mortgage desk and the person on the gold desk wins a lot more, that doesn't mean they traded better. The question you could ask is, what would happen if they switched places? A different question is, how did people on the gold desk and the mortgage desk at another firm do, because, for example, there might have been more volatility to trade in gold than in mortgages, so you should be looking at the process there.

If someone's in the bottom quartile, they're likely to be displaying this tilt behavior of seeking out volatility, and you'll get the opposite on the top quartile. You see this all the time in traders who have now gotten out of the position because they were losing, and all of a sudden they went from being a good trader to suffering a losing streak. And what you'll generally see if you dig into it is that they're making choices that are way too conservative, trying to avoid that state of paying.

Sometimes it's correct to take the more conservative line. We know it's not right all the time, but in a given instance, I can probably give you a good explanation of why I might be making a choice that's conservative—in poker, in trading, in whatever it might be. The only way for someone from the outside to spot it is to watch what has happened over time and see that every time I'm given a choice between higher volatility and lower volatility, I'm always choosing the low-ball line, and then they can see that I'm on tilt. But it takes a long time to understand, and the person has to know what information I'm seeing. If someone's observing me, they don't have complete information—they don't have the information that I have as I'm making the decision. They can't see my cards. My line might look totally reasonable unless you saw my cards every single time. And the low-vol choice doesn't necessarily look like a bad choice, I'm just not maximizing my expected value.

Michael: You've brought up low-vol multiple times. I keep thinking of something I say to myself when I see a long-term track record of 1% gain each month, every month, year after year: "We either have Bernard Madoff or Long-Term Capital Management"—the hedge fund that went belly-up in the 1990s. The idea of consistency raises a red flag to me.

Annie: Exactly. People don't understand why that should raise a red flag. And in fact, when people are looking for places to invest, they tend to be looking for consistency, which is exactly where they shouldn't be looking. I can name tons of poker players who consistently won a little. I would've never invested in them. I would much rather invest in somebody who had higher volatility but they're always going to win more. It's not always about somebody playing a positive expectancy; it's maximizing that expectancy.

Some people are temperamentally low-vol types. They don't like risk. They should probably find a different business than the kinds we're in. But a lot of times people are smart and they understand how to manage risk well, and then they lose, but they emotionally don't handle losing well and they don't recover from it, and all of a sudden they're low-vol types. It takes a long time to spot, and it's incredibly hard to repair.

The other kind of tilt you can see. It's easier to clamp somebody down than ramp them up. It's easier to get them to go from being too crazy to a little more conservative. And it's easier to say to somebody, "Hey, dude, you're out of your mind right now. Walk away from the table. Calm down. Stop playing. Get off that position. What are you doing?" Because I can see it the moment. I don't need to see a pattern over a long time in order to know that the first thing is happening. So, that's much less dangerous.

Michael: You've taught people poker. You're now helping executives outside the poker world—men and women. Talk about how this dense, layered subject that includes math, psychology, game theory translates from a teaching perspective to men and women. I'm guessing there might be less interest from women—maybe you're going to correct me on that? But being an accomplished female in all these subjects, do you find yourself having an advantage in getting these points across to women?

Annie: That's an interesting question. I've been asked a lot of different things about stereotypes—for example, how women should deal with being in a man's world in the way that they're perceived, and that kind of thing. But I've never been asked whether I deliver these concepts better to women because I'm a woman.

Michael: One of the most successful hedge fund managers in the world right now, I think she runs around $10bn, is all quantitative. If we were to have her in this conversation, she would be talking expected value too. Clearly there's some successful female minds in these areas, but in my experience so far, there's fewer. I wonder if that's an exposure issue?

Annie: I would say that it's two issues—or a combination. Men's and women's brains are different. We had different roles as we evolved as a species. Math and space are related to each other—that's obvious from geometry. Men were hunting and women were gathering, in general. The way they deal with space is different between the two. In general, women's brains are going to be built more for communication, verbal stuff, because they're talking to each other and raising the babies and that kind of thing. And no way is this sexist—I'm not saying this is what they're supposed to do. This is a million years ago. The females in the group were staying closer to the camp, and the men were doing the big hunts—that kind of mathematical relationship of how to organize that. Obviously, there's tremendous variation, and there are lots of incredibly brilliantly verbal men, and there are incredibly brilliantly mathematical women. What we don't have enough of is that interaction—what's the base rate of abilities, then you add society on top of it and what's encouraged.

I know that in my case, when I was growing up, I was doing a lot of math in high school. I took calculus in 11th grade, calculus 2 in 12th grade, and went to college and one of my majors was English—which was fine, I read a lot of good books—but someone should have said to me at some point, "Hey, did you notice that you're the only girl in this calculus 2 class? That's an advantage for you. And when you go to college, you might want to continue in something mathematical." I wish that I could have gone back and been a finance major or something to do with math. But instead, I got told, "Don't let anybody know that you're smart at this because they don't like girls like that," which sounds crazy!

And whether people are saying that out loud now, there's still this idea that if you're a mathy girl you're somehow unattractive or a nerd. It's not a desirable quality. It is terrible, but it's certainly not anywhere as bad as when I was growing up. And that was better than, say, when my mother was growing up. We're making a lot of progress, but there is still this big divide in what people think are the jobs that women should do. Women should be in PR, marketing or human resources, that kind of thing. I don't think people are pushing women to study finance or accounting, or to be a math major.

Michael: In the last couple years, I've been in the boardrooms of major mutual funds and hedge funds from all across Asia—Singapore, Kuala Lumpur, Beijing. Each time I was in those rooms giving a presentation, it was 50/50, men and women. I find it different in Asia.

Annie: That's why I say there's this cultural issue; that the question is what are you encouraged to be doing. I'm sure you've been in boardrooms in the U.S. and I'm guessing it wasn't 50/50.

Michael: Do you find that when you introduce your way of thinking to women, you connect better than a male teacher would? Or is that tough to say off the top of your head?

Annie: It's a little tough to say off the top of my head, but certainly, I've talked to rooms that are entirely women, and I think that they do hear my message well. They see this woman who went into a world that's predominantly men—in fact, among professionals, 97%—and did well, was at the top of that world, and here's the way that she thinks. I think it is an easier message for them to hear. Whether it's explicitly said or not, women are frustrated by "You're going to go over and do the art, and these guys over here are going to do the experiments." The more that we can get women going into STEM, I think women bring a different kind of thinking that is important for advancement. When you apply a woman's mind to the same problem as a man's mind, you get both perspectives working. You get more precise thinking and more innovation when you combine the two mindsets. I'm hoping it will be 50/50 in the U.S. soon. And I'm happy that I could be contributing to that at all.

Michael: I can tell you right now, the trading world will eat this stuff up.

Annie: I speak to a lot of traders and investment firms on these topics; I do a lot of hedge fund retreats. There's so much overlap in terms of the kinds of problems that traders are facing.

Here's a funny story. I was doing my PhD at Penn and I decided right at the end that I wanted more time to think about whether I wanted to go into academia. I ended up becoming a poker player, and started playing professionally in 1994. In 2002, a friend of mine, Erik Seidel—one of the best poker players ever—got asked by a friend of his named Roger Low, who had a hedge fund out in San Francisco called the Parallax Fund, to come on a retreat with his traders. He knew Erik because he had at one point done some trading. Erik doesn't much like being in front of audiences, so he said, "I don't like speaking, but I know someone who used to be a teacher, and you should have her come and talk to your group." I hadn't thought about teaching these concepts of poker that are a crossover with the behavioral economics and behavioral finance world. This was completely accidental. Erik called me up and said, "Hey, I've got this friend. He wants someone to come speak to his traders. Will you do that?" I was two weeks from the due date of my last child, but I said, "Sure!" I couldn't wear shoes because my feet were so swollen at that point. So, I waddled in barefoot, incredibly pregnant.

From there, Roger recommended me out to people, and I started to quietly build this other business of going and talking about the collision between life decision making and poker decision making. In 2012, I retired from poker, as that particular part of the business started to grow. And since then, that's what I've done exclusively.

The first talk I ever gave was on tilt—this issue that I talked to you about of how you can see extroverted tilt that's on the outside, but the long-term tilt that's internal is hard to see. I remember the example that I used was a head coach who's calling a short pass all the time, and he's never throwing it all the way down the field, so he's always handing it off to the running back or doing the short out. Obviously, you wouldn't want that person as a head coach, but he's going to be completing a lot of plays, right? He's going to be gaining yards. It's just that that's not the guy you want.

If I could change one thing in the world, it would be to get people to think more probabilistically.

As I was building up this business, it was the first time that I'd thought with real clarity about how I would express these concepts. And I realized that you have the normative guys and the behavioral guys, and obviously, as a poker player, I was sitting over in the behavioral camp—because in a game where people are exchanging money hand to hand in front of their competitors with 30 seconds to make every decision, all you see is the behavioral stuff, the irrationalities. You've got this underlying math happening, which is certainly normative, as you're trying to figure out if you're getting the right return on investment. But mostly you're thinking about this person's set of behaviors and irrationalities and how to exploit them to best advantage. You naturally become a behaviorist when you're in that world. But it was the first time that I thought about it with any clarity and in any real way.

I have to say, I'm incredibly passionate about these topics and I love talking about them. If I could change one thing in the world, it would be to get people to think more probabilistically. And the more that I can get that message out, and the more that I get to discuss these concepts with people, it brings me incredible happiness.

PART 2
Living in Uncertainty

Michael Covel: I saw this great piece of insight from you where you happened to use a modern-day political character: Donald Trump. I don't know your politics, and frankly, it's not relevant for the point that you were trying to make, which is that he went aggressive with his cabinet picks. They weren't middle-of-the-road people; they had specific views. They were either going to go down in flames or get nominated and win.

Can you speak to this notion of aggression and perhaps bring it over to other disciplines too, because you made the point that the aggressive posture of his nomination picks is tough to defend?

Annie Duke: I thought it was interesting that he was taking such an aggressive stance with the cabinet choices, particularly when somebody has lost the popular vote and has not won an electoral landslide—I think it was the 12th lowest in history, in terms of electoral college margin. One might expect him to make choices that were much more acceptable to the other side, particularly because the other side in this particular election was close.

If you think about George W. Bush's cabinet choices, Clinton's, Obama's, and so forth, they usually tend to be somewhat middle-of-the-road. Sometimes they'll pick people from the other side. And then once in a while, they'll pick somebody who is very far on the spectrum of whatever political party that they're in. An example would be Van Jones, who was on Obama's staff and was considered pretty far left.

I think about Trump's aggressive choices from a game theory standpoint. One of the hardest things to defend against is someone who's being aggressive across the board. Generally, in poker, you're playing against somebody and they'll make an aggressive play every once in a while, and you'll figure out what the quality of your hand is against the backdrop of the way they normally play, so you decide whether to defend against that or not and play proceeds as normal.

Other times you'll have someone come into the game who's aggressive all the time. In general, people's first instinct in that situation is to say, well, they're putting all my chips at risk, every single hand, so I'm going to wait until I have a good hand and then I'm going to choose to defend against it. Then I'll show them!

The problem with that is twofold. One is that by the time you've gotten a hand that you can defend against them, you may not feel strong enough to actually risk all your chips. They've got a five-to-one chip advantage on you because they've won every hand in between. So, even now when you win that hand, they're still kind of beating you. The other thing is, you could actually lose because when you get your money and you're probably not 100%, then you have a choice. You can say, well, I'm going to continue on this way and allow them to run over me and only defend occasionally, or I'm going to decide that I'm going to show them. And I'm going to start calling them all the time, which means that you're going to be putting your chips at risk with hands that are much weaker than you normally might if play were proceeding as normal.

It's in your long-term best interest generally to take the second strategy, but it's an incredibly risky strategy because you burn up a lot of capital. In the meantime, you can get taken down with the person you're trying to defend against.

I was thinking about that in terms of these cabinet choices and the subsequent confirmation hearings. Does the opposition start going after every single person? If they do that, they're going to be perceived as oppositional. They're going to be burning up political capital—there's PR risk to standing in the way of allowing the government to proceed. You have to decide, is my base going to be okay with that? How much is the other side's base going to come after us for that? How much political capital am I willing to burn? In the process of burning all this political capital, am I even going get what I want, which is to stop some of these people getting through, or am I going to focus on one person, to look at what my strongest case is and try to stop them from getting through?

At the time I wrote about it, it looked like the Democrats were going to use Rex Tillerson. But as I watched the confirmation hearings unfold, I saw they took a second tactic, which was to be oppositional to everybody. It was going to be difficult for them to stand in the way, but the hearings were also difficult for pretty much everyone that they had an objection to. That's probably a better strategy in the long run, because they're not in the majority.

Michael: Aggression meets aggression.

Annie: Aggression has to meet aggression, in order to stop that from happening in the long run. Let's say you're negotiating against somebody who's aggressive every single time you're in a negotiation, who takes this incredible stance and says take it or leave it. I'm assuming this is someone you have to continue to negotiate with until you have a good position, and then you'll stand up to them. They're going to be getting extra equity repeatedly, and whatever you get that one time you stand up to them is probably not going to make up for it. So, instead of making the decision to take it or leave it, allowing every deal to break until they understand that you're standing up to them in the long run is going to serve you better, if you have room to be able to do that.

Michael: What we're talking about, the foundation of these moves, is game theory.

Annie: Correct. Game theory is looking at games where you're playing against opponents over time. You'll notice that a lot of what I'm talking about is the conundrum of what you are doing over time. If you're in one negotiation and you don't have to continue to negotiate with that person, you'll likely take a different response to someone being aggressive than if you have to negotiate with them over and over again. If it's a one-time negotiation then first of all, you're not sure if they're being aggressive or if that's generally their stance. You don't necessarily have enough data and because you're never going to come across them again, you don't have to worry about any signaling for the future.

Michael: I was going through your Twitter feed and it feels like you're channeling decision theorists, behaviorists, and game theorists. You love the idea of taking these complicated foundations rooted in math and getting them across to people in all walks of life, to try to help them understand your perspective on dealing with skill, luck, uncertainty, expected value, and risk management.

Annie: Absolutely. One of the things I'm trying to address is that we walk around as if the world is a much more certain place than it is. It's about how, when you're under these uncertain circumstances, you make rational decisions.

We try to deal with uncertainty by ignoring it or removing it. That is not a particularly good method for making good decisions. It's actually the embracing of uncertainty—acknowledging that it's there from two sources. One is plain luck. I can know that a coin will land heads 50% of the time and tails 50% of the time, but I don't know what it will land on the next try. I only know what it is over the long run. The other source of uncertainty is hidden information. If I don't know what the coin looks like, if I don't know how many sides it has or whether it might be weighted, for example, it makes it much harder to figure out what it means when the coin lands heads.

> **We try to deal with uncertainty by ignoring it or removing it.**

We want to walk around like life is a game of chess, which is a pretty certain game, with no hidden information, and not much of a luck element. If I were to ask you, "What's the worst loss you ever had at chess?" it doesn't mean that you would find the worst decision there, but you would certainly find many terrible decisions in a game that you got pounded in, because there's a tight connection between the quality of the outcome and the quality of the decisions that are made.

But in poker, that's an unreasonable strategy. To go and look at a hand I lost is not necessarily the best place for me to find a bad decision. Outcomes and decision quality in poker are not that closely tied because there's lots of uncertainty in poker, lots of hidden information: I don't know what other people's cards are. And there's certainly an element of luck: I don't know what the next flip is going to land on, even if I know the odds in the long run. If I only look at losses for bad decisions, there's lots of hands that I could have played, or I played the hand perfectly reasonably and I lost anyway. And likewise, there's lots of hands where I played the hand perfectly unreasonably and I won regardless, because the

When you're going to be making multiple decisions over time with someone, you have to balance equity in the moment with equity in the future.

coin happened to flip well for me. That's much more like life, but we like to act as if we're on a chess board.

Michael: Let's talk about bad outcomes. What are some of the ways that you get people to understand that bad is not quite the right word, because outcomes are going to vary—it's more about how you get emotionally aligned with variance and outcome.

Annie: There's a few problems with how we interpret the quality of an outcome. The first has to do with the fact that we don't accept uncertainty very well, so we think about things as right or wrong, good or bad. We are not particularly comfortable or adept at thinking probabilistically—in other words, calling something 60% as opposed to 100%.

Going back to the 2016 presidential election, one of the places where you can see that is in people's reaction to Donald Trump's win. I was looking at Nate Silver and in the last week of the election his calculator had Trump anywhere between 60:40 to about 70:30 on the day. For me as a poker player, 30% is a lot—I've lost a tremendous number of poker tournaments on 30% shots. I was looking at the odds and I was less shocked when Trump won, because we have this tendency when something's 70:30 to default it to 100:0. As you pointed out, there's little that's completely all good or all bad, but we tend to succumb to this kind of black-and-white thinking.

That's problem number one. Problem number two is the fact that we all want to look back at the narrative of our life and see it as positive. This leads to processing outcomes by connecting them to decision quality in a way that preserves the positive side. If we categorize something as a bad outcome, we want it to not be our fault, so we offload responsibility for it. It was bad luck. If we have a good outcome, we do the reverse, and we say, look at how great I am.

We're missing a lot of opportunities to learn when we put something into the luck category, because it means it wasn't in your control, so there's not much for you to improve about your decision-making. And obviously if you're taking credit for all the good stuff, you're going to reinforce and repeat behaviors that aren't necessarily causal to the outcome. We want to try to disconnect outcome quality from decision quality and look at decisions independent of a single outcome. Once you collect enough data, you can start tying in outcomes a little more, but that takes a long time.

There are a few strategies you can do. First of all, you can create some trigger words. For example, anytime I automatically say something was luck, that should be a cue for me to say, "Wait a minute—that's a reflex." Likewise, when I have that urge to take credit, that should be a cue for me as well.

Then you can do all sorts of perspective-taking exercises. You can imagine: What if that happened to somebody else? Would I still feel that bad result was luck? Would I still feel that good result was all down to them? The way you process information about other people can help you to examine, what if the world were a different way? You can stop and think, what if it were because of my decision-making? What kind of case could I make for that? What kind of decisions could I have made that might have contributed to the outcome, or what if it wasn't all because of me? What if there were some luck elements involved? If I had to make a case for that, what would it be? That allows you to explore the other side.

There's lots of people in cognitive science who recommend that kind of perspective taking—the 10, 10, 10 rule: 10 minutes, 10 months, 10 years. When things like this have happened in the past and I can view them in retrospect, have I ever thought I could take credit for something that I could offload to bad luck? Those kinds of things can help you take perspective. And generally you'll start to realize, first of all, nothing's all luck or all skill. So, some things were luck and I should try to figure out what those are. And some things are skill, some things were due to my decisions, and I should try to figure out what those are. Then you also start to realize that there were some good things and some bad things about the outcome, that it was a mixed bag. Through that you start to move toward the middle, and start to represent the world in a more accurate way, which is essentially realizing it's uncertain and it's not all one thing or another, and it gets you away from black-and-white thinking.

Michael: Many times people get fixated on one decision instead of realizing that it can be adjusted next time. We all need to learn that if we make one decision and it's wrong, we can move on. There's going to be another chance.

Annie: One of the things that poker trains you to do is to not fixate on particular decisions. Because if you do that, you can go on what poker players refer to as tilt. Anyone who's played pinball can imagine what that looks like, right? It's the cartoon guy with the smoke coming out of his ears and his head exploding. When you're in that state of emotional distress, fixating on bad outcomes, or where you think other people are victimizing you with their bad play—that kind of thing can get you emotionally off kilter. And when you're emotionally off kilter, you tend to make poor decisions.

We are not particularly comfortable or adept at thinking probabilistically.

Then the whole thing snowballs and becomes a self-fulfilling prophesy, because you're not playing well, then you're losing, then that's making you more emotionally upset, and it becomes a loop. It's important you try to figure out how to deal with that, because poker has this unusual component whereby you make a decision and, unlike in most situations, about 30 seconds later you get a result, but in a tight, fast feedback loop. Then you have to make more decisions right after that. Then you get more results and then there's more decisions. Then there's more results.

This is not when you're playing on the computer, but when you're playing with live people. If you have a good dealer, you could be playing 35 hands an hour, and you could potentially be making about 20 decisions. That's a lot of stuff going on at the table in a short period of time with lots of results bombarding you, and you have to learn to deal with that. You have to learn to move on from that hand because you've got to play the next one. I might obsess about it later when I'm not sitting at the table to try to work through what my decision quality was, but you have to get good at letting it go in the moment and moving on and saying, all right, that's done, on to the next one. I have an opportunity to do better going forward, but if I allow myself to get caught up, then it's going to affect the next decision I have to make. The next decision is right now, with the next result about 30 seconds later, so I don't have the luxury of the rumination. Pretty much anybody who's become a successful poker player figures out how to get that under control.

Michael: You have this unique academic understanding that involves math, cognitive science, and also the gritty aspects of Vegas. Maybe you're going to tell me I'm completely wrong, but you've had this great success in what would be described as a man's world.

Annie: If you look at the main event of the World Series of Poker, the number of women playing in that event generally is hovering around 3–5% of the field. There's been an explosion in the popularity of poker over the last 15 years or so, and along with that, certainly the absolute number of women who are playing has gone up, as has the absolute number of men. What hasn't changed is the percentage of women who are playing—and it's small. Most tables I played at, I was the only woman. There are some amazing, great, successful female players who are incredible—Vanessa Selbst, for example; Vanessa Rousso; Olivia Boeree; Jennifer Harman has been playing since I started and she's amazing—I've probably left some out but people can go look them up. They're great, but it's a handful of people compared to the men.

When I started, I was playing in Billings, Montana, which is stereotyped in other ways. I was pretty much always the only woman at the table, and there's no sexual harassment laws at the poker table and no discrimination laws. Poker is one of the few business transactions where you're face to face with your opponent in person, and you're passing money back and forth as you win or lose. That doesn't happen in most business settings, and it creates some emotional context in the game, because people are losing amounts that matter to them.

When somebody was looking around the table thinking, "Well, I've got all these emotions building up in me and I have to figure out how to offload them. Should I offload them on that big guy across the table? Or should I offload them on her?" I found that I was often the receptacle for some offloading of the emotions. Aside from the fact that there were some people who were plain chauvinist and were expressive about that, who felt that I shouldn't be at the table, that I was ruining in their game by invading it. Why wasn't I at home?

Michael: You being there literally sent some guys into tilt.

Annie: Yes, exactly. You're going off to your poker game with your buddies and now there's some chick sitting at the table. Then the other thing is that poker's kind of a testosterone-driven game. Maybe less so now, but certainly when I started playing. It's an aggressive competition. Men don't want to be pushed around by women, and certainly they don't like to be out-negotiated by a woman or out-strategized or outplayed or see their chips go into her pile—that made a lot of them mad.

Then there was another type of person who didn't think that you could think that deeply, have that amount of creativity of thought, or underestimated how deep you get into your strategic thinking or how aggressive you might be. I want to be clear, there were also plenty of people who were none of those things, who were not chauvinistic at all and were wonderful people and treated me with respect and took every opponent as they came. But that wasn't true of everyone, just as it's not true of everyone out in the world.

Michael: You've described a fairly aggressive posture towards you on things that are frankly not fair. It's not fair for you to be singled out because you are a woman. How did you handle that?

Annie: It's germane to what we've been talking about—how you focus on the best strategic choice as opposed to the emotion. The mistake a lot of people make is they try to prove the other person wrong. Either they want the other person to like them, or they want to get back at them, but both of those responses are allowing your emotions to drive the train. Any time you're making emotional decisions it's going to affect the way that you play. And you're probably going to lose because of it.

It's about focusing on the purpose of me sitting at the table: Am I sitting at this table because I'm trying to get all these people to like me? I hope the answer is no. Once you make it explicit that your purpose is to win this game, that helps offload a lot of the emotion, because if your purpose is not to get people to like you, what follows from that is it shouldn't matter whether they like you or not.

Then you can take that thinking one step further and realize, well, if they don't like me, if they're having this kind of response to me that is primal and emotional, I can probably use that to my advantage in figuring out the strategy to play against them, because that means they're thinking with their hearts as opposed to their heads. Once you refocus, it takes emotion out of it because you're sitting in your frontal cortex. You're thinking strategically, okay, my job here is not to make friends, my job here is to win money and win bets, so I need to focus on the best way to do that. The fact that these people are behaving this way toward me is to my advantage because it means that there's something I can strategically leverage.

An example that I would give is if someone would find it to be the worst thing that ever happened to them to lose their chips to a woman. There's a certain type of player who feels that way. There are certain things that follow from that in terms of the way

The great things we accomplish in our life are because we overcome adversity.

they play against you. Generally, it has to do with being overly aggressive. What they're going to do emotionally is what poker players would term, "trying to run over you." They're going to try to bluff you a lot to assert themselves over you and then, guaranteed, when they bluff you, they're going to show you their cards. And they're going to say, "Haha, little lady, look at what I did to you." We already talked about what the response to that is, right? You call them, you don't allow them to do that.

Likewise, there's a flip side to that, which is that they're going to want to make sure you never bluff them because that would be a slight to their masculinity. If you know that somebody wants to make sure that you never bluff them, it means they're going to be calling you a lot. The strategy to that is don't bluff them, bet a lot of money, more than you otherwise would be able to with hands that are quite good, because they're going to be inclined to call you much more often.

Now, when people are in that sort of chauvinistic mindset, that's not the only way they can express, and you have to know which kind of person you're dealing with. But if you're dealing with that particular kind of person who doesn't want to ever allow a woman to bluff them and who's interested in bluffing a woman, you can come up with a strategic way to take care of that. Now you have a mindset shift where you're not so upset that you're not making friends at the table with them and maybe they don't view you in the most positive light. But you're happy because if they didn't react to you that way, if you weren't a woman sitting at that table, they wouldn't make those strategic errors that are easy to dig into. And once you do that, it takes you out of the game and it becomes fun. It becomes a problem-solving exercise—exactly what are the strategic goals that are being expressed because of the way that this person views me and doesn't like me—and then you're not so upset by it.

That's not to say there weren't times when I got upset at a table because someone was treating me poorly, but I would usually get up and leave, and it was rare. Normally I was able to focus on strategic choices. Then maybe once I got home and I was done with the game, I would let off steam to my husband, but I would let it out in other ways that didn't affect my play at the table. That particular kind of mindset—female lawyers, female businesspeople, CEOs, managers, whatever—we're all going to come across people who don't take us at face value. Their view is, you're a woman and I don't like women and I don't want you to succeed, or I don't particularly respect your intellect.

One of the big mistakes that women make in that situation is that they're upset because they want the other person to respect them. They want to prove, "I'm as smart as you are." They want that person to like them. If you take a step back and realize, no, wait, the way this person views me is good for me—it means I can make good strategic choices against them, because I can understand the kind of error that they're likely to make against me—then it's no longer about their approval. You can be better at your job because it moves you out of the emotional part of the brain into the strategic part. It's a good mindset shift that's going to make you less unhappy.

Michael: Let me build on that with something you linked to on your Twitter feed. The main headline was why growth most often occurs when we fall apart. And the subhead, which I liked, is why the avoidance of adversity causes more harm than good. You walked into this world where a certain adversity came to you, but you plowed into it. Plenty of other people might have wanted nothing to do with it.

Annie: The great things we accomplish in our life are because we overcome adversity, right? First off, throughout your life, you're always going to be dealing with adversity. *The Obstacle Is the Way* by Ryan Holiday is a book that I would highly recommend. It's about stoicism, powering through adversity, and taking that as a challenge to succeed. When you look at a lot of the great successes—people like John Rockefeller, for example— what you see is they came across an obstacle. There was adversity in their life and they didn't back away; it made them try harder.

It helps to work through, how do I not have a negative frame on this? How do I see the good in this? How do I strategically solve for this? Once you've gotten through that process, once you've faced the adversity, you've figured out in your least emotional mind possible with your most rational self, how do I deal with this? What's my contribution to why this adversity happened? How much of it is due to luck? What can I change about my decision-making, going forward?

As you said, it's not like you never get to make another decision. You can make a decision about, okay, I'm in this situation, what do I do next? How do I keep plowing through? How do I make the next decision? When you've done that and come out the other side, you're much stronger for it. You're much more prepared for the next thing that might happen to you.

You're much less likely to experience adversity when you've powered through it, by not avoiding it; it's less likely to happen because your decision-making improves, but also your mindset improves. You flip the script, you don't view it as adverse anymore, you view it as a challenge. When you view something as a challenge in your life, you come out the other side clearly a stronger person. You're stronger emotionally. You're a stronger decision maker. In the end, that is one of the most powerful ways to create that positive narrative about your life.

Shying away from adversity is a way to avoid those bad feelings in the moment, but in the long run we regret giving in to it. "Oh, this happened to me. I'm a victim and can't do anything about it," is not positive. But "I overcame," is one of the most positive things a person can think about themselves. As much as you can create that mindset, that shift, you're going to be a better, happier person for it.

Michael: You always give me gold!

Annie: I'm lucky that I get to spend every day thinking about these topics and trying to figure out how to convey them in a way that someone who is not a game theorist, who doesn't have a degree in economics or behavioral economics or psychology, can incorporate them into everyday life.

I believe if you can live these concepts, live in the uncertainty, learn how to make decisions under those circumstances and deeply de-bias yourself in those kinds of things, you will be more successful and happier, and I'm trying to get that across to as many people as possible.

PART 3
Thinking in Bets

Michael Covel: I'm watching an entire generation, the millennials, go gaga over cryptocurrencies and weed stocks. What's interesting is that the topics that you talk about, which are foundational to making decisions for what they are putting their money into, are getting only a cursory analysis across social media. These aren't necessarily unwise or dumb people, but they seem to have no comprehension of the issues, starting with, "It's a bet, and you've got to think that it might not turn out exactly as you expect."

Annie Duke: I was asked what I thought about cryptocurrency recently. I haven't looked at it that much; it's not something that I'm particularly interested in. I have no plans to invest in it; I have other things that I'm using my knowledge base for. But if I had to give a cursory opinion, the minute I see people saying it's impossible for cryptocurrency to bubble, I would be cautious, for exactly the reasons that you said.

The cryptocurrency community on Twitter seems to be an echo chamber of confirmation bias, with a lot of bandwagoning. I don't see a whole lot of dissenting voices saying, "Hey, wait a minute, this is high volatility." I also see tribalism with cryptocurrency—I'm a Bitcoin person, and because I'm into Bitcoin, I'm going to run down your cryptocurrency. There seems to be cognitive bias coming to the surface around that particular issue.

Michael: You say it's not your area of expertise, but thinking about bets, we could be talking about widgets, it doesn't have to be cryptocurrencies. Decision-making is decision-making. Uncertainty, luck, skill, and all this stuff you talk about, are the foundational precepts that we as human beings should probably be thinking about if we want to be successful in the long run.

Annie: I haven't studied cryptocurrency deeply enough that I would feel comfortable giving someone financial advice about it, but what I do see is a lot of people talking about it being a sure thing, as if it can't bubble, or that it couldn't go down—this tribalism where people are attacking each other and not understanding they're investing in something that's high volatility.

Michael: Let's talk about NFL head coach Pete Carroll. I remember debating this with friends at the time, and I had strong opinions about it. But there's a different way of looking at this, and the way you lay it out is probably how we all should be thinking about it.

Annie: Let me remind everybody of the decision you're talking about. In the Super Bowl in 2015, the Seahawks are on the one-yard line, they're four points behind. Now, it's important to know that the Seahawks have only one time out here. At this time Marshawn Lynch is considered to be the best running back in the NFL. In general, people were expecting that Pete Carroll was going to call a run play, Russell Wilson was going to hand the ball off to Marshawn Lynch and try to drive it across the goal line. But he didn't do that. Carroll called for Wilson to pass the ball. And as pretty much everybody will remember, the ball got intercepted in the end zone, end of the game, Patriots won. Maybe you could recall for me some of the headlines from the next day?

Michael: "Pete Carroll Doesn't Know What He's Doing," etc., etc.

Annie: Things like, "Worst Call in Super Bowl History." There were a lot of big exclamation points. I think the word idiot was used—actually, I think it was effing idiot in one of the online sites. People were really, really, really, really upset about this call. We should ask a simple question: "What do you think those headlines would've looked like if the ball were caught in that end zone?"

Michael: Genius.

Annie: They probably would've said something like, he outsmarted Bill

Belichick because now the unexpectedness of the play would've been considered brilliant. This is the most brilliant call in Super Bowl history. Everybody was expecting the ball to be handed off to Marshawn Lynch, and Pete Carroll outsmarted Belichick in having Russell Wilson pass.

It takes a simple thought experiment to see that there's a problem here in the way that analysis was done, which mainly had to do with people deriving the quality of Pete Carroll's decision from the quality of the outcome. Obviously, it was a bad-quality outcome. They lost the game on an interception. And people were using that as a tightly correlated signal to what the decision quality was. In poker we call it resulting. And resulting is a wonderful word to have in your vocabulary. In cognitive science, you would call it outcome bias. I like the word resulting better because I feel it's self-explanatory—you're using the result in order to figure out whether the decision was good.

I'll walk you quickly through the analysis that shows that actually the call was mathematically pretty good. There's 26 seconds left. The Seahawks have one time out on the one-yard line. If they call a run play and Marshawn Lynch doesn't get it to the end zone, they can call exactly one time out and then hand it off to Marshawn Lynch one more time, so they get two plays. It's second down, by the way. If they pass it, here's what happens most of the time. Sometimes it's caught and sometimes it's dropped, that accounts for 99% of the occurrences. In the case that it's caught, the game is over and the Seahawks win. In the case that it's dropped, what happens? The

Decisions and outcomes are only loosely correlated.

clock stops, at which point they can hand it off to Marshawn Lynch. If he doesn't get into the end zone, they can call a time out that they now have left and hand it off to Marshawn Lynch again. So people understand that pass was essentially a free option. About 1% of the time, it's going to get intercepted. There are some other things that can happen like a fumble or a sack, but those can happen on the running play anyway. So about 1% of the time, that pass is going to get intercepted.

In that sense, you can see that it's a nearly free option to get it into the end zone, preserving the option to run the two running plays also. You may agree or not agree with this analysis. But what is interesting is that the outcome was so bad that people didn't even give Pete Carroll the credit of having thought it through. And once you run through the analysis, it actually starts to look like a pretty good decision. And that's aside from the fact that you don't always want to hand it off because then you're too easy to defend against. You can see that clearly Pete Carroll was thinking it through, and the chorus of people yelling that this was the most idiotic play ever were guilty of resulting.

Michael: What's tricky about it is that there's so much on the line with the last play of the Super Bowl, but then you think of the thousands and thousands of play calls that Pete Carroll has made in his career, and he's had a lot of success. He clearly knows something about NFL play calls, and he knows not every call is going to be successful, and he's comfortable with that.

Annie: Interestingly enough, on big stages like the Super Bowl, it's been shown that coaches get more conservative and they roll back to a more old-school play calling style. I think it's because they're worried that fans, newspapers and pundits are all going to be resulting if one of these calls that isn't quite so obvious doesn't work out. Kudos to Pete Carroll for saying, "I know it's the Super Bowl, and I understand I'm risking that people are going to result on me and say it's the worst call in Super Bowl history, or scream that I'm an idiot, but I'm willing to do what's mathematically correct here." That makes him a much greater coach.

Michael: He was unlucky.

Annie: He went on *Good Morning America* and said, "It was the worst result of a call in Super Bowl history." So clearly, Pete Carroll knows something about resulting!

Michael: For so much of modern life, we are Monday morning quarterbacks, whether that's watching poker on TV, or football, or whatever it might be. There is such a difference between being in the game, spending your life to get the understanding of this whole process, making decisions, many not working out, some working out, having that edge, versus going down more of the headline-grabbing direction: "Let's see if Pete Carroll will say he was an idiot."

ANNIE DUKE

Annie: One of the problems with resulting is that you do feel smart once you know the outcome. The decisions that we make every day in our own lives are made under conditions of uncertainty. We don't have all the information that we need in order to make the decision and there's a lot of luck. So we have two sources of uncertainty: we can make a perfect decision and it can work out badly, or we can make a terrible decision and it can work out well. Decisions and outcomes are only loosely correlated. And then we have this problem with hidden information.

In poker, for example, the cards are face down and you're trying to decide what to do against your opponent when you can't see their cards. And even if you could see their cards, you could get unlucky because you can have things not work out.

A simple example of that from life is, I can run a red light and not get a ticket and not get in an accident, but I think we can all agree that running a red light is not a good decision. And I can go through a green light following all the traffic rules, the speed limit, my car can in perfect condition, weather conditions are good—I can be as careful and as good a decision-maker as possible going through a green light—and I can still get T-boned.

It is easy to be a Monday morning quarterback if you make this mistake of saying, "I know the outcome, so therefore the decision must have been bad," or, "I know the outcome, so therefore the decision must have been good."

That's not a bad strategy if you're playing chess, for example, because if you lose a game of chess, you made some bad decisions. The reason for that is that chess, unlike life, is a game that doesn't have any hidden information—you can see all the pieces—and it has little luck. In chess, it's a lot easier to do that derivation from the way that the game turned out. But in poker, that's a bad thing to do—just because I lost the hand does not mean I played it poorly, and just because I won the hand does not mean I played it well. If I make the mistake of connecting those together too tightly, my decision-making is going to be messed up. I'm not going to learn well from the way that things are turning out, I'm not going to use my experience well to become an expert.

Part of the problem is that in life, we treat it like we're playing a game of chess when we're not—we're playing a game of poker. We say, "Oh, look at what a smart decision-maker he is, he's playing three-dimensional chess," and I want to yell to the world, "No, if they're a good decision-maker, they're not playing three-dimensional chess, they're playing three-dimensional poker."

Michael: For those out there who might be thinking, "Poker's only a game…" Explain the connection to game theory.

Annie: This is a fun thing I do when I give my talks. I ask the audience, "Does anybody in the audience know who John von Neumann is?" I speak to pretty large audiences and a hand or two will go up, which is fine because not a lot of people know who he is.

Then I'll follow the question with, "Okay, that's average for the audiences that I talk in front of. Does anybody know who John Nash is?" I'll get a few more hands. Then I'll ask if anybody knows who Russell Crowe is, and of course I get the whole audience. Then I'll say, "Okay, so anybody seen the movie *A Beautiful Mind*?" and then I'll walk them back from that.

A Beautiful Mind was about John Nash, who won the Nobel Prize for game theory—a famously schizophrenic but brilliant mathematician. He studied at the Institute for Advanced Study and his mentor was John von Neumann. And John von Neumann was, among other things, the father of the modern computer and worked on the Manhattan Project. He ran our Cold War strategy—he's the one who came up with the idea of mutually assured destruction.

> We have to be good belief updaters.

While he was working on the Manhattan Project, he was moonlighting with Oskar Morgenstern on a book called *Theory of Games and Economic Behavior*, which was incredibly influential. He's considered, along with Morgenstern, the father of modern game theory. The way that we think about decisions under conditions of uncertainty over time, which is a loose definition of game theory, is based on Von Neumann's work.

If I were to define poker, that definition would align well. In poker, I'm making decisions under conditions of uncertainty—again, cards face down, this element of luck. And it's over time—when I make a decision against you, it's not the only decision I'll make against you, I have to make future decisions as well.

The fact that those definitions align is not accidental, because it turns out that John von Neumann started thinking about this work based on a stripped-down version of poker. There's a wonderful anecdote about von Neumann that comes from Jacob Bronowski. He asked him, "This theory of games, it's interesting"—and I'm paraphrasing here—"but how come you didn't base it on chess? Isn't chess the ultimate game?"

And von Neumann's answer went something like, "Chess isn't even a game, it's a calculation; poker is a game." What he's getting at is that because chess has no hidden information and little luck, it's a game that is solvable in the same way that checkers is solvable, or tic-tac-toe, which all 10-year-olds have solved. As long as you have enough computing power, you should be able to solve the game of chess, meaning you should be able to create a decision tree that gets you all the way out to the end of the game, all possible moves and counter-moves. But poker's a much more difficult problem to solve because you have hidden information and you have this luck element.

So von Neumann was basing the decisions that we're studying in game theory on poker. He was an important guy and I'm a little sad that people don't remember who he was. In, I think it was 1950, *Time* magazine named him the most brilliant mathematician of the 20th century. He got lost in the history of science, except they're pretty sure he was one of the models for Dr. Strangelove. That seems to be the mark he left on the popular culture world at any rate. He was around at the same time as Einstein, but Einstein had the advantage of the crazy hair, the mustache and the bicycle, I guess.

Michael: Thomas Schelling and Robert Aumann shared a Nobel Prize in game theory as well. I spoke to Aumann when he was around 80 years old, and he was so fantastically lucid in mapping out the thinking behind mutually assured destruction. Listening to someone like that makes you realize that in his mind, there's math going on at a level that I probably will not have a chance to understand my whole life. I agree with you, Von Neumann, Nash, Schelling—these guys would all be so fascinating to talk to.

Annie: If people want to see an example of mutually assured destruction, I highly recommend the movie *WarGames*, starring Matthew Broderick. They start playing tic-tac-toe and the computer figures out that you can't win. And then they move on to thermonuclear war to try to figure that problem out. It's a wonderful movie about game theory.

Michael: It all starts with the belief, then you make the bet, then you get your set of outcomes. If you don't have the belief set in the right way, you're going to have trouble with your betting, and then the negative outcome's going to be predictable.

Annie: It goes back to where we started: Bitcoin. What are your beliefs about Bitcoin? How good are you at updating your beliefs and checking against what the objective truth might be?

It's hard to know the objective truth of anything, but our goal should be to get closer and closer to that. In order to do that, we have to be good belief updaters. Our beliefs drive the bets we make, and they drive the decisions we make about what we think the possible future is going to look like. We have this set of beliefs that we form, and if your beliefs are bad, you're going to make bad bets around them.

We all need to remember that whatever we're betting on, whatever decisions we make, this is driven by our beliefs, so we would do well to always be double-checking those beliefs.

Our basic problem is that there's a lot of luck involved in the way things turn out. When we consider that beliefs inform the bets we make, that then results in a set of possible outcomes, but now we have to take the way that the future unfolds for us—the outcome that actually occurs— and figure out how to use that information to loop that back in, to update our beliefs, so that we can be a better decision-maker going forward.

The problem is that we can't see into the underlying cause of a particular outcome. It could be because of bad luck. If I go through a green light and I get in a car accident, I got unlucky. In that case, that outcome is not going to inform my beliefs about whether I should drive through green lights again. I'm going to throw it into the luck bucket and say, "That particular result shouldn't inform what my future decisions are going to be."

Now, if I go through a red light and I get in a car accident, hopefully I'm saying, "You know what, I should be sorting that into the skill bucket, I should use that to update my belief about whether I should go through red lights or not." But if you can get in an accident going through a green light or going through a red light, how can we tell?

Another example is when you go to the doctor with a cough. You could have a viral infection, you could have inflammation in the back of your throat that doesn't have anything to do with the virus, you could have some bacterial infection, you could have cancer, you could have a neurological problem, you could have allergies. There are all sorts of reasons that you could be coughing, and to a layman they're all going to look relatively the same, so how do you sort through when someone's coughing and try to derive the underlying cause?

That's a hard problem, and to make it worse, there are few outcomes that are solely luck or solely skill. Normally, it's some combination of the two, and we're trying to sort out what was in our control, which would be in the skill bucket, and what wasn't in our control in the luck bucket. And that decision is a second bet. We make this initial bet that results in a set of outcomes, and then once the outcome occurs, we have to make **We would do well to always be double-checking those beliefs.** a second bet about what part of it was in our control due to skill so that we can become good learners about it, and what part of it was due to luck, which we would just offload.

Here's the problem. Because this relationship between the outcomes that we have and the decisions we make is so loose, we have a lot of leeway when we're examining our own outcomes to take the bad stuff and say, "That was bad luck," and to take the good stuff and say, "That's because I'm such a genius." That's the tendency when we're examining why things turned out the way they did.

This is different than when we're an observer of Pete Carroll and we're saying, "You had this bad outcome, you must be such a bad decision-maker." That doesn't have to do with our own ego, our own life story. Once it becomes about our own life story, we make this consistent error known as self-serving bias. The bad stuff is because of luck, the good stuff is because of skill. And that becomes a big problem for learning.

That brings me to the story about Phil Ivey, who is one of the best poker players on earth. He's incredibly good at every single form of poker. He won a big tournament against an all-star final table. The other players at the table were brilliant poker players in their own right. After he won the tournament, he went off and had dinner with my brother.

Instead of saying, "Can you believe how great I am? Look at how well

I played. Of course, I deserve to win because I outplayed everybody. I'm so great," all he talked about was how poorly he had played. Not in the sense of, "Look, I'm a bad poker player," but he wanted to go through every single spot where he felt that he could have made a better decision. He was deconstructing all the hands that he thought were difficult, that maybe there was a different line of play he could have taken. And he was doing that with someone who he felt was going to give him good feedback. My brother, of course, was one of the best poker players in the world in his own right. He wanted to use it all as a learning opportunity as opposed to basking in the glow of the win. That shows you a different mindset and we can see it's probably not accidental that he's so good. He's not feeding his ego. He's making sure that he's learning as much as he can from every experience so that he has better and better results going forward.

Michael: We can all think of our lives in that way.

Annie: The conclusion that I come to, partly from looking at a lot of the literature, is it's hard to not be biased; it's too ingrained. Daniel Kahneman talks about this in *Thinking, Fast and Slow*. He's not specifically trying to offer a lot of solutions, but one thing he does say in the book is that he's starting to think that maybe better water-cooler conversations might be the way to go. And the idea behind this is we're all biased so we need to form constructive decision groups, because if we're trying to make decisions on our own, we're naturally always going to default to this self-serving view of the world where in general our beliefs are correct, we're smart, we take credit for the things that happen in our lives that are good, and we offload the things that don't turn out so good.

We tend to process the world in a way that supports a positive self-narrative and we process the world in the moment. One of the things that becomes obvious when you think about this is, if you take a little bit of pain now and say, "I don't deserve credit for that great thing that happened" or "There were decisions I made that led to this poor outcome that I could go back and change," surely you would become a better decision-maker going forward and the quality of your results would start to shift right on the distribution. You would get a lot of positive feedback going forward. But none of us are good at imagining the future and we don't want to take

Life is like the happiness stock where we're playing for the long run and we're trying to get a positive slope.

the pain in the moment. Left to our own devices, we're going to tend to default to that biased interpretation of the world.

Michael: It's beliefs versus facts.

Annie: Exactly. Being in a good decision group is the way to become better at this. One thing that happens a lot is that people think, "Do I need a strong decision group? Because if I acknowledge these biases and I'm a smart person who knows how to analyze data, isn't it true that I'm going to inoculate myself against the biases?" The answer is no.

It turns out that in a lot of ways being smart makes it worse. Smart people tend to have stronger blind spots to their biases, according to Keith Stanovich. And the work of Dan Kahan at Yale shows us that the more numerate you are, the better you are at analyzing statistics in a way that will support your prior position.

Jon Haidt said something to this effect that resonated with me: "I've realized that people are so biased that unless you have the clash of ideas out in the open square, we're all doomed."

Michael: We don't have the clash of ideas. On almost every issue these days, it seems like a partisan perspective gets in front of the idea. I feel bad for young people who are growing up in such a hyper-partisan world where they don't get a chance to say to themselves, "I don't know anything about Annie's politics, but look at the way she plays poker, I can learn from that."

Annie: You're getting a lot of the halo effect—if you're good at one thing, you're good at all sorts of other things that aren't necessarily related to the thing that you're good at. The reverse of that would be, if I don't like something about you in one domain, then I'm going to dismiss you across all domains. When we're talking about what's happening in the political world, if I disagree with your politics, I tend to dismiss you altogether and think your opinions have no value and you have nothing to teach me, and that's terrifying.

Michael: How interesting is it for you that you have been in the poker world and now you're coming back to the academic path?

Annie: For a long time, I felt like I was circling back. But I'm actually going to push back on that description of circling back; I'm going to make the argument that I never left. And here's why. I'm in graduate school, I'm going off to give my job talks. I ended up with a physical illness that caused me to delay going out onto the job market for a year and I started playing poker while I took time off to get healthy. I joke that my brief respite turned into 20 years!

In 2002, I started doing talks, but I still viewed myself as a full-time poker player. In 2012, academic work started to take a much bigger place in my life. If you had asked me around 2012, I would've said, "Well, I've circled back around. I've come back home to what I was doing in the first place."

But then I realized that actually I never left. When I was in graduate school studying cognitive psychology and language acquisition, that seems far afield from poker. But no, it's actually the exact same thing. If you think about a child learning their first language, there's this noisy system in the sense that there are these words flying around, there's all sorts of objects and actions and qualities that are out in the world, and the question that I was always asking myself is, "How does this baby decipher some unknown word?" They have to figure out that word refers to the chair over in the corner as opposed to any of the other objects that might be in the room, or some quality of the chair, like soft or brown or striped, or some action that's occurring, like somebody sitting in the chair.

Every single decision we make is a bet.

It's a noisy system to try to map these words onto actions, qualities, things, people, sounds, and all of that stuff. Then, once you've done that, you've got to take the feedback that that's being offered to you about whether you landed on the right idea and feed that back into the loop, and this is a hard problem. Kids have this solved by the time they're about two—it's remarkable. I was thinking about these problems and how do you learn in these noisy systems with noisy feedback.

Something I learned in psychology is that learning occurs when there's lots of feedback tied closely in time, decisions, and actions. A poker table is about the best play-out of that particular sentence that you can see.

A hand of poker takes maybe two minutes, including the shuffle and the deal, and can contain up to 20 decisions. Lots and lots of actions and decisions are occurring in a compressed period of time, and you're getting feedback right away, in this chip exchange that's occurring. I realized people should be learning very, very quickly when they're sitting at a poker table. In fact, it should be quite hard to make a living at poker, because there is so much feedback and so many decisions and actions that are occurring, and you're getting the feedback within 30 seconds.

But I came in and I was able to win. As I continued in the game over the course of 20 years, I saw people stalled in their learning, despite the fact that they were getting lots of feedback that maybe the things they were doing at the table were not necessarily optimal decisions. Most people are not Phil Ivey. Most people aren't winning a tournament and talking about every single mistake they made and trying to deconstruct every single hand that they played. Most people are not using the feedback that's being given to them.

I realized it's because the feedback is so noisy. I can have aces, the best possible hand, you could have a seven and a two, the worst possible hand, and you can still win and I can still lose. As you're sorting those outcomes out, I noticed there was a strong tendency not only in the people that I was playing against, but certainly in myself as well, when I lost, to say, "That was bad luck," and when I won, to say, "Look what a genius I am."

That feels good in the moment, but it's bad for the long run. What I realized is these problems that I was thinking about when I was at graduate school never went away, because this is the exact same problem: how do you learn when these things that you're trying to learn about are only loosely correlated with each other and there is a lot of noise in the system?

Michael: How does the word "bets" resonate with the masses?

Annie: The problem is that we don't think of our decisions as bets in an explicit way. I have certain limited resources—money, time, happiness, health, whatever—and I have to invest these limited resources in some decision that's going to drive me towards some set of possible futures, but those futures are only possible and there's a set of them. There's also an uncertain future that I'm driving myself towards. That's exactly what a bet is.

We tend to think about bets in the traditional sense—things that occur in a casino where I take my money. In that case, that would be the limited resource, and I bet on, say, a hand in blackjack. And there's some set of possible futures in which I win the hand, some in which I lose the hand, some in which I double down on my bet and that branches off into win or lose, some in which I split my cards and that branches off into win or lose. And we're betting against somebody, in this case the house. If I were to say to somebody, "What's a bet?" that's what they would think.

We need to realize that every single decision we make is a bet, because we're taking whatever limited resources we have—and again, it doesn't have to be money—and we're driving toward a set of possible futures. And we're mostly betting against ourselves. What that means is that there's some version of future Annie that occurs when future A happens, and there's some version of future Annie that occurs when future B happens, and some version of future Annie that occurs when future C happens, and so on.

When I make a decision that's driving me toward a particular set of futures, I'm saying that the Annie that exists in that particular set of futures will be better off than the Annie that exists in the set of futures that some other decision might have driven me toward. They're bets against ourselves, bets against alternative versions of future you.

We can all feel that deeply under circumstances where we had difficult decisions to make, and we're trying to decide between the options. And we decided on, say, option A, and we've hitched ourselves to a future that happened not to have worked out. Then we say to ourselves, "Argh, I knew it. I should have chosen option B. Why did I choose option A?" That's the alternative future version of us saying, "I told you."

Michael: People have trouble placing one bet and then quickly placing another, and adjusting the first bet with the second bet and moving on down the chain. Life becomes a bet that constantly compounds upon itself. That's a tricky thing for a lot of people, because it's not something that is brought up in the average high school or, frankly, most colleges.

Annie: Not at all. This is a self-compassionate way to look at things, which is your point, because everything is a bet and they compound on each other. We have to bet on whether some outcome was because of a lack of skill, so we can feed it back into the learning loop so that our beliefs can get updated, so we can make a better bet going forward.

One of the things we don't like to think about is that there's a lot of uncertainty in the world. We don't know what the future holds. We can't know with 100% certainty whether the bet we made is the right one. All we're trying to do is figure out what's the highest probability that I'm going to have a good outcome here. None of it is ever 100% or 0%, and that's scary for people.

In *Thinking in Bets*, I talk about how we're bad at saying, "I'm not sure." Partly because when you're in school, if you put "I'm not sure" on a test answer, you would get it wrong. Which is too bad, because we should be able to say, "I'm not sure, but here's what I do know, and let me show you some of my work. I'm not sure if this is right." You should get extra credit for that, because if we were to model the world, "I'm not sure" is almost the right answer to pretty much everything. Is this the fastest way to get to the airport? The answer would be, "I'm not sure. It depends on traffic. I don't know whether there's going to be a semi that's turned over in the middle of the road. I can tell you that given my past experiences, this tends to be the fastest way to get to the airport, but I'm not sure today if it is." That would be a better answer to that question, for example.

Michael: When you say, "I don't know," and you're comfortable with it, biologically, physiologically, there's a lot of good things happening inside of us. But when you think you have to know, it's creating an unsolvable stress.

Annie: A lot of the paralysis people feel when they're making decisions is they think that they have to be certain. One of the questions I get asked is, "Well, if I approach the world from the standpoint of uncertainty, that's saying, 'Hey, I don't know how it's going to turn out. I'm betting on it.' How do you ever make a decision then?"

'I'm not sure' is almost the right answer to pretty much everything.

And I say, "That's exactly how you make a decision, because you know that you can't be certain, and so you get much better at strategizing as opposed to always trying to maximize, which is hard to do when there's hidden information and luck." You're much more willing to say, "Okay, I've done my homework, I've figured out what I know, I've gone to the people around me who I trust, who are of the right category to give me a good opinion. I've gotten their opinion to try to check my biases, to try to check my beliefs and update those as best as I can, and run the decision by them. Look, I think this is going to have the highest probability of working out."

What's wonderful is that you've now wrapped uncertainty into that. You think it's going to get you to the best place, and you've done your best work to get there, so when it doesn't work out, it doesn't feel so bad because you thought about it beforehand. And when we have a good outcome, we aren't as likely to sit there and go, "Let me bask in the glory at this because I'm so brilliant," because the brilliance was already wrapped into the decision in the first place and we knew that there was some possibility that outcome would occur.

You could say, "I had these outcomes, I knew that there was this possible set. Now, let me go back and see if there is some way that I can improve this decision going forward. Was the good outcome more or less likely than maybe I thought? Was the bad outcome more or less likely than I thought it was now that I have this little bit of data here?" Because one data point doesn't tell us enough to make big changes, but we can start to refine based on that.

What's lovely about that is not just that we're much less likely to be swatting these things away when they don't feel good or onboarding them when they do. We're much less likely to get emotionally distressed by a bad outcome because we've wrapped it into the decision process in the first place. Also, it allows us to be more decisive. The thing that scares people the most is they think, "Oh, this sounds like I'm just out there. What does it mean if I'm not certain that it's going to work out? It feels more like guessing."

The problem is that you are already guessing because you can't be 100% certain of anything—that's completely impossible. If you know that you're already guessing but you're walking through the world pretending you're not, number one, you don't have an accurate view of the world, and that's going to degrade your decision quality, and number two, it's likely to cause you to be paralyzed because you feel like you have to get to certainty in order to actually make a decision.

Michael: I think your confidence is scary for people who are not familiar with thinking of bets as a way of life.

Annie: The confidence comes from the fact that I acknowledge that I don't know, which hopefully will help people feel better about it. If I'm in a restaurant and I'm trying to decide between two dishes or I'm at a grocery store and I'm trying to decide between which line I'm going to get into, I know that's a bet. I'm betting that line A is going to be faster than line B, and I might be wrong—not wrong in the sense of I made a poor bet because I'm looking at how many things are in the person's grocery cart and how fast the checker is, but I could end up in a line that's slower even though I've gone through the decision process. I don't know whether this line will be faster. All I'm trying to do is use my best judgment here, and given what I do know, and the presence of luck, trying to get myself to the best possible future—in this case, being in the fastest grocery line. The other thing that I recognize is that I never need to get anywhere near perfection in order to have this stuff work out.

These things compound over time, and small changes will make a big difference. If you think about it like this, you have some distribution of the quality of decisions that you make, and there's some decisions that are way out at the left tail. Those will be terrible decisions. Some decisions that are way out at the right tail, those are excellent decisions. And then you have what your average decision quality looks like. What we're trying to do is get more of our decisions out to the right tail, maybe make the tails a little fatter. And then eventually, we're trying to shift the whole distribution, but let's start with getting more of our decisions out to the right tail. I can do that, for example, by forming a good decision group, then with their help I can make sure that I'm executing more decisions that are at the right tail of my own distribution. Now, when I do that, I only have to make each decision marginally better than what it otherwise might've been, because that creates a better probability that I'm going to have a good outcome, which is then going to put me in a better position for the next decision that I have to make, which hopefully will be a little bit more to the right of my distribution, which will then create a marginally better chance that I have a good outcome, and so on and so forth.

And over your lifetime, like compounding interest, that's going to create a much higher likelihood of having good outcomes.

An example that I give in *Thinking in Bets* comes from poker. We have all of this feedback happening, so let's say I'm playing in a game and I have 100 learning opportunities that got dumped into my lap. We know that it's a noisy system, so I'm going to miss a lot of them. Let's say that if I'm running on my own, left to my own devices without doing this work or thinking in bets, maybe I catch five out of the 100 learning opportunities. So, I'm missing 95% of my chances to learn. And now let's say that I do the hard work of thinking in bets and I manage to now catch 10 of the learning opportunities as opposed to five. Now, notice that I'm still missing 90% of the learning opportunities that are being dumped in my lap, but I'm going to do a lot better. The outcomes for Annie who catches 10 are going to be much better because those are going to compound over time.

> **Confidence comes from the fact that I acknowledge that I don't know.**

Think about how wonderful it is to think in bets, because if you're thinking from a standpoint of certainty, not catching all 100 of those learning opportunities is considered failure. But by understanding that we're in this noisy system, trying to do the best we can to hitch ourselves to the most likely good outcome that we can find, then Annie who's only catching 10 is now a huge success because I'm doing better than I was before.

Michael: I would guess that for a certain number of people in the population that get down and perhaps suffer from depression, some of it comes from this incorrect view that they are supposed to navigate life in this certain way, and that there is perfection. Whereas if someone's listening to you with an open mind, they can hear that you are comfortable not knowing.

Annie: In particular types of therapy, such as cognitive behavioral therapy, some of these concepts are wrapped into that—the idea that we shouldn't be overgeneralizing, that we can't know for certain how things are going to work out, that you can't possibly achieve certainty, that when things don't work out it's not necessarily your fault.

What has to go along with that is that sometimes there are decisions that can be improved and sometimes the good stuff isn't because you're such a genius, and sometimes it is.

You approach your outcomes in a much less emotionally charged way when you recognize that a single outcome doesn't have a lot to say about what your life narrative should look like, whether that narrative is positive or negative, whether you're smart, whether you're a good actor, whether you're a good decision-maker. You can view your life outcomes more from the standpoint of an observer, rather than someone who is so incredibly emotionally invested in every single thing that happens to you. Once you step back, you notice that the emotional charge isn't there anymore. There's a lot more self-compassion that comes from that, because we aren't getting yanked around by the momentary fluctuations.

Life is more like the happiness stock where we're playing for the long run and we're trying to get a positive slope. If we drill down and we take a zoom lens onto what that function looks like, as we look at that happiness stock, we're going to see these momentary fluctuations. We know that when we're investing in a stock for the long run, all we're looking for is a positive slope, and what happens at 11:30 on a Tuesday is pretty irrelevant. If we can get to that place where we're thinking about our lives in that way, it's going to create a lot more happiness for us; it's going to make us a lot warmer, a lot less hard on ourselves.

Michael: Social media pushes the opposite of what you push.

Annie: You can be smart about the way you approach social media, which is, as Jon Haidt said, to expose yourself to the clash of ideas in the public square. It's bad if you're only following people you agree with. That's not to say that you should necessarily be following people who are at the extreme (although taking a look at subreddits occasionally is actually quite helpful to gain an understanding that those worlds exist), but it would be good if everybody went and looked at their Twitter in this way: If I say I am liberal, am I only following people with liberal opinions? Or am I following some people with conservative opinions? If you're a conservative, are you following people with liberal opinions?

You can do that about anything. There are all sorts of different theories in investing. There are people who are pro-Bitcoin or people who are anti-Bitcoin and cryptocurrencies, and you should make sure that you have a slate. Obviously you want to get the more thoughtful people from each slate—that's the way I use social media.

CHAPTER 8
BRETT STEENBARGER

PART 1
The State of Flow

BRETT N. STEENBARGER is Clinical Associate Professor of Psychiatry and Behavioral Sciences at State University of New York (SUNY) Upstate Medical University in Syracuse, New York. An active trader and author of the popular TraderFeed blog, Brett coaches traders in hedge funds, proprietary trading groups, and investment bank settings. He is also the author of the Wiley titles *Enhancing Trader Performance* and *The Psychology of Trading*. Brett received a BS from Duke University and a PhD in Clinical Psychology from the University of Kansas.

Michael note

Brett Steenbarger is one of my favorite guests. The ability to break us human beings down to the understandable is a serious skill. He has published a series of books and too many papers to count. He also writes a great blog you must check out.

Michael Covel: The first thing I wanted to jump into is the flow state. Michael Jordan, being in the zone, that type of thing.

Brett Steenbarger: That is a good analogy. Being in the zone is what people mean when they talk about a flow state. The flow concept was popularized by the psychologist/researcher Mihaly Csikszentmihalyi. He talked about states of consciousness in which people become fully and totally absorbed in what they are doing. They lose track of time. During those states, not only do they feel most fulfilled, but they also report their most creative work. And he found, in his studies, that this state is most likely to occur when there is a match between the challenges of a task and the skill level of the individual, so that when we are challenged by something we enjoy doing, but not overwhelmed by it, we become fully absorbed. If we're insufficiently challenged, we become bored. If we're overly challenged, we become overwhelmed. He proposed that learning in any discipline is most likely to occur effectively if we can sustain a state of flow.

Michael: How have you seen this manifested in the trading world?

Brett: One thing you emphasized in your *Trend Following* book was the idea of the importance of position sizing. It's something I find many traders don't consider adequately. For instance, if a trader is taking too much risk on a trade for their ultimate level of emotional tolerance, they're creating a mismatch. The challenge of the profit and loss state overwhelms them, so they can't remain in that flow state where they will optimally process market data. We're most likely to experience flow when we are not frustrated. If we set perfectionistic expectations that we won't experience whipsaws or we won't experience drawdowns, we set ourselves up for frustration that can nudge us out of that flow state.

Michael: Let's talk about risk tolerance. This is how much you should risk in whatever trading approach you might be taking. Of course, you can go too far to one side, and that's a pretty easy mathematical certitude. But when you start to risk those small amounts, it's such a personal choice. What are your views about how to get people to think about risk tolerance? It's not one size fits all.

Brett: There are two facets of risk management. One is the logical side, and one is the psychological side. And in a purely logical sense, you can determine, for a given or expected sharp ratio, what kind of risk you would need to take in order to generate a particular target return. Like you say, that's a fairly structured determination. The other question is, how much risk can a person tolerate psychologically? Is that a level of risk that investors are ultimately willing to tolerate?

There is a tremendous mandate among investors to make money and not lose it. And the world is not exactly constructed that way. What happens is that a level of risk taking may be appropriate for achieving a particular target return, and may even fit with a person's psychological risk tolerance, but could fall outside of the mandates of the owners of a firm, if it's a proprietary trading firm, or the investors in the firm. That can create conflicting problems. Many times I find that people are most able to manage capital effectively if their risk taking is less than what might be logically optimal—that by minimizing drawdowns and containing them, they are able to maintain a psychological state closer to the flow state that works for them. Many successful portfolio managers I've worked with are not high risk takers, but they end up being consistent and achieve good risk-adjusted returns.

> Learning is most likely to occur effectively if we can sustain a state of flow.

Michael: No risk, no return. You have to put your foot outside the boat, so to speak—you can't expect a return for not doing anything. Even astute institutional investors that maybe work with some of the largest public pension funds that put a lot of money with assorted hedge funds around the world, I sometimes wonder about their decision-making. It looks like a political crap shoot in there and it's often not the most astute investing decisions that are being made.

Brett: It can be political. It can be simply a function of cognitive bias. Investors, many times, are attracted to recent returns. And so, someone who's had a big year might be more likely to attract capital than someone who's had a more modest year, despite length of track record.

Michael: But we're also talking about institutional investors. These folks should be aware by now, for some of the largest funds in the world, where their alpha comes from.

Brett: I would agree and there are certainly more and less sophisticated investors. And again, this applies not only to institutional investors, but to anyone who is allocating capital to someone for trading. I see it happening within proprietary trading firms, hedge funds, and commodity trading advisors (CTAs). It's common to be drawn to eye-popping returns and overweight those.

Michael: I saw a quote on your site from Mario Andretti: "If you have everything under control, you're not moving fast enough."

Brett: It's interesting you picked that up. Obviously, you can't be completely out of control in your trading and in your risk taking; however,

> There are two facets of risk management: the logical side, and the psychological side.

we don't grow as people if we stay within our comfort zones. We have to push the envelope, to some degree, to expand our boundaries, to expand ourselves. I always want to be pushing, moving harder, moving faster, doing more, and pursuing opportunities that are uncertain, because those are the ones I find that lead to the greatest personal payoffs. If I'm feeling completely comfortable, completely in control in my personal life, then I probably am relatively stagnant.

Michael: How would you advise a client when you see this in their behavior? They think they're progressing, but they're too under control. They've lost the edge.

Brett: It gets back to that principle of what psychologists do, and that is comforting the afflicted and afflicting the comfortable. When things are going well, it's easy to take the eye off the performance ball. I will look for occasions where, even within that comfort zone, a trader or a portfolio manager might be missing opportunities, and bring that to their attention. I act as a mirror to the trader. Most of the professional traders I work with have enough of a competitive mindset that if you put them in front of that mirror and help them see that they are performing suboptimally, they often will pick up on that. But it takes that nudge.

Michael: You've worked with some of the top traders. Even though they might have hired you to give them the straight talk, do some of them still push back? Do some of them get to the point where they don't like that mirror?

Brett: Oh my goodness, yes. And I would go even further. There are some who want the trading coach to augment or support their own confirmation bias. They don't want to hear what's uncomfortable. They're looking for more of a cheerleader than a coach. That becomes difficult. There have been occasions where I've had to turn down coaching assignments because what the person was asking for would've required less than full integrity on my part.

Michael: I often see statements such as "95% of traders lose," or "entry is only 10% of the success," or "90% of trading comes down to the psychological component." What immediately comes to mind when you see those percentages tossed around?

Brett: What comes to mind is the distinction between what is necessary and what is sufficient. Having a focused and disciplined mindset is necessary for trading success, but it's not sufficient. If a relatively emotionless mindset were all that were needed to succeed in trading, then probably there would never be any losing algorithmic trading systems. The computer doesn't have emotions and it executes flawlessly, and in a disciplined fashion, and yet we all know that it can overfit and not perform. It takes focus and discipline, but it takes something more. That's commonly referred to as an edge in markets. You have to be trading patterns and concepts that reflect a true and objective, positive, expected return. The idea that psychology is 90% of trading is maybe true, but it takes an objective edge in order to succeed.

Michael: I first saw a process versus outcome chart from Michael Mauboussin. It showed that with a good process, a good outcome is

If I'm feeling completely comfortable, completely in control in my personal life, then I probably am relatively stagnant.

deserved. With a good process and bad outcome, that's a bad break. A bad process and a good outcome is dumb luck. And a bad process and a bad outcome is poetic justice. Process versus outcome. So many people are fixated on outcome that process gets lost in the shuffle.

Brett: We all know that there are going to be occasions, even with that edge, where there are a series of losing trades, or there is a losing period in markets. During these drawdown periods people begin to doubt their methods and make random changes in their processes. And so, the drawdown turns into a slump. It's like the baseball hitter who strikes out again, begins to doubt themself, and now changes their swing and proceeds to have several games of poor performance.

It is important to distinguish between process and outcome, and to be able to accept that, at times, there will be frustrating outcomes from good processes. We are not guaranteed success. Drawdowns are inevitable. By accepting that and focusing on process, we can stay as true as possible to whatever edge we have in markets.

Michael: Speaking with so many different fund managers over the years, I've seen many that have done well as trend following traders. And then the clients come to them, they see those results and they want a part of it. That still doesn't make it easy for people to accept what goes along with that style of trading. But in conversations over the years I've heard how the in and out of flow of money keeps even some of the best traders on edge. There are many men and women that you and I respect who have made fantastic fortunes and made their clients lots of money with 2 and 20 type fee structures. But those fee structures carry a psychological burden, don't they?

Brett: They certainly can. Worry is a two-edged sword. I've seen worry work in the favor of a trader in terms of keeping them prudent about risk management and act as a break on overconfidence biases. And I've seen worry act as one of those frustrations that take people out of the zone, out of that flow state. It becomes particularly challenging when the worries of investors end up becoming the worries of trading firms and money managers.

Michael: That defeats the whole purpose of why the investor actually wanted the expertise of that trader to begin with.

Brett: Your point is a good one, that it's one thing to intellectually accept a degree of uncertainty and potential drawdown from trading. It's another thing emotionally to accept that, and to be in that drawdown state, and be able to stick with a sound process.

Michael: What are some of the common characteristics of successful traders that you've seen?

Brett: There is an important distinction between short-term traders, most notably day traders, and longer-term traders, most notably investors.

I would mention *Thinking, Fast and Slow* by Daniel Kahneman here. My experience is that Kahneman's ideas are important—that there's a vital distinction between slow thinking, deep thinking, and fast thinking, quick pattern recognition. The shorter the timeframe of the market participant, the more I see fast thinking and quick pattern recognition as essential to success. The more I see longer timeframes and investing as important to the trader, the more I see the slow thinking, the deep thinking, the explicit analysis as important to success. There are hybrids too—people who I've known and worked with who have skills on both sides. But generally there are important skill differences between the short-term trader and the longer-term market participant.

It's common to be drawn to eye-popping returns and overweight those.

That being said, I do find some personality commonalities. One of the personality traits that is emphasized in the "big five" research, as it's called, is conscientiousness. Conscientiousness is attentiveness to detail, process orientation, and a sense of responsibility. People who are high in conscientiousness, who are detail-oriented, who are focused on responsibility, end up being more reliable followers of a particular system than people who are low in conscientiousness, who can be impulsive.

Another dimension that ends up being relatively important is emotional stability, or sometimes the opposite, neuroticism—people who are relatively steady in their emotional makeup versus people who have lots of emotional ups and downs. It's easiest to make decisions under conditions of risk and uncertainty if your flight and fight responses aren't roiling. I have found that successful traders either have this emotionally steady, stable makeup, or they find some mechanisms to provide them with a high degree of conscientiousness so that they can be detail-oriented and responsible. If they aren't grounded in a state where they are relatively steady emotionally and relatively reliable in their performance, they often don't follow whatever talents or skills they may have with consistency.

And that brings me to the last characteristic, which underscores one of the findings from Jack Schwager's research, that successful money managers are different from one another in their

Having a focused and disciplined mindset is necessary for trading success, but it's not sufficient.

personalities and in their trading styles, and they trade in a fashion that is consistent with their personality strengths. The person who is quantitatively oriented and analytically skilled might have different strengths than the person who has that fast-thinking pattern recognition. Each finds a way, through their trading, to be who they are in terms of those strengths.

Michael: I've an outside-the-box-type question. Given your background, and given the epidemic overuse and misuse of prescription drugs related to the mind, where are we headed? It seems like that we've passed the threshold of those people that need medical help, and we're at a point where a lot of issues of the mind are being treated primarily pharmaceutically.

Brett: As you know, I have a clinical faculty appointment at the medical school in Syracuse, New York. I'm a clinical psychologist by training, but I work closely with my colleagues in the department of psychiatry. I've seen both sides of this issue. I've seen people with lifelong debilitating depression or anxiety disorders benefit tremendously from the appropriate medications. It has turned their lives around. And I've seen people who have been overly quick to turn to pharmaceutical solutions, when in fact other ways of dealing with behavioral problems—for example, in children—could be found. There are habit-forming medications that can be quite dangerous, that end up being prescribed. I've seen this with the minor tranquilizers, benzodiazepines, that people take to calm themselves down or help themselves sleep. On a temporary basis, they can work. But used to excess over time, they create a dangerous dependence.

Michael: One more quote that I saw on your site that I love was from basketball coach Bob Knight: "Your biggest opponent isn't the other guy, it's human nature."

Brett: I am a Bob Knight fan. I admit it publicly and proudly! We all have our moments, and we have our flaws. But what coach Knight exemplified was the importance of preparation—the drive to not just win, but to prepare to win. Human nature is such that we like to avoid effort. We like comfort. And as I mentioned before, we don't grow—certainly not as a basketball player—unless we push our limits. Human nature keeps us out of the gym. It keeps us away from practice. It keeps us from researching markets and from developing fresh sources of edge. It's important to push past that.

Michael: I'd like to talk about two different trading strategies: trend trading versus mean reversion.

Brett: Many times traders, trading firms, and investors have trouble tolerating drawdown. Even though they may end up conceptualizing a macro market in terms of trend, they find themselves unable to fully participate in that trend and trade with it because it always involves some degree of retracement. And so what happens, ironically, is that people who think of their trades in terms of trend will end up trading in a way that

> How people actually behave and how they describe their behavior can be very, very different things.

looks more mean reverting. As a result, their participation in any trend that manifests is suboptimal.

One of the cornerstones of my own thinking about markets is a philosophical tradition called contextualism. Contextualism emphasizes that events are the result of the context of situations that we are in. There are situations in markets that lead to more directional persistence and there are situations that lead to less directional persistence. We call those situations regimes. They're stable periods in which patterns within markets will persist and then change with changing economic conditions, changing social conditions, and so forth.

I like to think of trend not only in terms of price movement, but in terms of regime persistence. Now, that persistence of regime may or may not implicate directional persistence of price movement. You could have a mean reverting pattern that is part of a stable regime, that itself will persist over time. And so the trend that you're trading in that situation is not trend of price movement, but trend of regime, if that makes sense. From my perspective, trend following is a broader and more important concept than simply whether markets will go up or down day after day.

Michael: You are, perhaps inadvertently, bringing up an even more important issue, which is definitions in the trading and market space. Terms get tossed around with different meanings. One I've seen recently that's hotly debated is trend following and momentum trading getting put into the same camp.

Brett: Yes. And a hell of a lot of emotional attachment to terms like momentum or value. And the discussions end up being more ones of ideological affiliation than real understanding.

Michael: That's true. Somebody could criticize my world and say, "You do that for trend following." What I have tried to do, though, is find particular traders who often weren't associated with each other but were trading in similar ways, making or losing money in the same months, which I thought was unique data to have and to analyze. With bigger terms like value, you could say, well, Warren Buffett and Seth Klarman are both value traders, but they don't behave necessarily in the same way.

Brett: How people actually behave and how they describe their behavior can be very, very different things. And that's the bedevilment of every psychologist, that when you look at what people do as opposed to what they say they do, you see some important differences. There's a whole tradition in psychotherapy called integration perspective, which looks at what the common characteristics are of good therapies. So, if you look at successful therapists, what are they doing in common? Even though some might say they're a behaviorist, and some might say they're a Freudian, and some might say they're a humanist, what are they doing similarly that might account for their positive outcomes? It turns out there are common, effective ingredients of therapies. I suspect, as you're alluding to, that's true for trading as well.

Michael: I've seen people who describe themselves in certain terms, and they're honest and accurate, while other traders don't want to use the term that would best describe them. I often figure it's for client purposes or marketing purposes, because it's clear they're doing what they say they're not doing.

Brett: One of the areas of research that fascinates me is the role of creativity in successful trading. And the process of thinking aloud, talking aloud, writing, processing information explicitly, and then reading over or listening to what you have said ends up being one of the techniques that can lead to fresh perspectives and creative outcomes.

Michael: My podcast is like that for me. It's like going to a never-ending school with very, very bright people. It's quite fun.

Brett: It's a tremendous resource that you've assembled. I think of each podcast as a kind of prism. You're putting on a different set of lenses, so to speak, so that you're seeing the world from a different angle. And eventually, with enough good people giving you enough good lenses, you start to see fresh angles and fresh directions. That's what leads to creative insights and promising directions in trading or in other areas of life.

PART 2
The Principles of Performance

Michael Covel: Do people have a burning desire to succeed?

Brett Steenbarger: That's a great question. I do believe the majority of traders go into trading with ideas of success. Now, those ideas may be fantasies or they may be plans, but they're drawn to trading in large part for the outcomes. The problem that often occurs—and I see this more among beginning traders than experienced ones—is that part of what draws them to trading is the allure of not working a standard 9-to-5 job, and it seems this could provide relatively easy riches. Of course, as you and I know, it's much more than a 9-to-5 job when you do it right. The fantasy of the easy riches collides with the reality of what you need to do to prepare to win, and that creates quite a dissonance for many beginning traders and ultimately leads them to leave the field.

Michael: There's a burning desire for the outcome, but not too many people will take the step back and say, "Okay, hold on, we can't just focus on the outcome or we will go crazy. We must break this down. We must look more at our process." I would love for you to draw some distinctions here from process to practice, practice to process.

Brett: The distinction I like to make is between those who have a self-proclaimed passion for trading and those who have an enduring passion for markets. Those two are very different. The person with the passion for trading wants to trade and ultimately ends up over-trading. But when markets are closed, there's nothing to generate passion. That's different than the person who has a passion for markets, where it's more about process, an interest in understanding, unraveling, reverse-engineering what's going on in markets and figuring out ways to better exploit that. Those are different motivations that end up with different consequences for traders.

Your question about practice and process to me is essential. Often you hear traders talk—and again, I see it more with the beginning traders— about finding your edge, and sticking to your edge. All well and good. However, that doesn't take into account the reality that markets are ever-changing and finding your edge is a continual process, so we have to be continually evolving. The way that happens in the medical world, where I came from, is through identification of best practices that lead to the best outcomes and then turning those best practices into robust processes so that they become habit patterns—they become automatic.

> **Markets are ever-changing and finding your edge is a continual process.**

The analogy of evidence-based medicine is quite apt for trading. We want to find the drivers of our success and turn those into processes that become replicable.

Michael: Markets are always changing and one of the lessons that you talk about is adaptability. We can't control the markets, so whatever the markets must do—and they will do something—adaptability is number one, isn't it?

Brett: Absolutely. A great example that I've written about is in trend following. Trend following as it occurred in the late 1990s is quite different from trend following right now (late 2015). There are portfolio managers and traders I work with who are trading trends, who are trying to identify trends to trade, but the way they are executing on their trend trading is more similar to what happened in the late 1990s, whereby they are confusing trend with momentum. So, if they're long, they're buying strength; if they're short, they're selling weakness. What we've seen recently are markets that show anti-momentum in the short run, even as they are trending.

A different way of saying that is the trends have a lower Sharpe ratio.

How you implement a trend following approach requires adaptability. You may stick to your basic orientation to markets, i.e., trend following, but how you make that happen, how you put it into practice, has to be based on outcomes and your study of markets. That's where the adaptability comes in.

Michael: It gets even more complicated when you read about a large fund that's managing billions of dollars, and let's say they started off as a trend following fund and perhaps they still have billions of dollars as a pure trend following trader, but they're adding other strategies. That raises a whole different issue, which is not about markets and more about clients. When I talk to the pro-trend following traders on the record, they're going to talk in a certain way to appeal to clients. You get them off the record, they say, "Oh my gosh, it's such a pain in the neck to deal with clients that don't understand our strategy."

Brett: For a fund, diversification makes sense. There may be trend following approaches, and there may be relative value approaches, and so on. Having diversified sources of return is a good thing for investors. One of the things I've seen in the fund world is that investors have limited appetite for the downside—that's been true ever since the 2008 debacle—so funds are managing risk much more tightly than in the past. So, even though in name they may be trend followers, any wiggles against the trend—that lower Sharpe ratio that I mentioned—ends up getting them out, often at the worst possible time. Sometimes it's the business pressures and the pressures of risk management that make it difficult for a trader to implement their strategy.

Michael: Track records often contain remarkably insightful data. It's incumbent on individuals to do their homework, because sometimes the public pronouncements don't match the performance data.

Brett: One of the downsides of having so much computing power now is that it's relatively easy to back test strategies. With enough iterations, you can randomly find a strategy that will look good not only on the back test, but on out-of-sample performance. It looks like a smooth, wonderful, ideal profit-and-loss curve, but of course that doesn't match the reality of real-time returns.

Michael: So much of elite performance starts at that research level, that back test level. The ultimate execution often can be quick, but it's all that prep time where the gold is made, so to speak.

Brett: The key in performance fields is that elite performers spend more time in preparation than in actual competitive performance. There's a lot of practice time that goes into the curtains being raised on a Broadway play. There's a lot of practice time that goes into the first game of a chess tournament. Preparation works at two different levels: it helps develop a strategy and approach, and it helps prepare the performer mentally, psychologically, emotionally. That preparation time, I found, is correlated with success to the degree that it pushes the trader to expand their horizons and develop the best of what they're doing.

Michael: There are some pro traders at the highest levels, perhaps with long track records, perhaps a lot of money under management, and the way they go about practice might not be nearly as good as one of their peers who might have deliberate practice down to a science. There's some contrast, even at the highest levels.

Brett: Very much so. I'm blessed by being able to work with a number of talented traders and successful firms. In fact, the smallest firm that I work with has about $3bn under management. Traders in those kind of firms have to do something right, and have to have some real strengths to get to that point of managing significant capital. But even within those funds between portfolio managers, there are real differences in the preparation approach.

I would say there are two sources of difference. One is the difference between repeated experience and deliberate practice. Some traders try to learn rigorously from their trading—What did I do wrong? What could I improve? How am I going to improve it tomorrow? Next week?—and they're constantly setting goals and then keeping score about whether they reach those goals or not. That's the essence of deliberate practice.

The second thing that distinguishes the successful traders is the emphasis on what they do right: their strengths. Positive psychology research tells us is that it's leveraging our strengths, not just showing our weaknesses, that accounts for elite performance. We want to figure out what are we doing well, because those are the practices that will anchor our best processes.

So, in two different respects—identifying what we're doing wrong, correcting that rigorously, and identifying what we're doing right, and turning that into best practices—that is real preparation.

Michael: Let's say we're giving advice to the new trader at the table. Let's say we're talking more of a system mindset. As a systems trader, you need to have entry/exit criteria. You have to know how you're going to manage your portfolio. What's the risk management strategy? You can't leave that out.

Brett: I do believe that the strengths that make a good systems trader are different from the strengths that make a good discretionary trader. Much of the success of systems pertains to the quality of the research that's conducted. In some ways, the strengths that are relevant to a systems trader are not so different from those that are relevant to a medical researcher. The information you take in, how you process that information, how many variables you consider at one time, and how you weight them—those are all part of what can be best practices.

> **Elite performers spend more time in preparation than in actual competitive performance.**

There are also strengths interpersonally. Many times, the research is too complex to be conducted individually. I work with some people who develop relatively high-frequency systems, and those systems are developed in teams. There are programmers, there are quants, there are traders. Being able to work well with others is a strength that is highly relevant to best practices and to ultimate outcomes. In the systems world, for discretionary traders, strengths are different and often pertain to the amount and type of information that's taken in, how that information is translated into tradeable ideas, how those ideas are expressed and managed as positions, including the risk management, and of course there are best practices related to not only risk management and position management, but self-management—how we take care of ourselves. All of those go into making someone successful. There's no single process of trading. Trading consists of multiple intersecting processes.

Michael: Talk about creativity. I have a feeling that many traders, entrepreneurs, and venture capitalists think of creativity as instinctive. But defining creativity like you've done changes the ballgame a little. It forces us to think about the word itself. I don't know that a lot of people would necessarily think, "I have to be creative to be a trader."

Brett: Yes, to the degree that we regard trading as a business. But it makes sense to say, "We have to be doing something unique in order to be superlatively successful at this business." If I open a hamburger stand that's like every other hamburger purveyor, then how am I going to achieve a significant degree of economic success? I have to do something different, unique, and it's in that difference, that uniqueness, that creativity comes into play. We see that in financial markets, because many times the herd is following a similar set of strategies, looking at the same information and processing it the same way. That's why you see swings in sentiment that often end up being relatively good contrary measures. That's why you see many people getting hurt at the relative tops and bottoms of markets because they are doing things that are not unique, not creative.

It's particularly an issue in professional money management, where there tends to be a high correlation among financial markets. There also, as a result, tends to be a high correlation of returns among portfolio managers within a firm and across firms. That is a problem for investors. Investors want to diversify their capital. A trader who has the creativity to examine tests and implement new strategies is going to be appealing to anyone who invests and wants that diversification.

Michael: You point out in your work, hurting a little, or maybe even a lot, is where the reward often is. In some perverse way, that desire for comfort can set one up for a black swan event. So, comfort's often an illusion, isn't it?

Brett: I agree with you and it's hard to imagine us extending our boundaries, transcending who we are, if we aren't willing to go outside

Asset management is all about achieving smoother returns, more unique returns, rather than chasing beta from any given market.

our comfort zone. That can be done in a variety of ways. It can be done by looking at new markets. It can be looking at existing markets in new ways. It could be looking at new and different timeframes for implementing our trading.

One example from my own recent trading has been a redefinition of volatility. I find that volatility is important to market returns and in the models that I create, volatility ends up being an important variable. As we know with stocks in particular, volume and volatility are highly correlated, so that markets move more when there's more participation, which makes sense. But I got it in my head, "Well, what if I looked at volatility a different way? What if I looked at the volatility of a given amount of volume in the market?"

> We have to be doing something unique in order to be superlatively successful.

If X number of shares trade or X number of contracts trade in the market, how much movement is associated with that amount of volume? You're disaggregating the relationship between volume and volatility, which I call pure volatility, and it turns out that has real value as a variable for understanding markets. Because when you see volume expanding, and when you see the movement per unit of volume expanding, you can get some big moves. That's an example of creativity—looking at something similar in a unique way.

Michael: We've all got a certain personality. We've come to the game with something. We behave in a certain way. We think in a certain way. We react in a certain way. Our emotions go in a certain direction. Jack Schwager has said it for a long time: "You got to trade your personality."

For a lot of people, that might be hard to digest. Why don't you break apart the word personality from your perspective and give some guidance to the audience out there that's thinking, "Man, I might not even be sure what my personality is. And if I do know, how do I make the decision which direction to go?" It's a conundrum.

Brett: It's even more complex than your question implies, because as you mentioned earlier, it's not only personality traits, it's also our cognitive style—how we think about things. We want to leverage our strengths in both of those domains. Again, reverse-engineering the success of our trading can provide real clues as to some of those signature personality and cognitive strengths that would contribute to our success.

What I've found from the research I've done with traders is that average holding period ends up being an important variable, particularly on the cognitive side. I would make a distinction psychologically between a trader and an investor. The longer timeframe necessitates a higher degree of underlying research, and the longer-term research becomes the focus, not the day-to-day movements of the underlying assets.

That's a different set of strengths from the active day trader, who is looking at markets moving rapidly, seeing patterns set up quickly in markets, and trading those patterns. There's little explicit research, reading, calculation. It's all about fast pattern recognition. The distinction that has been made between thinking fast and thinking slow is relevant here—the deeper the thinking, the faster the pattern recognition. As Kahneman states, those are two different brain functions and two different modes of processing information.

Now, in addition to that, we could distinguish two types of trader or investor personality-wise. One is highly risk-taking. They tend to be more outgoing, more extroverted, more stimulation-seeking, more aggressive, and are willing to take more risks in the pursuit of higher returns. The second group of traders is less interested in absolute returns than in risk-adjusted returns. They're less risk-taking, they're seeking smoother profit and loss curves, higher Sharpe ratios, and often are seeking what we would call alpha rather than beta. They tend to be more analytical in their cognitive style and more introverted in their personality style, so a different approach to markets. Those two dimensions, the holding period, the research orientation versus pattern recognition orientation, and the elements of risk-seeking versus risk-adjusted return-seeking are a few ways people could think about personality and cognitive style, and how that might relate to some of their strengths.

Michael: If somebody says to me they want to be a trend following trader and they want a smooth curve, I would say, "You've got the wrong strategy. There's no such thing." Is there a smooth curve for anybody?

Brett: Not at all. For any single strategy, the profit and loss curves are likely to be bumpy, if one were simply an index trader. However, the idea of smoother profit and loss curves is all about diversification, portfolio construction, and combining different approaches to markets to balance the returns. The basic risk parity notion of buying a volatility-weighted basket of interest rate instruments and equity instruments would be a case in point, in that in recent years, that basket has had a smoother profit and loss curve than either asset individually. You could expand that more broadly to a basic asset management approach.

For instance, if you think about returns as being generated by certain factors, trend or momentum could be one factor, value could be one factor, carry could be another factor, then you can combine investments or trades that express those different factors, and harvest returns from those factors in a smoother way than if you were trading one strategy in isolation. Asset management is all about achieving smoother returns, more unique returns, rather than chasing beta from any given market.

Michael: Of course, you're right. Once you add in multiple strategies, trying to find a smooth curve is the goal—that's what many people do. But trying to find a smooth equity curve from one strategy in isolation might be difficult.

Brett: I agree with you. Probably the bible of the asset management world would be Antti Ilmanen's book, *Expected Returns*, which is worth reading. I do think that there are things that individual traders can do to improve the smoothness of their returns. A simple example would be trade expression, that a given view in a given market may have more favorable risk-reward if traded with an option structure than if traded with an asset outright. There are ways of achieving better risk-reward, but that doesn't eliminate the potholes along the way.

Michael: Regardless of one's strategy, if there's no real emotional buy-in, success is never going to happen.

Brett: The emotional buy-in occurs because the trading approach is genuinely yours. You have researched it. You have thought about it. It springs from your creativity, it springs from your work, and it's the time and effort that generates the strategy and helps you understand it and believe in it. That's why it is perilous to borrow trading strategies from others. Because at the end of the day, you are not trading your strategy and it's unlikely you will have the conviction to stay in that strategy during those inevitable periods of drawdown.

Michael: If somebody gives you a strategy and you don't understand it, with your intention being to follow it like a black box and trust the signal that comes out, you're not going to make it. However, we all have to learn from somebody; we have to start somewhere. So, if you can get a head start, if you can move down the path, as long as you understand what's going on, that's how we all learn.

Brett: It's about mentorship and I see a lot of good mentoring at the firms where I work. In the beginning when you have a junior trader who is working at the side of a senior trader, the junior trader starts by mimicking the trading of his more senior colleague. That's what mentoring is all about in the earliest phases and it is a head start, as you point out. It's over time, as people make their own unique observations of markets and adapt their trading to their strengths, that they start to develop their own style and begin to express that approach to trading in their own manner.

> **It is perilous to borrow trading strategies from others.**

To take the example we've been talking about, someone may learn trend following at the feet of the master, and over time may implement it in new and different markets, may implement it on different timeframes, may implement it on relative price movement rather than absolute. There would be many ways to make the strategy one's own over time and develop that conviction that helps people stay in the strategy once it's theirs.

Michael: Let's talk checklists and ultimately moving towards a flowchart. Something concrete. It's standard operating procedure. But I have a feeling it comes naturally for you and it might not be natural for other people.

Brett: I wouldn't say it was natural and I think that for me it was part of an evolution. I think that's true for many people. Atul Gawande wrote *The Checklist Manifesto*, I think, because he saw that checklists were not standard operating procedure for most people, and yet they worked remarkably well for airline pilots, surgeons, and so forth. The idea of a checklist is to figure out those best practices, what you are supposed to be doing when you perform well, and you codify that in a list, and you don't risk your capital unless you do A, B, C, D, and E. Over time, you may discover new and different best practices and so your checklist will evolve, but it's a way of grounding yourself so that best practices turn into habit patterns, or processes.

Michael: How many traders come across you for the first time—maybe they've engaged you, maybe it's casual conversation—and they've got so much excitement? Maybe that excitement is unbridled, it's not necessarily focused. Your personality probably does a good job of calming people down; and if they can't calm down and take it to a checklist-type scenario, it's probably a pretty good self-reflect of saying, "Hey, you know what? Maybe this isn't for me."

Brett: Again, a good point. Many people are trading implicitly for action, for thrills. There's nothing worse for them than a quiet market. That approach to trading rubs against the grain of being more process-focused and keeping checklists.

I like people to be passionate about what they do. I like them to be excited about their work, what they discover, and what they trade in markets, but ultimately you want them doing what works best.

> When people develop checklists they figure out what they do best and turn that into a set of routines.

A great example in baseball history is Ted Williams. He diagrammed the strike zone and determined his batting average for every possible location of a pitch so that he knew where a pitch would have to appear on the plate for him to have the best odds of getting a hit. That's what people do when they develop best practices and checklists—they figure out what they do best and they turn that into a set of routines.

Michael: I want to talk about physical fitness. We can all think back to some article we read in our youth, or we saw a picture, maybe, of a trader or a successful person and they had an appearance that was clearly not healthy, which might get you thinking, "Oh, that guy, he made hundreds of millions of dollars and he's overweight and doesn't care about fitness."

Why don't you talk about health and fitness and perhaps even add in some of your views on yoga and the moment of now?

Brett: The research in psychology tells us that a positive emotional experience is associated with superior processing of information, superior productivity, superior creativity. Maximizing our positive experience in general is a way of preparing ourselves for trading performance. Part of that is our physical preparation, our energy level. Eating is part of that. Sleeping well is part of that. Physical exercise is part of that. Using yoga or meditation to help increase our focus and to help us stay calmly focused is part of that.

The training that we do on the physical side, on the personal side, fuels positive emotional experience and that ends up giving us greater focus, concentration, and energy level in our trading. I would say this same thing not only of exercise, but of the quality of our personal relationships, that maximizing our positive experience from those boosts our energy level and that ultimately fuels our trading.

Michael: Even though it's about trading, your work could apply to any discipline.

Brett: Trading happens to be the playing field that I've chosen, but the principles of performance are common across disciplines. Ultimately, we pursue the disciplines that speak to us.

CHAPTER 9

VAN THARP

PART 1
Trading Transformation

VAN THARP was the founder and president of the Van Tharp Institute, dedicated to offering high-quality education products and services for traders and investors around the globe. In the unique arena of professional trading coaches and consultants, he stood out as an international leader in the industry. Over the years, Tharp helped people overcome problems with system development, trading psychology, and success-related issues like self-sabotage.

Michael note

Van Tharp had a diverse career in the trading world. Many attribute the phrase "trading psychology" to Van. He also did heavy work in position sizing—what people often call money management. And for those that recall one of the best-selling market books of all time, Jack Schwager's *Market Wizards*, Van was in the classic first edition.

Michael Covel: What was Van doing as a 10-year-old boy? Where were you living at the time?

Van Tharp: By the time I was 21 years old, I had lived in 21 different houses in three different countries. I was probably in England in an Air Force dependent school at that time. My dad was an engineer attached to the Air Force, so I got to stay in England for 10 years. I had a nice British accent when I was five, then I went to Air Force dependent schools and I lost it.

Michael: Can you pinpoint the time where the love affair with markets, trading, psychology all started for you?

Van: I had two periods when I lost everything. The first one was while I was getting my PhD in psychology. It took the second one for me to begin to think, maybe it's me. Then I began a research project to figure out what was wrong with me. That's how it came together. The first thing I did was develop a test for traders and investors—a research tool to see what might be wrong with me, and if I could measure that in other people too. We did a pretty good job of that.

Michael: What time period?

Van: We're talking 1981 or 1982.

Michael: There were not many other people attempting to bring psychology into trading at that time.

Van: There were three or four people who would periodically write a book to do with psychology in those days, but it wasn't what they did. Mark Douglas and I pretty much started at the same time, around 1982. We were the first two to do this thing full-time.

Michael: Define "trading psychology," what it means to you, and how you've come to talk to others about it.

Van: I'm going to give you a different approach, because my mission is transformation through a trading metaphor. There are three levels of transformation.

The first level is the least psychological, but it's adopting the kind of beliefs you need to be a successful trader. It comes out of my neuro-linguistic programming (NLP) modeling work, working with lots of traders on the process of trading in developing systems, in modeling position sizing, even modeling wealth. The next level of transformation is making the personal changes you need to even be able to adopt and accept those models, because a lot of people won't or can't do it. And the third level is if you transform yourself enough, you actually change your level of consciousness where it's easy to trade in the now and do some of those things. That's my global definition of what we do now.

Michael: Talk about NLP.

Van: To me, NLP was always the science of modeling. How do you figure out what somebody does and how do they do it well? And how can you teach that to somebody else? One of the keys to that is you can't model one person; you have to model a number of successful people. Initially, all the courses I took were the trail of techniques that had been developed through NLP from modeling work rather than how to model.

It took a while to get a good modeling course, which I got through a guy named Wyatt Woodsmall. One of the things he said is, you need to ask a number of people what they do well and find out what they do in common. When you figure out what they do in common, then you need to find out three ingredients for each of the tasks that they do: Beliefs, mental states, and mental strategies. And since beliefs, mental states, and mental strategies are all psychological, it leads you to believe that almost everything is psychological.

Michael: Give an example of NLP in action.

Van: Let's say I ask 10 good traders, "What do you do?" The first thing they tell me is something about their system and the first conclusion I'd probably draw, since all 10 have different systems, is that the success has nothing to do with the system itself, it has to do with what common elements are in the system. The first thing I get out of that is to develop what we call tasks of trading, which are the common tasks that people do when they trade. I'm going to give you the simplest task, because it's obvious, everybody does it, but I can show you how those three ingredients apply.

The task would be the action phase where you press the button on your computer to buy, or call your broker on the phone to buy, or whatever it happens to be. The basic belief behind that is it's an action step, there should be no thinking whatsoever involved. But it's interesting when you look at the mental strategy behind it. Mental strategies are the way people sequence their thinking.

The first thing people do is look at computers or charts or whatever, because most people work visually—they have to see some signal that tells them this is their entry. Then it goes internal and they have to recognize that it is a familiar signal—that's the one they need to work from. Then typically people act from feeling good, so they need to feel good about it, and then they take action.

> It is through position sizing that you meet your objectives in trading.

To illustrate how you can totally mess that up, all you need to do is add an auditory component—because people don't normally make decisions that way—where after you see the signal and you recognize it, you maybe ask yourself the question, "What could go wrong?" Then you don't feel good, you get a whole series of pictures about what could go wrong. The next thing you know, you're in a mess. That's a common example of how I've used NLP and modeling on a simple task.

I can give you another example that's much more obvious and should seem intuitive to everybody. We always say, before you enter into a trade, you should know exactly where you're going to get out, and that's what defines your initial risk. And you should probably never enter into a trade unless you have some idea that you at least have a 2:1 reward to risk in your favor. To support that, I typically recommend that everybody keep track of their trading results as R-multiples (the amount that you profited or lost in terms of your initial risk). A lot of people think that's silly, but if you don't do it, you don't think in terms of risk to reward. And that's one of the key things for success.

Michael: When you have this almost stoic mentality where you're worried about the worst-case scenario, you can calm yourself, because if something bad happens, it's not a surprise. Many people go through their life not thinking about the worst-case scenario, then when it happens, they're debilitated, they can't handle it.

Van: I don't see it like that. I believe you're crazy to ever enter into a trade without knowing when you're wrong about it and where you're going to get out. Worst-case scenario is you never get out and you take a huge loss that's many times bigger than you originally planned. If you're following a large trend and you're going to be in it for a long time, you typically might want a fairly wide stop that's going to keep you in through the whipsaws, like three times the average true range, or the old version of buy and hold for stocks to me was a 25% trailing stop. Those things protected you while the thing was going on, you didn't have to pay too much attention to the trend, and you just followed that. But there's a lot of people now who are day trading, and you might be able to get by with knowing you're wrong if it moves 20 cents against you simply because of the methodology you used to get in, in the first place.

Michael: You make it sound so easy, but people don't get this as easily as you describe it.

Van: These are the basic concepts that I was talking about. That's why we have to take people through level two transformations to get them to accept that. One way to think about it is, most people have seen the movie *The Matrix*. I love the metaphor because I think it's actually true that we are robots—we're all programmed and we live in an illusory world that's made up of our beliefs.

The first way you can actually deprogram yourself is to begin to look at all the beliefs you have to see if they're useful or not. Some beliefs are obviously not useful. Some beliefs are useful. I have some paradigms that we can take people through to help them see that. What happens for a lot of non-useful beliefs is they're highly charged with emotion. You can't just decide it's not useful, I'll get something else. You have to release all the charge involved in it too, and that's another level of this transformation.

If you remember, in *The Matrix*, Neo took the red pill and learned to

You're crazy to
ever enter into
a trade without
knowing when
you're wrong about
it and where you're
going to get out.

reprogram himself. That's beginning to look at your beliefs and reprogram yourself as to whether they're useful or not. Then eventually, towards the end, he was able to go beyond those beliefs, at which point he got superhuman powers. That's when you go to level three and you've raised your level of consciousness a lot.

Michael: Describe level three. I've heard you describe it as the moment of now, and I use that expression a lot in my work.

Van: David Hawkins has a scale of consciousness which I find quite useful in his book *Power vs. Force*. The scale goes from 0 to 1,000 and it's a log scale. A thousand, that's the level of a Buddha or a Jesus, and 200 is the difference between negative consciousness and positive consciousness. Most of humanity for much of its existence has been below 200. You don't even have to believe this scale is true, but if you look at the emotions involved, if you're trading out of fear, hatred, anger, apathy, or hopelessness, which are all in those lower states, then you're not going to do well. It's not until you get up to what Hawkins says is about 350 on the scale, which is acceptance that you're going to have wins and you're going to have losses, that I would expect you'd begin to trade effectively. We measure it by happiness. I like happiness as a scale for where people are.

Michael: Is there a definition you use for happiness?

Van: We have a course that teaches happiness. It's one of my advanced peak performance courses. In that course, we have a scale that measures it. My super traders have an Excel spreadsheet where they can plot that scale for where they think they were in each year of their life and see where they are now.

Michael: Outline one or two points behind the measuring of happiness.

Van: There's levels of happiness. Most people think they will be happy if they get something or achieve something. They'll go, "My happiest moment was when I got married," or, "When I get this car, I'm going to be happy," or, "When I get super trading profits," or, "When I make a million dollars," and it isn't the case. You have to get to that state first.

But when people's level of consciousness is fairly high, they are happy for no reason, it just comes out. I have times now when I can burst into spontaneous laughter and not stop. It's fun!

Michael: Over the years I've used the phrases "money management" and "position sizing" interchangeably, but I know you've been dogmatic about it and probably were the one that was pushing it in the early to mid-1990s when you first introduced it.

Van: My definition of position sizing is it's the algorithm that tells you how much, throughout the course of a trade. It is through position sizing that you meet your objectives in trading, it has nothing to do with your system. All your system does is tell you, we have a measure; when you have the R-multiple distribution of your system, we can use something I call a system quality number to measure how good that system is. That tells you how easy it will be to meet your objectives using position sizing strategies, but it is through the strategies that people do it.

It's interesting, because even people who understand position sizing are clueless to the fact that it's what you use to meet your objectives. I'll hear somebody say, "Position sizing is critical to help you make as much money as you can and minimize the chances of ruin." That might be somebody's objectives. But I would say those objectives aren't too well thought out.

I've written a book called *The Definitive Guide to Position Sizing.* There's probably as many algorithms for position sizing and you could spend as much time on it as you could any sort of entry system. I have three heroes in position sizing that I've modeled. Ed Seykota, who introduced to me the concept of market's money—that you can call your profits on a period of time market's money and risk more of your profits, if you don't want to give up, say, your core equity that you started with. Tom Basso: I did lots of workshops with Tom and he was also in *Market Wizards.* He introduced the concept of constant risk and constant volatility throughout a trade. That's also a position sizing concept. And then Bill Eckhardt, whom I probably met and didn't realize it at the time, introduced the pyramiding aspect of the Turtles' concept, which was absolutely brilliant.

Michael: Some people might not know this, but you were one of the original 40 people that got called to go to Chicago and get interviewed to be a Turtle.

Van: Right. But my motives were different. I read this ad that said Richard Dennis wanted to interview people. I had already developed my test, so I sent him a couple of copies of my test and said, "You might find this useful." What I got in return was his test. I took it, and the next thing I know, they wanted me to come to Chicago for an interview. I went, but I had no real desire to go to Chicago in the wintertime and stay there. I had other things I was doing. Although, I must admit, when I was declined, I sort of wished I'd had the job.

Michael: Was there anything about the process that you recalled or learned? Or is it one of those interesting footnotes in a career for you?

Van: All I remember about it is one question they asked me at the time. I could answer it in a heartbeat now, but at the time I didn't know the answer because I hadn't even done much of my modeling work. I was pretty new. I'd done a lot of the psychological work that we'd started out. Somebody there asked me, "If the markets are random, how can you make any money?" I didn't know. Then I got to thinking about it and I had all sorts of ideas and I wrote them a letter back and said, "This is my thought on that." I still don't remember what I said, but it's an easy answer now.

Michael: Is it something you wish you had the opportunity to do in hindsight?

Van: I didn't want the job; I was going out of curiosity. I'd have had a hard time accepting it had it been offered. But I had a kind of buyer's regret, maybe I should have tried harder, like getting turned down for admittance to a school that you didn't plan to go to anyway—when you get turned down, you go, "How could they do that?"

Michael: How did Ed Seykota's view of the market's money influence you?

Van: There's hundreds of position sizing algorithms you could use, all of which could be formulas for determining when market's money becomes your money. But let's say your goal is not to lose too much, but you want to make a lot of money. Ed's genius was that he was a computerized trend follower who totally understood position sizing at a time when nobody was a computerized trend follower, and most people didn't understand position sizing, and in a period when there were big trends in commodities. That's a huge edge that comes along maybe once in a lifetime, and different people pick up on different edges.

Within that particular model, you don't want to give back a lot of your initial cash, but let's say your goal is to make 100% in a year. You start out, you're going to risk maybe half a percent, but when you make profits, you're willing to risk, say, 10% of your profits. If you have a $100,000 account, you'd be risking $500. But let's say you're up to $110,000, now you can risk $500 on the initial $100,000 and $1,000 on the $10,000. Now your risk is triple, or your position sizing has tripled with a small increase in profits. You're going to have big fluctuations in your own position or in your own equity once you start doing that. But you can have ways to smooth that out too. At the end of the month, all the profits become yours, which is what I'd recommend for people who have to report to clients once a month.

Michael: Why do you think Tom Basso had success?

Van: I know Tom well. He was involved in a whole bunch of our workshops for four or five years. It was due to me introducing him to Jack Schwager that got him into the second *Market Wizards*. Jack Schwager and I were friends and he came to one of our workshops and I recommended that he interview Tom. Jack wasn't sure about Tom's track record, but once he had met Tom he had to include him.

Way back, probably in the early or late 1980s, I gave a talk to maybe 300 money managers. I have a test for self-esteem that shows how you feel about yourself. If you get a score of 5 or less, your self-esteem is off the charts or you lie a lot, and there was one person in that room who had a score of less than 5, and that was Tom. I got to know him and realized that was a genuine score, and he and I became good friends. He was a guest speaker in all my peak performances and he helped in my systems workshops.

Michael: What did Jack not like about Tom's track record?

Van: He'd written *Market Wizards*. He was looking for phenomenal performance, not necessarily somebody who's making 10% or 20% a year. But Tom had some phenomenal years. He started trading forex before it became a common thing. And he was one of the first people with 24-hour data, because he'd collected it. Data can be a valuable thing if you have a lot of it that nobody else has. Tom found all the systems that he used automatically could be used on the forex data. He opened up a fund and it did well in the first years—I think he went from 50 million to half a billion under management. Then they probably had some bad years and he ended up getting out of that particular aspect of trading. But he did have some fantastic years.

There's one more irony about that story, because when Jack wrote *Stock Market Wizards*, I think after the first year he formed a hedge fund, and one of the guys in there went bankrupt. I have no idea who it was, and that fund didn't do too well. Jack gave it up, but who did he give it to? He gave it to Tom Basso.

Tom was probably the most mechanical trader I've ever seen. He said, "I'm a businessman first and a trader second, that's how I look at everything. If a human being does it multiple times, then I can automate it, and that's what I tend to do." He had three or four systems going. I have no idea what exactly those systems were, but I remember at one point we talked about random entry. He plugged random entry into his systems and still could make money with them, so proving it was all exits and position sizing.

In my book on position sizing, all the things on constant volatility and scaling out came from Tom, and probably the most interesting thing about him was his mental rehearsal. One time he was in St. Louis running his company, and I called him on the phone, and Tom said, "I can't talk now, Van. We're having an earthquake." I'm thinking, "St. Louis? Earthquakes?"

> I have three heroes in position sizing that I've modeled: Ed Seykota, Tom Basso, and Bill Eckhardt.

Then later on it turned out he was running his entire operation on his laptop and cell phone, because they were having an earthquake drill. One of the biggest stressors for traders typically is when they move, and Tom moved his whole operation from St. Louis to Scottsdale, Arizona, and they didn't miss a beat because they rehearsed everything ahead of time.

Tom had a thing. He developed an exceptional mental skill, because for many years—I think he started as a teenager—he would watch himself do things at the end of the day. At the end of the day, he'd play a movie of his day and how it went. Because he did that every day, he soon developed the ability to do what is known in NLP as associate and disassociate. Most of the time you're in your body experiencing it like you're in your body, but he could also be an observer outside of his body watching himself at the same time. He was the only person I ever knew who had that ability. Then I discovered that if you did that technique of watching yourself or playing a movie of yourself at the end of every day as a review of the day, that skill tended to develop. Those are a few of the interesting things about Tom.

Michael: You mentioned that he said he was a businessman first and a trader second. Can you clarify?

Van: This is the meaning I give it, which is not necessarily the meaning he would give it. For one thing, he was a business owner, which meant he thought about it all as a business rather than as a trader. I have all of our super traders make business plans that are 150 pages long, planning out everything, understanding everything.

Another aspect of being a business is the fact that Tom could take off time from trading and do workshops with me, for example, and know that his business would be running smoothly. He could probably take a month off and know that the business would be running smoothly, because it was a bunch of automated systems. I think that was the way he viewed it.

Michael: Is there anybody else in the trading world you learned from?

Van: Most of the people I've learned the most from are relatively unknown, but because I've worked with them and they've been good, I've watched them grow and do some other things. The fellow who wrote the foreword in the second edition of *Trade Your Way to Financial Freedom*, his name's Chuck Whitman. I worked with Chuck in the early 1990s and then he decided to form a company. At one point they occupied a full floor on the Board of Trade building, and then they got too big for that, and now it's like 60,000 square feet someplace. All his traders have treadmills that they can walk on and trade at the same time, to keep their minds going. Chuck's a superb floor trader—he understands risk and he understands options enough to be scary. If you realize that you're competing with Chuck on options, you either need that level of knowledge or you need to give up options. Chuck's been an interesting model over the years for what he's done. He was a successful floor trader, but he adopted almost every principle that we teach.

Michael: Describe self-sabotage.

Van: I'll give you several definitions and the first one is easy for everyone to understand. I'll give you a way that you can measure your own self-sabotage. I would define making a mistake as not following your rules. If you're a no-rules discretionary trader, then everything you do is a mistake. If you have rules, then it's pretty obvious when you make a mistake, because you don't follow them. Your rules should be detailed enough that you can follow them. If you say, I'm never going to take a trade unless I can see the reward to risk is at least 3:1, that's discretionary—you still have to somehow figure it out that you have that kind of edge when you get into the trade.

If you understand that definition of mistake, you can start keeping track of your mistakes and you see what each mistake costs you. I've talked about R-multiples before, and I recommend that you compute the value of your mistakes in terms of R-multiples. For example, you heard a rumor and you got into a trade. Well, you had no business taking that trade. It wasn't part of your thing. Maybe you did have a stop, you got out at a half-R loss, so that's a half-R mistake. You get into a trade, you have your stop, and then somehow in the middle of it, you get distracted and you get out early and miss out on 10 R of profits that you would've had otherwise. Even though you made money on it, that's a 10 R mistake. You might get into a trade accidentally and make money. Well, that might be a one R on the plus side.

Overall, you can figure out the negative value of your mistakes and your efficiency. Say you make one mistake in 10 trades, you are 90% efficient. If you make three mistakes in 10 trades, you are 70% efficient. My guess is that most traders are 70% or less efficient. When you start doing that, you realize that if you keep making the same mistake over and over again, that's self-sabotage. Most people don't realize they make mistakes and they get what they want, because they're not aware enough of their thought process and what they go through. This is an obvious way to become aware.

Michael: There's an article in one of your newsletters titled "Book Smarts versus Smart Position Sizing Strategies." There was an experiment that Ralph Vince did years ago.

Van: This came out of an old newsletter Chuck LeBeau and David Lucas used to write. The experiment was that Ralph didn't like PhDs. He got 40 PhDs who didn't have a background in trading, math, or statistics—so maybe PhDs in literature, religion, language, or who knows what, but that was the criterion. He had them each trade a system with a hundred trades. To best describe the system, it was one R winners and one R losers, but it was 60% winners. Theoretically at the end of the trade, they should be up a hundred trades, they should be up 20 R.

> **I define making a mistake as not following your rules.**

The idea was, "How many of them made money?" The answer is four of them made money. That's four out of 40, or 10%. What would typically happen is, this is a 60% system, so let's say they start out and they're betting 10%. That's probably way too much, but let's say they're betting 10%. Let's say there's $1,000 so they're betting $100. This streak could be anywhere in the run. They bet 10% and they lose one R. Now they're down to $900. They bet 10% of the initial stake and they lose again, they're down to $800. They bet 10% again, and they lose, they're down to $700.

Now they start thinking to themselves, we've had three losses in a row, this is a 60% system, I'm due. So they risk 30%. They have their fourth loss. Now they're down $400 from $1,000. They're down 60%. And now they go, well, four R losses in a row, it's got to be right now. They bet another $300 of the $400 that's remaining. And that loses as well. Now they're down to $100—they're down 90%. They're only playing a game that gives you R losses. Once you're down 90%, you have to make 900% to get back to break-even. With one R gains, you're never going to do it. That's typically how they lost money.

Michael: I had a chance to interview Mike Aponte, the once team leader of the Massachusetts Institute of Technology (MIT) blackjack team. I think he would've smiled at that whole story you told, because it would've been the polar opposite of what he had to do to make his millions playing blackjack.

Van: If you do things like card counting, it takes your odds to 52%. That's not too good. And boy, you better understand position sizing.

Michael: Indeed.

Van: I've been watching traders over the years and I've been careful about what I'd say. Even some of the things I've said today, if I'd said them in 1990 people would've gotten upset, but I find I can say a lot more things today than I ever could about metaphysics and changing levels of consciousness. I'm a oneness trainer, for example, and we do a blessing that's supposed to change your levels of consciousness. Since I've been doing that, the changes I've seen in the people who do our workshops and everything is absolutely amazing. My super traders make more progress in a year than I used to see in five years. I think some interesting things are happening in the world.

Michael: What are the things that you're talking about today that would've been rejected in 1990?

Van: People are more open to these things. David Hawkins said that human consciousness was about 197 as a whole up until around 1989, which actually is when the oneness phenomenon was born. And then it started going up and his latest data says maybe it's 207 or something like that. I think that's what the shift is.

PART 2

Beliefs About
Trading

Michael Covel: Define belief in the context of trading and investing.

Van Tharp: There's a lot of definitions for that. I would call a belief any thought that flows through your mind that you attach to, and the more you attach to it the more serious it becomes.

There are two different hierarchies for beliefs. For example, Don Miguel Ruiz has a book called *The Five Levels of Attachment*. He has things where you are not attached at all, it just flows through, and then things where you develop a preference and then where it becomes part of your identity. And then you internalize it and you become fanatical about it.

For example, let's say you went to a football game and you didn't care who the teams were or anything, you just enjoyed watching it. That would be probably at the first level—it didn't matter what was happening, you appreciated the skill of the players, everything else. At the second level, you have a preference that one team will win over the other, but you don't care at the end who wins. You say, I'd like the green team to win. And at the third level, you identify with one of the teams, then it becomes important for them to win. At the fourth level it becomes more like your identity. I am the red team and if they don't win my self-esteem is damaged, and I feel better about myself if they do win. At the last level you want to go to war with anybody who doesn't believe in your team, fans from other teams, everything like that. It's about the amount of attachment.

Then there's a hierarchy of beliefs, according to Robert Dilts. There are beliefs about environment—so you could say something like markets tend to trend. It's a statement about the environment. Or you could say, at the next level, it becomes a belief about behavior—so, it's something that you do: I trade trending markets. And then at the third level it becomes what you're capable of doing or not—so, I can or cannot trade trending markets; it has the word "can" in there. And then at the fourth level it becomes values—so, it's important to find a good trend. And then it becomes a belief about yourself: I am a trend follower. Finally, it becomes a belief about you and the universe where you might say: Trend followers go to heaven, and those who don't follow trends are doomed to eternal hell.

Michael: A certain amount of belief is important in our lives, but can you take it to an extreme where it becomes a negative belief system?

Van: Yes. Let's say, for example, you have some sort of prejudice. The prejudice might be that people of a certain color are inferior, or people of a certain behavior type are inferior, or somebody with a certain blood type is inferior. Let's say you have the idea somebody with a certain blood type is inferior. But you don't know whether they have that blood type or not, you just have that belief. And then you have relationships with people and you have to get to the point where you're pretty intimate with them before they'll tell you their blood type. But as soon as you discover that the blood type isn't what you consider perfect, you decide to break off this relationship and maybe it hurts you, it hurts them, all because you have this funny belief. Maybe you decide to marry a woman and you're sure she has the right blood type, and then you find out later that she got a partial transfusion with a blood type that in your opinion is bad. Suddenly she's impure and the rest of your life you feel betrayed by her. It affects your whole relationship. And all because of a silly belief that's not true in the first place.

> You don't trade the markets; you trade your beliefs about the markets.

Michael: The analogies you're using can easily be applied to money, investing, and trading.

Van: Right. You don't trade the markets; you trade your beliefs about the markets. You might think a chart represents the markets. It doesn't—it's all the ticks and stuff and it's your way of looking at it. There are other people who can't look at ticks and things, so they have moving averages or bars of a certain size, and then they don't like even the moving averages. They may adjust the moving averages with time and do all sorts of funny things to that. And then maybe they go four or five more steps removed from reality and add other indicators in there. It's all belief.

Michael: One of the most powerful beliefs is the moment of right now. One of the great examples is the Navajo and their idea that there's no future, but a never-ending present. There's also references to Eckhart Tolle in your work.

Van: The best way to trade is to look at what the market is doing right now. You can relate it to the past a little bit. It's going up and right now it's still going up and that tells you something. Can you predict that it's going to keep going up? No, you can hope that. If it stops going up, it's pretty obvious and you can get out and hopefully you don't lose much money. And if it keeps going up a lot longer than where you'd have gotten out, you tend to make money. Again, it's paying attention to what's going on now.

Michael: What are some of the first steps for getting rid of non-useful beliefs?

Van: I have something called the belief examination paradigm. You take any belief you have, any statement I've said could be called a belief, and you find out, where did you get that? Why do you have that as a belief? Then you ask two different sets of questions. One is, what happens when I have that belief, or what does it get me into? You list 5–10 things about that particular belief. Then you ask the opposite question, what does it get me out of, or who would I be without the belief? You list 5–10 things on that. Then you can look at it and say, is this useful? Which means it's a global judgment, because at some level maybe no belief is true, but you have to operate in the world and you have to operate through your beliefs.

In terms of an operating environment—and trading is an operating environment—some beliefs are much more useful than others. When you decide a belief is not that useful, then you can change it and do another belief—with one exception, and that's when there is a lot of stored emotion in the belief itself. For example, a belief like "I'm not worthwhile,"

I consider a lot of things that go on in the world as a game. Money is basically a game.

obviously you don't have to do that exercise to say that's not a useful belief, but there is probably a lot of anger, shame, guilt, fear, or who knows what tied up in that belief. To get rid of it, you have to do much more extensive stuff of releasing the feeling and then the belief can move on. If you have a belief like "I'm not worthwhile," chances are you're not going to make any money trading.

Michael: You cover a lot of different areas: system aspects, R-multiples, position sizing, etc. But I notice that you have certain references to Hindu, Christian, and Buddhist beliefs. Many of these are foundational things that I think most people in the world can agree with, but others might view as controversial. Some people might be thinking, "What if I'm not a religious person? Can I still benefit from Van's work? Or is Van saying that I can't get to a certain level of success if I don't have that religious belief?"

Van: First, I would not call myself religious, I'm spiritual. I don't have any particular faith that I believe in, but I do believe in the idea of oneness—the same thing as quantum physics. Because at some level everything's one and it all relates together. It doesn't matter whether you have strong faith in a particular religion or you're an atheist, you still have spiritual beliefs. The spiritual beliefs of an atheist might be that everything's random and mechanical and that's going to influence how you perceive the world.

The best way to trade is to look at what the market is doing right now.

To give you an example. I had a series of people write in and say how reading my book had changed their lives. Then one person objected to some of the spiritual stuff in there, especially the idea about chakras, and he made some statement about how he used to believe in positive attitude, the law of attraction, abundance, and all those sorts of things, but it never worked for him. The reality was that he was a limited human being living on a rock hurtling through space. I looked at that and I thought to myself, wow, if I had that belief I'd be depressed. But that's his belief and that's the way he operates in the world—if you believe it, it's true for you.

Michael: So much of life takes place in our mind, but given that we have such a short time on the planet, it's better to take a positive direction than hold on to more negative options.

Van: Let me give you another big-picture example. If you look at our economy, the debt is awful. The debt is isotonic and you think it's got to totally collapse or we're going to have hyperinflation. Maybe the US government's going to collapse. You read newsletters that talk about the end of the world tomorrow. There's one set of newsletters that's pointed out a new law is coming into effect where foreign institutions have to report on the holdings of US citizens, and that's going to end the dollar and all that stuff. It's real doom and gloom.

You can let all that shape you and then you're always looking for chances to go short, and you miss the fact that the market is setting new highs almost every other day. You could say, "It's a bull market, how come I'm not making much money?" Then if you look at the range of the S&P over the last 100 days, it's probably less than 5%. So, the market's making new highs while over the last 100 days the S&P's up less than 5%. It's a sideways, quiet market that's setting new highs. That's what's actually going on. You can make money in that market if you're aware of what's going on, but not if you're shaped by doom and gloom.

Looking at it fundamentally, the debt is a lot like the price of the Nasdaq in 1999. I was saying that when it first hit a billion dollars or maybe even a trillion dollars. That seemed high, but you look at our unfunded debt and it's over a hundred trillion. Almost logically it seems like it has to crash someday. There'll be plenty of opportunities when it does, but right now it's still going up and that's the reality of it.

Michael: What do you mean by *big money*?

Van: I consider a lot of things that go on in the world as a game. Money is a game. If you try to learn the rules of the game and you're not very aware, you come to the idea, maybe if I'm a millionaire I'll be happy. Then you get to millionaire status and you think, maybe I need to be a billionaire to be happy. Since that rules out all but about one person in a million in the United States, then you might say, if I have the right to the most toys, then I'll be happy. So, you get this rule: you win the game by having the most money or the most toys or something like that.

In all games, somebody invents the rules and does it in a way that typically benefits them, but you could change the rules. The way to change the wealth game is deciding you win when your passive income is greater than your expenses. Passive income is income that requires some work, but let's say it doesn't require more than two hours a week, or two hours a day, which means you could day trade for an hour every morning and call that passive income. When your passive income is greater than your expenses, then that's it. Two hours a day is all you have to work. That's a different way of perceiving the money game.

But when I talk about the money game and big money, it's pretty obvious that big money lines things up so that they win and you lose. The way I view it is, if trading were really, really easy, big money would have it all tied up. They would make it impossible for you to trade. You'd have to go through all sorts of hoops to get a license to trade. Like brokers have to go through a Series 7, which has nothing to do with trading. It's a ridiculous memorization of facts that don't have anything to do with anything, but they have to do it. However, the fact is trading isn't that easy, so it's easy to enter into the trading arena.

Michael: To be successful at anything, ultimately you have to dedicate some time and effort. Good trading is a profession. This isn't the money tree that delivers free fruit.

Van: I consider trading as much a profession as anything else. A doctor goes to premed, then four years of medical school, then an internship and residency. They make a lot of money and they go in the markets and think they know how to trade. Usually, they have a disastrous result. Whereas if they put in four to six years learning how to be a trader and learning the right way, they'd probably have different results.

Michael: One expression I noticed in your work that I had not seen before is "trader jail." Could you explain it and give an example?

Van: There's a large hedge fund that had a psychological coach working for them and he set up something where if someone had a drawdown that was about 50% of what they were allowed by the company, they were put in trader jail. This meant half their money was taken from them and they were in a position where they would be fired if they didn't get that back. I worked with a client who had gone through this. It put him in freeze mode where he couldn't do anything.

Michael: It was an irrational drawdown number, picked from something unrelated to what the markets were even giving.

Van: It was a concept. You might call it an invented belief that was not useful at all. It probably didn't help anybody, but hindered a lot of people.

Michael: Most fear the unknown. They fear what's going to happen next. How do you move people to start conquering this fear?

Van: I'll do it from a belief standpoint. That comes right into a spiritual belief. If you believe that everything's perfect as it is, then you're never going to have a fear like that. But if you believe the universe is a random place and bad things happen to good people, then you could easily have that fear. Or worse yet, if you believe that the world is an evil place, then you're always building up defensive walls to protect yourself from that sort of thing. You're not going to have that belief unless it's a fundamental spiritual belief that's behind it.

> I consider trading as much a profession as anything else.

I have workshops that deal with things like this, but typically in my super trader program people are going through one to three years of doing massive psychological work where they're looking at maybe 500 beliefs and putting them through that belief examination paradigm that I talked about. A lot of those will have attached feelings that they have to get rid of so they can release the beliefs. When you've done that stuff enough, it's going to change your approach totally.

Michael: The idea of sleep. People try to do so much: I'm going to exercise, I'm going to do this, I'm going to work hard. There's a lot of people that are going through life on three or four hours of sleep a night, and the body and the mind don't function optimally on three, four or five hours of sleep. Do you discuss sleep in your work at all?

Van: Not much, but I was a sleep researcher in the days when I was into biological psychology. I know a little bit about it. When my wife was a nurse in Singapore they put her on four days of day shift and then she'd do maybe two days of shift that started at 4:00 p.m. or 6:00 p.m. and went to midnight. Then they put her on the evening shift that started at midnight and went to 8:00 a.m., and then she'd get a day or two off, which is what you need to recover. That's considered her weekend or her time off from the schedule. Living that way is ridiculous. People can't do it. I sometimes only sleep three or four hours, but I usually get eight hours for the day, because I take naps.

PART 3
Modeling the Process of Trading

Michael Covel: They awarded the Nobel Prize to Eugene Fama and Robert Shiller, which seems contradictory: one the leader of the efficient market hypothesis and the other a behavioralist.

Van Tharp: I have a longstanding theory on what happens to Nobel Prizes, which is that the Nobel Prize in economics is awarded to the person who comes up with some theory that supports the status quo, which allows people in the market to say, "This is how the market works." You get from efficient portfolio theory to who knows what.

I'm not an economist, but I have all sorts of unique things in the market, and you have this great approach that you've been talking about trend following for a long time, but neither one of us will ever win Nobel Prizes in economics, because we don't do anything to support the status quo.

Michael: Why would anybody show up to learn from you if the efficient market theory was valid?

Van: Correct.

Michael: Why do people use so much energy to propagate things like the efficient market theory and maintain the status quo?

Van: I'm going to move this in a slightly different direction. I have a workshop on systems thinking, and the importance of systems thinking is that about 20% of the population can do it. Part of the reason you need to do it is that we all have these models of the world, which are made up. Even something like the market, we have no clue what the market really is.

Somebody might show you a chart and say, "That's the market" and you go, "Okay." Then you look at the assumptions behind it, and you find it's a bar chart, and it takes the open, high, low close of a specific period of time. If you look at the ticks on that, you might find they're all distributed around a certain time, and maybe that's all in the top third of the bar. Then there was one tick that was way down. That was the low of that period.

> Your map of the market is not the market. It's not the territory at all.

We decide, "We're going to express all those ticks for that time period as a bar and say that represents the market for that period of time." Some people can't accept that and they say, "I need a candlestick," or maybe, "I need a line that goes through the bar," or, "I need some sort of indicator that tells me what the bar's really doing."

In my opinion, all this stuff is made up. Because it's made up, you have to realize it is, so your map of the market is not the market. It's not the territory at all. You better hope it's useful, which means that the structure of your map is somewhat related to the market, because the more useful it is, the better and more effective you'll be as a trader. But people can make up all sorts of things and then assume it's real.

Systems theory is important because systems theory realizes that the map is not the territory, that what we say something is isn't that thing, and can shape its thinking around that.

Michael: What does that leave us with?

Van: In my book, *Trading Beyond the Matrix*, I say there's a matrix that's all made up. If you understand that, then you can figure out what's useful and what's not useful for functioning in the matrix, reprogram yourself to be superefficient, and perhaps one day even go beyond the matrix.

Michael: When somebody first comes to you who's a bright person—they know what's going on, but they haven't been exposed to something like position sizing—what's it like to observe things come into focus for them?

Van: Let me explain what I've been doing over the years. I've been modeling good traders and what they do. I've modeled the process of trading. I've modeled how to develop a system that fits you. I've modeled how to position size to meet your objectives. I've modeled what we call the infinite wealth factor. A lot of stuff about market type, because your system has to fit the market type in order for you to be able to make money. If the market's sidewise and you're jumping in the market to go long all the time and nothing's happening, you're not going to make money, and if the market's going down and you're trying to go up, go long, you're not going to make money either. All of those things factor in.

When I'm looking at a new person, there's a number of steps. They've got to learn the various models. There's a bunch of beliefs that I call Tharp Think that are in the book *Trading Beyond the Matrix*—they are useful, and those need to get into your neurology. You need to not simply say, "Oh, I agree with him." You need to get to the point where the models are in your muscles and you think, "Yes, this is the way things are." You've also got to raise your consciousness enough so that once you know those models, you can follow them. That's our whole process that we do in the super trader program, which is raising people's consciousness from, say, fear and greed to at least acceptance, where they can accept profits and accept losses when they come up.

Michael: Pick one or two of the typical biases that a new trader walks in with that you need to reprogram.

Van: The first thing is that they need to understand that they have to take total responsibility for what happens to them in the markets. It's easy to think there's some magic secret to making money in the markets. If you find that secret, that's it. That's not the case at all. For example, I could teach you a good system, and then you'd start trading it and maybe make three mistakes every 10 trades. If you're making three mistakes every 10 trades, you're trading at 70% efficiency. Let's say that trading system has an expectancy of 0.8 R, which means in 10 trades it's going to make 8 R. Let's say that three mistakes cost you 2 R each time. That means you've taken 8 R and turned it into 2 R, and that might mean you decide the system's no good.

Superstars typically find some sort of edge that becomes unique for them and that they are willing to really exploit.

You've got to get to a point where you understand that it's what you do that produces the results, including the mistakes. That's number one, beyond everything. And there's another level of that, which is, your responses produce the thoughts you have. You give meaning to everything. If I say a particular word, you determine what that word means to you. My guess is if 10 people read what I'm saying here, they'll each give a different interpretation to it. You've got to accept responsibility. That's right at the beginning.

Michael: But when people understand your world, they don't have a different interpretation. It's just those that have not been exposed yet.

Van: Not necessarily true. I could say, "Think of a dog." What do you picture when I say, "Think of a dog?"

Michael: My first dog, a big black Labrador.

Van: Right. I was picturing my little Papillons that I have upstairs. Somebody else is picturing a German Shepherd. Somebody else is picturing their own dog. Maybe somebody else is picturing the dog that bit them. They're all giving a different meaning to the same word, "dog."

Michael: Let's say we change dog to position sizing. There can be different ways that one can go about position sizing, but once everyone has the understanding about what the different choices are, that's fairly concrete.

Van: Well, sure. I coined the phrase "position sizing," because everybody was using the phrase "money management" at the time.

Michael: Me included.

Van: There were so many different connotations to that, so I said, "Let's call this position sizing so it gets down to the factor of how much."
If you look at the world of investors, they think about asset allocation, which comes from studies which look at a set of portfolio managers over a number of years and find the variability of the performance is a function of how much is in bonds, how much is in cash, and how much is in stocks.

That's my definition of position sizing. Once you make sure people have the same meaning that you do, then you can begin to communicate.

Michael: Give the backstory about when were you exposed to the "how much" question for the first time.

Van: I think my second peak performance workshop was with Ed Seykota. We did a retreat in Hawaii, and I had him present a couple of things. He presented the example of a coin flip where it came up heads 75% of the time and tails 25% of the time. And the question was, "What was the most important factor in your trading?" Of course, I said, "It's you," and Ed goes, "No, it's how much." I've been thinking about that ever since. This was the late 1980s.

Michael: Is there anything else that you found interesting about your involvement with Ed?

Van: The first time I used him as part of our modeling, we did a video of the interview. The interview was me asking him questions for about an hour and a half. When I looked back at the video, he didn't blink in the whole hour and a half. I don't know anybody who doesn't blink for a whole hour and a half, but I had somebody watching it later, and that woman said he was channeling something. I always knew Ed did things like that. That was kind of interesting about him. He dabbled in all sorts of things that were quite different.

Michael: Was it intense concentration?

Van: My opinion is that he was channeling somebody who was answering my questions. Let me put it in a different perspective and talk about why Ed was one of the greatest traders ever, because he had a super edge at a time when he was maybe the only person who had that edge. He was a computerized trend follower. I looked at his computer at one point. All his programs were written in assembly language. Nobody writes in assembly language, but I guess at MIT in the 1960s, he did. He was a computerized trend follower with all these programs written in assembly language, who understood position sizing about as well as anybody. When nobody else was doing that, that was a huge, huge edge.

Michael: Was it Malcolm Gladwell who made the point in one of his books that there is a built-in advantage if you happen to come along at a certain point in time? You can look at certain years and say, "That was the perfect time to be there."

Van: You can see a lot of these. Like John Templeton—when he retired from Franklin Templeton in 1999, he took his entire net worth and shorted the dot-coms. In 1999 those things were jumping as much as 50 bucks a day in price, and to have a position in something like that and be able to stay the course was amazing.

There are certain things where people have a huge edge that comes out of nowhere. They have the insight, and then they become one of the all-time greats and geniuses. They had the right thing at the right time. Warren Buffett, for example, figured out how to buy an insurance agency and trade through the insurance agency and not have to pay taxes on what he was trading, because he was an insurance agent. Again, a huge edge.

Michael: I can remember the first time I entered Bill Dunn's office in the mid-1990s and there were no screens on anyone's desks. It felt like I was in a accountancy office or a law firm. So many people approach the markets with that extra kind of excitement coming from the greed side of them, but the reality is, when you meet the superstars, it's not about that in any way, shape, or form.

Van: The superstars typically find some sort of edge that becomes unique for them, that they are willing to exploit. They understand that there's certain fundamental principles that are unique to success, and they operate within those principles.

Michael: With most trading simulations, back testing, using computers, this is something where you are putting rules into code and testing its math. There's not much room for discretion, except perhaps at the initial choices. But even if there is so much success in the systematic mindset when it comes to trading, many people still believe there are market wizards out there with a discretionary and intuitive gene, or an extra something. I don't know if you're a pure discretionary trader, but it seems to me it'd be difficult to implement some of the position sizing methodologies that are in your work.

Van: You have to know when something's not working anymore, so that's definitely discretionary. For example, the market type may have changed, and the system. It's the late 1990s, you're making a ton of money buying growth stocks, and you think you're a genius. Then 2000 comes along, and the market's totally changed. If you're not aware of that, you're not going to do well. But there are also subtle things that happen within the market that make it so that things no longer work.

Let's talk about a trend following example. Maybe in the mid-1990s, I have a guy who teaches at the Army War College, and he's got a master's degree in Systems Thinking and a PhD in Decision-Making Under Stress. He developed a fairly simple mutual fund switching system, where he had a basket of mutual funds and every month he ranked them on their relative strength over the last six months, three months and one month, with the biggest ranking being the last month. He'd buy the three strongest, and he'd put a 10% stop on them. Then at the end of the month, if he wasn't stopped out, he'd see if he should keep those, or if there were three stronger, or whatever. That was a great system. It outperformed the market, at least during the time it worked. He never had a losing year, and it's a pure trend following system, so you go, "Great."

The first thing that changed was suddenly mutual funds decided that they didn't want you trading in and out. So suddenly his system totally died. He couldn't do it anymore. Exchange-traded funds (ETFs) were in the process then, so he switched to an ETF strategy. In *Trading Beyond the Matrix*, he describes the performance of that system, and I think it had some losing years, but it still always outperformed the market and did well.

If I look at the same system now, I can't even trade it, because it's a fairly automated system. Once a month you calculate it, you put in your orders, have a 10% stop loss. At the end of the month, you either switch or buy something else. But what happens now is, if you look at the current track record and you test that, you have at least a 20% drawdown with about 40 months to get out of it. What's happened? Lots and lots of people with big money are doing things with ETFs that make it so that system doesn't work anymore, and there's a new version of it that works that requires a much shorter timeframe. Systems stop working too.

Michael: Why are you still doing this? Why are you so passionate about what you do at this stage of your life?

Van: It goes back to that thing people would say: "If Van knows so much about trading, why does he coach and why doesn't he make money trading?" That makes the assumption that the be-all and end-all in my life is making money. It's not. My passion is helping other people, especially helping them make transformations that change their lives. Our mission for our company is, "Transformation through a trading metaphor." Our whole company thrives on it. We're always getting letters and phone calls from people saying how we changed their life. I get a lot of joy out of that. I see no reason to ever retire, because I love what I do, I'm good at it, and I help a lot of people, and hopefully we'll keep doing that.

Michael: Somebody probably had to give you something in terms of an insight or an inspiration to send you down your path. How did that happen?

Van: I started this business around 1982. It's fuzzy as to what exactly happened, but around that period, it was probably the low point in my life, and I was psychologically dead. But I remember going to a Religious Science church, and I remember somebody saying to the minister, "I don't believe in God," and the minister said, "What kind of God don't you believe in?" They talked about

> **Traders have to take total responsibility for what happens to them in the markets.**

this man up in the sky who passes judgment on us and decides whether you're good or bad, whether you're going to go to hell or heaven or whatever. The minister said, "I don't believe in that kind of God either, but maybe there's something else."

At that point I found a course in miracles. I didn't understand everything it said, but it totally matches up with personal responsibility, about how it's all illusion, and you create things through your thoughts. The first course took me four years, and I never got that it was all made up.

It took me a second or third time to figure that one out, even though it's obvious. It was through that process of working on myself that I started to find myself, and a mission developed: My job is to help transform traders through a trading metaphor.

I also had the belief that I couldn't help transform anybody any further than I managed to transform myself. It has been and it still is a lifelong goal to transform myself. For example, I'm currently taking a Siddha yoga course that requires me to go to India once or twice a year. They say in about 10 years I'll become a Siddha yogi. We'll see that when it happens. Interesting things have happened as a result of doing that, and it's certainly helped me be able to produce transformations much quicker than 10–15 years ago. I can't put it down to a specific thing, but that in a nutshell is what happened.

CHAPTER 10

ALEXANDER ELDER

PART 1
The Stages of Trader Development

ALEXANDER ELDER, M.D. is a professional trader and a teacher of traders. His books, including *The New Trading for a Living*, are international bestsellers among private and institutional traders, and are translated into 17 languages. Alexander trained as a psychiatrist and served on the faculty of Columbia University. Now, he is a full-time trader who shares his hard-earned lessons with his students. Alexander is the originator of Traders' Camps, week-long classes for traders, and the founder of SpikeTrade, a worldwide group of traders. He is also a sought-after speaker at conferences in the United States and abroad.

Michael note

Just about everybody involved in the trading space has Dr. Elder's international bestseller, *Trading for a Living*, on their shelf. His story of overcoming obstacles on the way to success is an inspiration to be cherished.

Michael Covel: Was your background in psychiatry your entry route into trading?

Alexander Elder: I love psychiatry. I began reading Sigmund Freud when I was 15 or 16 years old. Psychiatry made me into who I am. I did my residency back in the old country, and when I came to New York I got accepted into the Albert Einstein Program, which was at that time the best residency in the city. Then I got a job and I was working as a psychiatrist and developing a private practice. But by my mid-30s, I felt that I was about as good as people get—that it was no longer a huge adventure, it was grinding and polishing, grinding and polishing. I was looking for something to get involved in. And meanwhile, I'd been trading a little on the side. I wouldn't even call it trading; I was gambling. I didn't know anything. But trading fascinated me, and I got deeper and deeper into it. I would have a $3,000 account and I would bust it out and go back to work and put some money together again and open a $5,000 account, until I finally figured out the game. It took many years.

People often ask, "What do psychiatry and trading have in common?" They're both based in reality. You look at a chart and you're trying to see what you want to see there, but the chart is doing what it's doing. Do you have the ability to brush away your fantasies and look at the chart with the eyes of a child? Up is up and down is down and sideways is sideways, without fantasizing too much, without saying, "That's what it should do." That's the parallel between psychiatry and trading.

To finish the topic, I practice little psychiatry now—one or two hours a month, that's about it. But lately I got this fascinating patient coming in. This guy is a super-serious professional trader, runs an eight-figure account. He came to me because he was depressed. He lost a lot of money because of poor risk control. First, we dealt with his depression and now we're dealing with his personality and also looking at markets together. The guy is coming in and saying, "I made $45,000 last week after our session, I made $78,000 the previous week. Therapy is paid for; I'm coming here forever!" That's my ongoing psychotherapy now.

Michael: How did you make the transition? You're working with patients and you start to get into trading, but how did you make the transition to being this helper, educator, and mentor to others?

Alexander: It began when I was a kid. I had a sister who was 10 years younger than me, completely different generation, so I was caring of her and showed her this and that. Ever since then I have had this typical older brother attitude towards teaching. Plus, my parents were serious career people who had this idea that the pinnacle of creation was a professor chairman of department. So of course, I had to rebel against that. I escaped from academic medicine, and lo and behold, I started my own school, Elder.com. It's funny how it goes from childhood to now.

> **Money management is as needed in trading as a life jacket on a boat.**

But in any case, the transition from mostly psychiatry to almost exclusively trading came gradually. People often ask me, "How do I transit from my current profession to trading?" Don't jump, don't do it right away. Start cutting hours in what you're doing in your primary work, and start adding hours to trading and follow the trend. As trading picks up, allocate more and more hours to it. That's what I did.

Michael: How do you see the stages of trader development?

Alexander: I feel sorry for some poor idiot who reads an advertisement in a newspaper that says, "You can triple your money in here working 15 minutes a day with no math." That's fantasy life. Somebody who is not looking for magic, somebody who is looking seriously to learn to trade and to become a trader, has to put time and energy into it. I often say to people that learning to be a trader will probably take as long and cost as much as getting a college degree. It's a process: You have to read, you have to acquire a body of knowledge. You have to practice on a small learning account, like having a bicycle with training wheels, and then you have to start gradually adding equity to it.

In terms of stages of development, I would say that stage one is when a person is completely green coming to the markets and trying to figure out which end is up. If during this stage a person can lose no more than 10%, that's a wonderful result.

Michael: Most people hear that and say, "You're telling me a wonderful result is to only lose 10% a year?"

Alexander: Michael, suppose you decide that it was a huge mistake to become a trader and a writer, and you're going to become a dentist, so you go to dental school. Are you going to make money in your first year of dental school? I mean, you can be brilliant, but you're not going to make any money as a dentist. It is going to cost you money. You're going to pay for education. You're going to read, study, and spend time in the lab. You're not going to make money as a dentist in the first year. If I was a recruiter for dental school and I said to you, "Michael, come, join our school. You're going to be making money within months of joining us," you would know that I'm bullshitting you, that I have some hidden agenda.

> The stock market doesn't operate on dynamic causality, it operates on statistic causality.

It's the same with trading. If you are going to learn how to trade, you should anticipate it will take time. When a beginning trader goes against somebody like Michael Covel—the two of you are putting on a trade—make a wild guess who is going to walk away with money?

As a beginner you should anticipate that you will lose some. The idea is to lose as little as possible—to have a small account to practice tight money management, which is one of my favorite topics. But at the first stage of development as a trader, it would be strange not to lose money. As a matter of fact, one of the worst things that happened to me when I first began learning to trade, and I knew nothing, was that I made money on my first trade, and then I made money on my second trade. After that I got this delusional idea that trading was easy and I had it figured out. It took me a good couple of years to work out from under that delusion.

Michael: You got to be ready for that first year. You got to be willing to take your lumps; maybe you get lucky, but you can't count on that. Where do you progress after that stage?

Alexander: Remember my strong suggestion: At the first stage, trade with a small account. You certainly don't want to put all your savings into this new venture. Go easy in the beginning, this is a learning time. Stage two: You want to outperform riskless assets. In other words, you can put your money in the bank and buy certificates of deposit and get maybe a couple of percent, but can you consistently beat that in your trading? It's surprisingly difficult for a beginner. It's easy to do in a single trade, but over the course of several quarters it's hard.

Once you're outperforming riskless assets for a few quarters, you know you're in good shape. Now you can start adding capital to your account, step by step, not too much, maybe 50%. If you're trading a $20,000 account, you go to $30,000, but no more than that. If $30,000 goes well, maybe you will go to $45,000. Add capital every few months. Then you find out how good you are. Some people are very, very good. Some people are solid, some people are so-so, but that's stage three.

Michael: Three stages total?

Alexander: I would say as a rough division three stages. Stage one, don't lose more than 10% of your equity. Stage two, outperform riskless assets. Stage three, find out how good you are.

Michael: Were there books or other resources that helped to shape you early on?

Alexander: At the time I got into the field in the late 1970s, the body of trading literature was much smaller than it is now. There were maybe only a few hundred books about trading. Now my publisher alone produces at least 100 books a year, not to mention other publishers. Back then there were not too many books and I have read them all. I read everything there was to read. That's my background, my education, my personality. I want to get the complete background.

Michael: This concept of money management—what is it, and why is it needed?

Alexander: Money management is as needed in trading as a life jacket on a boat. You may be able to go sailing without a life jacket and come back safely. But if you keep going out often enough without a life jacket, trouble is there. I believe markets are fundamentally not predictable. In other words, I can say, "Based on my analysis, there is a high possibility that this stock will go up." And there is in fact a high possibility that this stock wants to go up, but I cannot tell you that with certainty. There is too much unknown in the markets.

Suppose my analysis is right, and the stock goes up, and I bet a quarter of my account in it. Then there is another stock and another stock. If you do three or four of those in a row, you feel like you can walk on water. Then you say, "My analysis says this stock is going to go up." But this time you're betting half of your account on it, and lo and behold, things fall apart. Suddenly all your winnings from the past are destroyed. And as a matter of fact, your entire equity is negative and you're in a deep hole and how are you going to dig yourself out of it?

Before I talk about money management, I want to say there are two kinds of causality: dynamic and statistic. You take a pencil and push it on your desk and whichever way you push it, that pencil is going to go. That's dynamic causality. You apply force, it goes in this direction—that simple.

But statistic causality is if I give you a box and I say, "Michael, there are 20 tennis balls in here: 12 of them are green and eight of them are yellow. What color do you want to bet on?" Of course you're going to bet on green. But when you put your hand in, there is a possibility that you will pull out two, three, four, five yellow balls in a row, right? If you are betting a large fraction of your account, by the time this bad run comes to an end, your account is demolished. That's why money management is needed—because the stock market doesn't operate on dynamic causality, it operates on statistic causality.

Michael: That's a huge insight. Many people never get past that, do they?

Alexander: I remember when I was learning to trade, I would run my equity up 50%, 80%, crash, 50%, 80%. I would have these wild equity swings and I had no clue why it was happening. To take an account and run it up 50% in several months, I have to know something about markets. How come I end up losing money? I was beating my head against the wall. And there was no book. There was nothing to explain how it was happening.

Then the strangest thing happened. I graduated, finished my residency, and I got a little more money and I started putting more money into trading. Once my account got up to $60,000, I started making money. Again, I was puzzled. I haven't changed a thing. I was trading the same method, but once I went north of 60, it turns from a losing to a winning

Learning to be
a trader will
probably take as
long and cost as
much as getting a
college degree.

account. It was only years later I figured out why that happened—because I continued to trade the same size. There was a certain size I was comfortable with. Once the account grew bigger, that size fell into money management rules, which I didn't even know existed.

Michael: What percentage of traders and investors do you think are even aware of what money management is?

Alexander: I tend to deal with people who read my books. I don't know who all of them are, but the people who come to my classes tend to be pretty high-end. I would say among high-end people maybe nine out of 10 know what it is. I sharpen it for them, but it's not news for them. Among people in general, it's low.

I published a little eBook, *To Trade or Not to Trade: A Beginner's Guide*, $8 on Amazon. I begin the book by saying, "Listen, you are coming into an extremely exciting area, an area that I love, which also happens to be highly dangerous. So let me begin by saying in advance, there are personality traits that will make you a loser, so if you have those traits, make this $8 the last expense ever in the stock market. Turn around and leave before you do any more damage. Now, if you have the personality traits that are suitable for trading, please continue to read. But remember, we're going to talk about risk management. We're going to talk about record keeping and all this 'boring' stuff that separates winners from losers."

Michael: The idea of having that exit strategy on the upside, but then being comfortable to not just hold on the downside, but to turn around and go the other way.

Alexander: Towards the end of 2007, I was having dinner with my publisher, and he was fishing for a project. I said, "There is no book on selling and selling short." He says, "Who do you think would write this?" I said, "I guess I could." It came out in May of 2008 when the bear market was picking up speed, so you would think it would become a bestseller. No such thing! People don't like selling and selling short. I love shorting.

My initial experience was trading commodities and, of course, in commodities everybody sells short. You have to do the same thing in stocks. The market is a two-way street. It goes up and it goes down. As a matter of fact, it goes down about twice as fast as it goes up. You can make money trading both ways.

People are afraid of shorting. The first thing they say is, "What happens if you sell short and it goes up against you—you can be wiped out?" Well, if you get wiped out by a short trade, you're an idiot and you deserve to be wiped out. It means that you're trading without a stop. Of course, you have to run at some point. You have to set a stop. Shorting is completely doable.

I sort of make a joke out of it and I say, "Contrary to what your mother may have told you, shorting can be pleasant, but use protection when you do it. Don't listen to your mother, go ahead, do it, but use protection."

I always tell people, you've got to sell short. Find a stock that you hate. Find a stock that if you buy, it's going to go down. Now go ahead and sell short. But don't short a lot. Sell short, I don't know, 100 shares, 50 shares, 20 shares, whatever—a small quantity; but get comfortable with the concept of shorting. Learn on the small side, but you have to learn how to sell short. Maybe you will say, "Look, I don't like shorting. I prefer buying long." That's fine. But you have to make that decision after you have shorted so you make it on the basis of your experience and not out of fear.

Michael: One of the interesting things that you do in your work is travel. You are reaching groups of traders in distant outposts. Talk about the contrast, if any, between some of the places that you've been to teach— Eastern European countries compared to, let's say, the United States. Is there a difference?

Alexander: There are definitely differences. Similarities of course, but differences as well. First of all, I want to say that technical analysis is a study of crowd psychology. And crowds behave quite similarly in all countries. If you look at chart patterns in New York, Moscow, Sydney, and Singapore, they'll look remarkably similar. If I removed identifying codes and prices, I doubt you would be able to say which is from which country. Crowds behave in similar ways, which is why technical analysis works around the globe.

In terms of individual traders, people are quite different. I find that in America traders tend to be older and more educated. According to statistics, the average trader is a 50-year-old college-educated male and often a business owner. It's an older group of people. Whenever I teach in Eastern Europe, it strikes me how amazingly young people in the classroom are. It's full of 20-somethings; to see somebody in class who is 50 or 60 is a treat. In Asia, more women are trading than in the United States. Plus in Asia there is a much stronger gambling component than in either the United States or Europe. So with individual traders there are certain kinds of personal colors, little psychological differences, but when you look at the charts, which are created by crowds, there's not much difference.

Michael: It always strikes me as odd when someone reaches out to me from Indonesia or Singapore, say, and wants to know if a certain style of trading is right for them. They may think that their country is unique in terms of the markets. But as you correctly say, the markets are people coming together and buying—it's crowd psychology, it's the same everywhere.

Alexander: It is. But in terms of trading and worldwide markets, I always advise people to try to trade where they live. Because the question I ask them is, where do you think the profits are coming from? Strangely enough, many people don't think about it. Then they realize that the only place from which profits will come are the pockets of other traders. Well, other traders are as smart as they are, and they have as good computers and they're as eager for the money. It's a tough fight to get money out of somebody else's pockets while paying commissions and suffering slippage.

When people ask me, "Do you trade in Australia? Do you trade in Russia?" I say, "Look, it's hard enough to trade when I am awake. I don't want people picking my pockets while I'm asleep." If you go to a market in a different time zone, you can't watch the market in the day, which is not a good thing.

Michael: I'm pretty sure this is a line of yours: "I think financial markets are like manic depressive patients."

Alexander: That's me.

Michael: What does that mean?

Alexander: I mean markets go up and markets go down, but let me be a little more specific. Benoit Mandelbrot was a mathematician who ended up winning a Nobel Prize. Many years ago, the Egyptian government hired him to study cotton prices, because cotton is the major export of Egypt and obviously they want to sell it high. So, one of the great mathematicians of the world studied cotton prices and came up with this conclusion: "Hold onto a seed. Prices oscillate above and below value." That's one of few facts about markets—not a rule of thumb, but a mathematical fact that prices oscillate above and below value.

> Technical analysis is a study of crowd psychology. And crowds behave quite similarly in all countries.

Now, we can define value. Of course, the fundamental analyst has their ways of defining value. As a technician, I use a pair of moving averages and I believe that value lives in the zone between those averages. When the market goes below value, that's when people start panicking and selling, and I'm looking to buy. And when prices return to value, I take profits. When prices start rising above value and people get happy and they start buying, well, I'm looking to sell short above value. I use envelopes of course to help identify value, plus a whole bunch of indicators. But that's the main depressive behavior to me. There is a joke: "A neurotic is a person who builds castles in the clouds, a psychotic lives in those castles, and the psychiatrist is the fellow who collects the rent." I want to profit from crazy behavior, I don't want to be a part of it, which most people are.

Michael: Let's assume someone has trained with you. They've been through education with you. They have a great understanding, they get it. Aren't there a certain number of people, though, who self-sabotage, even when they've come out on the other side?

Alexander: First of all, the number of people who train with me is small, because all I do is run traders' camps where we accept 25 people once or twice a year. I have given lots of public classes for a day, but you might not be able to learn to ride a bicycle in a day, much less to trade. Just orientation to give you some dos and don'ts. But there are people who will not succeed, who will never succeed.

That eBook I mentioned earlier, *To Trade or Not to Trade*, begins by saying, "Listen, some people will never succeed. For example, if you have an addiction problem, if you have any kind of substance problem, forget about trading. You will never make money if you're an addict." So no, not everybody can trade, just like not everybody can do anything. It's a big world.

Michael: What excites you?

Alexander: Last time I checked, we go through this vale of tears only once, so you might as well enjoy the journey. The thing that I am most excited about these days—it's a fantastic intellectual as well as emotional adventure—is this group that I run together with my friend and business partner, Kerry Lovvorn. Nobody else in the world does it; it doesn't exist anywhere else.

We have a group of 18 professional and semi-professional traders, and they're obligated to submit a pick of what they think is going to be their favorite best trade for the week ahead. It can be long, or it can be short. We only do US stocks at this point. Every week we have winners and losers, and at the end of the quarter we accumulate all the results and winners get paid and they get diplomas. We have elite people who are always up, and members who participate on a voluntary basis. It's a great pleasure to see how people get it, how people learn, how people get with the program and look at each other, ask each other questions in advance.

Michael: One more quick question. You live in New York City. Where's your favorite place to eat?

Alexander: There's a Michelin-rated sushi restaurant called Jewel Bako that's probably my favorite place. My partner, Kerry, through hanging out with me, developed a serious sushi addiction. He's based in Alabama, but he comes to New York and finds the best restaurants and then I follow him. There's also a wonderful restaurant around the corner from the apartment, where you sit next to this conveyor belt and this wonderful river of sushi is flowing at you and you take whatever appeals to you and eat it! Come to New York—we'll go, I'll show you.

Michael: Absolutely, I will definitely take you up on that!

PART 2
Trading Psychiatrist

Michael Covel: Talk about how long you've been skiing and what it does for you at a root level.

Alexander Elder: As a young child I began cross-country skiing. We had a lot of snow where I grew up, in Estonia. Sometimes I had to ski to school, but it was flat there. I didn't begin downhill skiing until I came to the United States when I was in my 20s. Soon after that I started having children and skis went out the window. Then when the kids became teenagers, I started taking them skiing and my own skiing returned. Now I love to ski. I live in Vermont, 12 minutes away from the ski lift. After this interview, I'm going to get dressed and go—it's a beautiful sunny day and ski season is still on. Two weeks ago, I was skiing in Austria with several friends.

It's a wonderful way to connect with nature. It's physical, it's challenging. It's sort of like trading where you should become a little better every time, every week, every year. I got this app that measures the speed of each ski and the distance covered. I keep an eye on that thing, always trying to become better, but also it's a wonderful way to be out, and breathe fresh air. I would say about one-third of the time I ski alone, and two-thirds either with friends or my wife. So there's also a company feel to it as well. It's a great sport.

Michael: Has it become your meditation? The reason I ask is that in the last four or five years, I've become addicted to yoga. It's the physical feeling that it gives me after—the cortisol changes, and stress reduction. Do you find something similar with skiing?

Alexander: Not at all, because when I ski, I have to completely concentrate on skiing and nothing else. I haven't taken any bad falls this season because I realized that every time I tumbled before, it was because the slope seemed easy or medium, and my thoughts drifted off into something else. I have to be totally, absolutely, 100% concentrated on the snow, on the position of my skis, and what's ahead of me. It's not a zone-out experience; it's a complete focus on the current moment.

Michael: When you're in that moment and you have to only concentrate on skiing, there's a nice part of that where you get to turn your brain off.

Alexander: You're absolutely right. It's only this moment and I can't think of anything else. I can't think of what's coming up later in the day. I can't think of what the euro or the dollar are doing. I can't think of anything like that. Now, here, in the moment.

Michael: I saw a great piece of research that showed stopping exercise increases the chance of depression.

Alexander: I have my exercises for summer. I bought myself a paddleboard. It's like a surfboard, but it has a cut in the middle, and you drop paddles into it and go. I live between two lakes. I also have a tractor, and I love working on the property. I was talking with my friends about going skiing in Norway in July or August. Apparently, they have a ski resort which is completely snowed in all year. I love skiing, but there are many other good things as well.

Michael: What is the biggest change in the landscape that you've seen since your first book came out? You've had 20-plus years to witness the constant 24/7 news on TV. Now it's Twitter, Facebook, and all that stuff. What's changed about human nature?

Alexander: Human nature hasn't changed much. The one change—and I don't think it's impacted trading all that much—is I think the world has become much less violent in, let's say, the last half-century. We don't think so because we hear all this horrible news all the time, but if you think about it, during the First World War, 50,000 people would get killed in a single day and it was sort of, yep, that's how the cookie crumbles. You read about the military in Iraq and Afghanistan, where 3,000 people died in the course of the entire war, and everybody is concerned about it. So the value of human life, I think, has become higher and the level of violence in society is lower. There is scientific evidence for that, as studies of human skulls for the last several hundred years have found that skulls are becoming thinner.

What everybody knows is not worth knowing.

The chances of someone getting hit on the head with a heavy object are becoming less, so evolution propels us towards thinner skull bones.

That's the big picture. In trading, people always look for some kind of magic, how to make money, working 15 minutes a week, no mathematics required, this kind of nonsense. It always existed. The magic always changes. It used to be that if you have a calculator, you can calculate an exponential moving average instead of a simple one. Then we got computers, which was a total golden key to success.

Now, it's algo trading. But in the end, all of that comes down to human beings with their emotions. One of the greatest fallacies of economists is that they assume that humans are logical beings. To an extent, we are, but not to a large extent. We're driven by emotions and that does not change a lot. That's not becoming any thinner like our skulls.

Michael: Let me take you back in time. For those folks who are not familiar with your story, you mentioned growing up in Estonia. And if I'm not mistaken, med school, age 16—that's a kid that's moving pretty quick! What was the drive that was pushing you at such a young age?

Alexander: I didn't have any great interest in medicine, but I wanted to go to university. I grew up in a medical family. Everybody was a physician for a couple of generations before me. I needed to get into university to avoid service in the Soviet army. This was the mid-1960s. I still remember we had blackouts all the time, because we were told that the Americans were coming any day to bomb the hell out of us, so we had bomb drills. Nasty times, completely repressed society, labor camps. It was brutal. I grew up to hate the system. So I went to medical school, but all I thought about was getting laid, getting girls. I also got some education in the process, and I graduated in the top 10% of my class.

Michael: How were you developing this desire to escape that was obviously building to something else, because you're in the middle of a repressed system with a control of information? There was no internet. What were you doing to get that insight beyond friends and family?

Alexander: My grandfather, who was a big influence in my life, was always listening to foreign radio broadcasts. Every Soviet city of any size was ringed by special antennas which suppressed the shortwave frequencies on which the Voice of America, Radio Liberty, and BBC were broadcasting. My grandfather gave me a radio which actually came from a German submarine—long story—and I would sit in front of that radio and move the dial, and there was this "Wow, wow, wow" noise from the suppression towers. I would try to get a little connection to the BBC or maybe Voice of America, dependent on weather conditions.

I also had a friend in the university who was the archive researcher for Aleksandr Solzhenitsyn when he was writing *The Gulag Archipelago*. He was completely fearless, he would speak his mind, and so I would hang around and listen. After Solzhenitsyn was exiled from the Soviet Union, my friend was sent to prison for many years. There was a sense that the system was completely false. The system was completely inhumane. The system was wrong. I got a sense of that. And the funniest thing is, I realized fairly early on that I have this nose for quality. I know what's good. And it's not that I worked at it, I have it. It works in trading, it works in human relations, and it works also in politics. I have a sense for that. Even if the good is suppressed, I can see it.

Michael: You get your medical degree, you're a doctor in your early 20s, then you make a break for it. How did you make it to America?

Alexander: There is a book that the Hoover Institution on War, Revolution and Peace at Stanford University put out, called *The KGB Wanted List*. I'm in that book twice. The KGB tried to catch me and they tried to kill me. Obviously they failed at that job, as well as at many others. I went to medical school at 16, but I got political early on and I hated the Communist system. I hated it so much that by the time I was in my late teens, I would not go out of the house on national holidays because they would have red flags out. It would disgust me to walk under the flags.

I got more and more involved in politics, and gradually my friends started going to prison and there was no question in my mind that's where I was going to end up, because whenever I get involved in something I like to take it far. I realized I didn't love that country enough to go to prison for it.

The Soviet Union borders at that time were absolutely locked. There was a tremendous military force guarding borders. I grew up in Estonia, I love swimming and I got into snorkeling. Well, you need a mask, a snorkel, and fins, right? But you were not allowed to have all three; you could have two, but not three. Why? Because Finland was 90 kilometers away. What if you swam to Finland? And that was the law, so if they caught you with all three, they would confiscate them and arrest you.

I wanted to get out. I got a job as a ship's doctor and when the ship was in Africa, I jumped ship and I ran away. I put on my running shoes and got going with the rest of the crew in hot pursuit, because nobody was going to go on shore alone. I had to dash.

We were docked in Abidjan, Ivory Coast. The country was the same as the Soviet Union—a completely isolated system, not only politically, but also economically. I was the fifth-best paid person on the ship and I was getting $10 a month plus some Russian money. It was cheaper for the Soviet government to put a doctor on a ship which only had maybe 80% crew than to take somebody to a harbor doctor if they got sick. We were allowed on shore leave, but only in groups, and the group was responsible for coming back together. If somebody tried to escape, the group was told to do anything, including kill him, and don't worry, the Soviet government would

The single most important factor in your success or lack of such is the quality of your records.

get you out of it. Of course, the group from which you ran away got punished, so I made sure I ran away from the group which was led by the secretary of the Communist Party for the ship. I did not run from any of my friends. I ran from the bad guy.

I was on the ship for about two months prior to this run. We were in Africa, as I said, and every night when the sun went down and it wasn't so hot, I would go to the upper deck and skip rope for two hours. When the running time came, I was not the biggest or the strongest man on that trip, but I was the one in best shape, and nobody caught me. I broke away from my pursuers, got a taxi and had it take me to the US embassy. The rest is history.

Michael: How irregular would that have been in the early 1970s, when this took place?

Alexander: Essentially once every few years they would have an escape like mine—maybe two or three times a decade. It was completely unusual. They did a pretty good job vetting who got a job on the ship and who didn't—it wasn't a simple thing.

Michael: I'm sure today you wear it a little bit as a badge of honor. With time to look back on it, it's pretty damn cool that you pulled it off, isn't it?

Alexander: I wouldn't have done it today. Today, I realize I was risking my life. It's so dangerous. As I get older, I value life a lot more, but back then I was living forever and I took a wild chance, and it worked out well for me. It was a kid stuff.

Michael: You say you took a wild chance, but it sounds from your description it was calculated. The reason I'm going down this path is because the way that you think is the useful takeaway from our conversation. Getting inside the mind of somebody who's making that decision—what's coursing through the veins?

Alexander: You have to be prepared. We're having this conversation early in the morning before the markets open. I've been up for the last hour and what am I doing? My morning homework, studying, researching, planning, scheming—what I will do and what I will not do today. That's what I did back then in Africa. Running from the ship with my crewmates in hot pursuit. That's like putting on a trade: the trade is on, but the work was done way before that.

Michael: Working on ourselves is the best way to work on anything, whether that's trading, entrepreneurship, whatever. The interior work is where it starts.

Let's move into the teaching of this, because you've done this for decades. People who haven't had these life-or-death experiences that you faced, who haven't necessarily had that chance to get those adrenaline rushes, have a wake-up call. Maybe if people hear Alexander Elder talking, they might think, "Do I have to work at it like that? Do I have to focus like that?"

Alexander: You have to work hard, and you have to find a place where you're emotionally stable, where you are not shaken by the market when you're making decisions, and not jumping like Pavlov's dog in response to the opening bell. For example, just yesterday, the Dow opened down 500 points and challenged recent important lows, and then it ended up 200 points. This is precisely the market where people who are not strong, skilled, and prepared will sell at the bottom. And then they will wait and wait for signals, and more signals, and more signals. Finally, all signals are good, now they are buying. By that time, I may be selling short already because the best buy signals occur at the market top. That's where everything is perfect, and everybody knows that this is a bullish market. Well, what everybody knows is not worth knowing.

Michael: You mention down/up volatility on the Dow. There are people across the planet watching every minute. It strikes me that if one has a choice to trade, widening your time horizon has resonance in terms of stress reduction. Being glued all day long to every piece of information seems difficult in the long term.

Alexander: It's also extremely counterproductive for trading. If someone is glued to the screen all day long, they inevitably start following the market instead of looking at it in an objective way.

Here's the concept that I keep repeating to anybody who will listen. It took me a long time to comprehend it, so I figure I have to repeat it often. Looking at the stock market, we all trade pretty much the same stocks, year in and year out, decade in and decade out. It's the same—Ford, General Motors, then Tesla comes in, and Facebook comes in—but the point is, we trade pretty much the same basket of stocks. Now, some stocks get taken over, some stocks go out of business, some new stocks, some initial public offerings (IPOs), but that's around the fringes. We trade the same things.

One of the
greatest fallacies
of economists is
that they assume
that humans are
logical beings.

There are strong hands who buy low and take profits high. And there are weak hands who panic at the lows and get enough assurance to buy at the highs. This constant see-saw goes on, from strong hands into weak hands during rallies. Then a decline begins, and now the weak hands start being shaken out, and at the bottom, the last weak hands panic and sell their stocks, and that's where I buy. The best buying opportunities occur at the point of maximum danger. It takes some technical knowledge to identify that maximum danger with a degree of precision. I don't claim to have 100%, but a reasonable degree to get the zone.

Michael: If you were to offer a composite explanation from new traders and experienced traders, what is the drive to want to be glued to the screen? What is the advantage for people who don't yet have your perspective?

Alexander: It's a great question. There are two parts to that answer. First of all, it's financial pornography. Seeing how this thing moves up and down is like watching a porno video. It's entertaining, especially for someone who is new to the system.

The other part is someone who is losing money and is becoming afraid, and feels that he's being buffeted by the market. He looks at it like a rabbit is looking at a snake, and the rabbit is frozen. "Look how that snake moves." "Oh, maybe it doesn't see me." "Oh, I think it's moving away." "It's coming closer."

It's partly entertainment, and partly feeling weak, dependent, fearful, and keeping your eyes on the snake. But neither of those things does you any good. Here I am before the opening, making my trade plans, and I like to hang around for the first 20 or 30 minutes to see how the market opens, and then I'm going to go ski, and then I'm going to come back, have my orders in. Then I'll come back again for the last hour before the market closes, see if any changes or adjustments are needed. I'll be glued to the slopes, not to the screen.

Michael: I don't take anything away from Michael Bloomberg (and his Bloomberg terminal) at all. I salute him. He's an entrepreneur. He's done well. But he is a billionaire because he has given people one of those screens of data that never stop. You have to try to get people to understand that it's not all about data. You've got to make some choices, right? Trying to take in all the data, I don't know how that fire hose approach works.

Alexander: Sometimes, I compare trading to medicine. Now in the 21st century, you cannot know all of medicine. You cannot be an ophthalmologist, dermatologist, surgeon, and psychiatrist. When you go into medicine, you've got to specialize. You choose a specialty where you aim to become very, very good. And anything outside of your specialty, you know enough to say, "That's not for me. I have a good referral for you."

It's the same thing in trading, between fundamental news, political news, technical developments, and the tremendous wealth of technical indicators. There is no way to learn everything that is to be learned about the markets. You have to be humble and say, "I am a simple person. I am going to find a sector of market expertise, and I will aim to become good in my sector. And anything outside of that sector, I'm going to raise my hands and say, 'Not for me.'"

Michael: I've seen you describe it as mind, method, and money. Why don't you apply some weights there for the audience? I would say the vast majority of market players who are first getting started put almost all the weight on method.

Alexander: I went through that stage myself. It's tremendously attractive. It's intellectually challenging. When I began to trade, that's all I did: learn technical analysis. Then I realized, wait a second, what's wrong with this picture? I know technical analysis pretty well, but my equity goes up 40% and down 80%. Same technical analysis, huge equity swings. That was decades ago.

Along with method, the mind—psychology—is second, and the third weight is money management. A trader with a system that's steadily making money, year after year, I would say that chances are high that this trader will burn himself with the system. Why? Because he will get greedy, trade a size that's too large. And meanwhile, there are specific formulas for how to control your trading size, because if you start piling on risk, the quality of your trading is going to go down. You mentioned mind, method, money. After several decades, they came up with a fourth M: management, primarily self-management.

It is absolutely essential to keep records. Show me a trader with good records and I'll show you a good trader. Because by keeping high-quality records—not simply writing down numbers, bought at five, sold at six, but keeping good-quality records with charts and explanations, why you did this and did that—you insert a learning loop into your progress. You are not just chasing stocks or futures, but you are looking back at yourself. How did you buy? How did you sell? You become your own teacher, so the self-management record keeping, I believe, is hugely important.

Years ago, when I was actively practicing psychiatry, I would ask patients about their drinking. Every once in a while you run into somebody who you suspect is an alcoholic, and I would say so to the patient. Some would accept and many would deny. If a guy denied that he was an alcoholic, I never argued. I would say, "Look, I want you to continue drinking for the next week exactly how you drink. Don't change a thing. Every time you take a drink, I want you to write down what you drank and how much. Come back with the record and we'll take a look at it." No alcoholic could ever come back with a complete record. They would be terrified looking at this thing.

Why? Because for people who are engaged in some kind of impulsive, stupid, self-distracting behavior, the last thing they want to do is look in the mirror. Creating records creates a mirror of your actions.

Now, moving from psychiatric office to trading, most traders run forward and keep making the same mistakes month after month, and year after year. There is a Russian expression, "Don't step on the same rake twice." The guy steps on the rake in the garden, it stands up and hits him in the forehead—can happen to anybody—but don't step on the same rake twice.

Keeping records creates a breaker mechanism in unproductive, bad, not useful behavior. Keeping records makes you alert to yourself. When you trade, you have several components of your trading. Obviously, you have your computer, you have your database, you have internet knowledge that you have acquired—all these wonderful things. But also your personality, moods, fears, likes and dislikes—these are part of trading. It's important to pay attention to yourself and to your decision-making process. That's why I keep saying to traders, "The single

The best buying opportunities occur at the point of maximum danger.

most important factor in your success or lack of such is the quality of your records. You've got to keep a diary of your trades."

I used to keep mine on paper. I used to keep it on a variety of computer forms. We now have an absolutely fantastic record-keeping system. As soon as I began keeping good records some years ago, I could see an improvement in my trading.

Every couple of months, when you have a free evening, go back and review all trades, because we all make our trading decisions at the right edge of the chart. How does this trade look when it migrates to the middle of the chart? Do you think I remember what I traded in May or June of a given year? I remember one or two spectacular trades, but 99% of what I did I have no recall.

I'm going to go through every single trade I closed. I'm going to pull up every closed trade. I'm going to pull up a current chart of where that stock or commodity stands today. And I'm going to draw a new chart with all the markings. I will see what I did right, what I did wrong. It's going to be a fantastic educational experience—like a class for one.

Michael: I want to hear your explanation around the concept of robustness. I'm always struck that smart people, when they first start to think about technical analysis, trend following, or systems trading, get this idea in their head, "An indicator says to do this at this level." They get so precise that it could only happen at that one variable. Now, of course, their application should be consistent, but the idea that it breaks and falls apart if it's not at that one precise point is such a blind spot for people.

Alexander: I absolutely agree with you, and you use the term that I was going to say: robustness. Good systems are robust, good methods are robust. Whatever moving average you use—there's 10, 11, 12, 13—it should give pretty much the same results. If 11 works and 12 doesn't, well, you're using your own method, toss it out the window, look for a new one.

It's like driving a car. You can drive a Mercedes-Benz or you can drive some 15-year-old Buick, or you can get behind the wheel of a Ferrari. As long as you know how to drive, you will drive them all about the same standard. Why? Because it's your personal skill. This idea that if you only had created a perfect system, the market will open up and start raining money on you, is a delusion. It comes from weakness. It comes from thinking that you are not strong enough. What about building a system that will make decisions for me? If this approach worked, then the guy with the biggest computer would've owned the exchange by now. It hasn't happened, because ultimately, it's the human being who makes the decision.

Michael: What was the pivotal moment early in your career?

Alexander: There was not a particular moment. It came slowly through a lot of painful experiences, losing money, and being stubborn. I was not going to give up. I hated to lose. I was going forward and making all these mistakes and losing. Eventually, I figured out how to change myself. I wish it was a fast process. There was a guy in Chicago, Brian Morrison, who said in an interview that a high level of education is an obstacle to success in trading. He said, "I have a PhD in mathematics, I specialized in cybernetics, but I was able to overcome these disadvantages and make money." I had those disadvantages. It took me an embarrassingly long time to overcome them, but overcome them I did, out of sheer cussedness. If I'd had a teacher like myself back in those days, I would've done it so much faster. I didn't have to spend so much time. Essentially, I was discovering, I was reinventing the bicycle, and today I can show somebody how the bicycle is constructed, and they can ride it as long as they're prepared to put a little bit of time into practice.

Michael: You said you hate to lose, you're stubborn, but that's an aspirational drive. When it comes to your trading, for example, if your stop has been hit, you're not about hating to lose, and you're not about being stubborn, you're taking that stop. When did this hate to lose thing start? I assume when you were a kid?

Alexander: It came a bit later. A turning point for me came, strangely enough, about a year after I came to the United States. I got a job as a research assistant at a psychiatric research center in the suburbs of New York and they gave me a room in a dorm. I had a black and white TV, and I had a car—a luxury. I thought I was on top of the world. Then I came down with a nasty cold, so I was laid up in my room for a few days, and my boss's secretary was coming over every day and bringing me chicken soup. When I'm lying in bed, I did a lot of thinking, and I realized that back in the old country I grew up in this successful family and if I turned out to be a total bum, they would be chewing my ear off, but I would still have a roof over my head and three square meals a day, all my life. And here I was in America. I didn't have a single relative here. I didn't have any support system. I realized that if I did not function, there was nothing between me and the abyss. I realized it was all completely up to me. That was a very, very useful discovery.

> **There is no way to learn everything that is to be learned about the markets.**

Years later, when I was practicing psychiatry, I realized that some of my alcoholic patients experienced the same feeling. When they're drinking to the point where they're hitting rock bottom, they ask themselves: Do I become a bum or do I turn my life around? That's one of the themes in my first book, *Trading for a Living*, which has a chapter on lessons from Alcoholics Anonymous. You hit rock bottom, you take a bunch of impulsive trades, you destroy your account. And now you decide whether to walk away from it forever, or to push away from rock bottom and start paddling up. I paddled up.

Michael: This is always a personal choice, isn't it? Those alcoholic patients could get all the treatment in the world, but it's up to them if they want to stop. We always think there's someone that can fix things for us. But the reality is when you're in the middle of whatever that addiction might be, it's up to you.

Alexander: You know how many psychiatrists it takes to change a light bulb? Only one, but the light bulb has got to want to change.

Michael: You could teach that for weeks and months, but so many people won't want to accept it.

Alexander: I can teach it for months, or I can say to the guy, the single best step for you to improve your trading at this point is to start keeping good records. Let me show you the format in which I keep my records—feel free to change it, adapt it to your needs. And I would like you to record every trade like that, let's say, for the next month. After that I'm going to teach you the next thing. I doubt that one person out of 10 will do that.

Michael: Even if they have a terrible system, you're saying, "Write it all down and let's see what you got."

Alexander: You need this toughness, and commitment to work, to change yourself. If somebody has that, I can teach them. It's wonderful for people to lose money trading, because when I trade, where are my profits going to come from? They're going to come from people who are impulsive, undisciplined, and ignorant, right? I'm not going to get any profits out of experienced traders like you, Mike; I'm going to get profits out of somebody who stumbles into the market and doesn't know anything about risk management, knows a few things about stochastics and moving averages. And now, he's out to beat me at the trading game. We need people like that to support the markets.

Michael: If Alexander Elder says, "You are acting impulsively. That is ignorant," more people feel their egos bruised today than they would in past years.

Alexander: Back when I was busy practicing psychiatry, a typical beginning of a case would be a patient comes in, we sit in the armchairs and the patient says, "The boss is an animal. The wife doesn't care. The kids only talk to me when they need money and life is generally miserable." And I sit there listening, listening, listening, taking it all in, occasionally asking little questions, and the patient slightly begins to relax. The first time in a long time somebody is listening to him. We make the next appointment.

He comes to the second session and by now, he feels more comfortable with me. He knows that somebody is listening, paying attention, serious. He tells me more about the animal of a boss and the wife who doesn't care. Then there's a pause and I say, "A man walks down the street and a dog bites him." The patient now is nudging me in compassion. He knows exactly what I mean and how it feels. The question I ask is, "There were 50 other men on the street. What signal did he give to the dog that he was okay to bite?" Now the hook is in, now we can talk.

Michael: That's what you have spent your career doing: passing on great pieces of insight, to help people understand what it might be like, a little bit, to be a psychiatrist.

CHAPTER 11

DANIEL CROSBY

PART 1
The Personal Benchmark

DANIEL CROSBY is a psychologist and behavioral finance expert who applies his study of market psychology to everything from financial product design to security selection. He is the co-author of *The New York Times* bestseller *Personal Benchmark: Integrating Behavioral Finance and Investment Management*. He is at the forefront of behavioralizing finance. His books are *The Laws of Wealth*, *The Behavioral Investor*, *You're Not That Great*, and *Personal Benchmark*.

Michael note

There's nothing easy about tearing apart how psychotic most people have become when it comes to investing and their money. Daniel rips the bandage off and dives deep into terribly complicated topics.

Michael Covel: Let's jump right in: The efficient market theory. This is not something every investor knows about, but they should.

I watched a fascinating video interview with Eugene Fama and Dick Thaler. As far as I could tell, they didn't agree about anything. They respected each other for their academic achievement, but they didn't agree on anything.

Daniel Crosby: In the simplest possible terms, the efficient market hypothesis says that the price is always right. The price that you see is the correct price, or at least the closest to the correct approximation of a price you'd ever get, and you can't beat the market. Those are the two legs to the efficient market hypothesis.

Michael: I've been at this for a little while and it sure looks to me there's a lot of evidence that you can beat the market, that there's momentum on that side. You've got Warren Buffett, Howard Marks, Seth Klarman—there's a whole army of people that have beaten the market. And then on top of that, I don't know how the efficient market hypothesis explains what happened in 2008.

Daniel: That's why you're starting to see it break down, in the face of these bubbles, panics, crashes. And the thing is to try to argue the other side because I don't believe in the strongest form of the efficient market hypothesis and I don't think many people do, frankly, any more. But the strong form efficient market theorist would say, "Look, you've got hundreds of millions of people in the market. Probability says, even if you have monkeys throwing darts at *The Wall Street Journal*, you're going to occasionally get a Warren Buffett, Seth Klarman or Howard Marks—you're going to get some winners in a system that big, there's nothing special about these folks."

But where that breaks down is certain types of investing have consistently outperformed—specifically a value and momentum strategy—which leads me to believe that maybe it's not monkeys throwing darts at stock, but maybe it's something about these strategies.

The reason these strategies have persisted is because there's a strong psychological underpinning. Looking at value and momentum approaches, these are hard to arbitrage away—it's hard to arbitrage away bad behavior.

Michael: Let's talk about rules for a moment. This is something that's big in your work. For me, I know about the trend following side. People can call it something else—they can call it time series, momentum, or whatnot—but most of these strategies are literally automatic. They're 100% systematic, it's all rules. And then also, you'll find the population of trades in some of these momentum strategies. There are so many more trades. For this to all be luck is crazy. But on the value side, are things as systematic? You could have a situation where a value player has made a half-dozen brilliant long-term bets in their career. And that alone can make you a superstar in investing.

Daniel: You bring up a gap that I've been trying to bridge. Typically, you've thought of trend followers—momentum folks—as quantitative higher-frequency traders, whereas the value folks have traded less, have had more concentrated positions, perhaps a discretionary mindset. I talk about rules-based behavior when investing, and one of my pillars of that is something I call consistency, or *just following rules*. And I do identify a sort of a combo value-momentum investor. But I think that anyone who's a behaviorally informed investor is going to fall down on the side of rules.

> In the simplest possible terms, the efficient market hypothesis says that the price is always right.

There is a meta-analysis of all the studies on following simple rules versus leaning on your own discretion. When we're talking about discretion in these studies, we're typically talking about expert discretion, PhD-level discretion in everything from prison recidivism studies, to stock picking, to making a medical diagnosis. And what they found in these over 200 studies is that expert discretion is beaten or matched by following simple rules 94% of time. And at big cost savings, of course, because you're not paying 10 chartered financial analysts (CFAs) to go out and meet with managers and try to make these discretionary decisions. And then there's also the headache savings—you can go live your life instead of being up at 2:00 in the morning to look at the Chinese soybeans futures or whatever. That makes a lot of sense. You can do it more cheaply and you can also do it with a higher quality of life. I hope this is where the industry is headed.

Michael: When I think about trend following strategies, which are way, way away from high-frequency stuff, it seems like the perfect example for showing the problems with efficient market theory and the benefits of the behavioral side of things. Because you have these 100% systematic strategies that are showing this long-term performance. You've seen the studies as much as I have—this works. It dovetails completely with everything that Daniel Kahneman and Amos Tversky did.

Daniel: There's a push towards a greater acceptance of trend following within what we'll loosely call the behavioral community. Because to be candid, there's two or three handfuls of people who I see as identifying as behavioral finance informed investors and most of them I would classify as high-conviction value. But increasingly you're seeing people come around towards trend following, towards acceptance of momentum, because we're beginning to recognize the psychological underpinnings of these things. We're recognizing that part of why momentum persists is people's tendency to overreact or underreact, update our preferences slowly, and project the now into the future indefinitely.

> **Value and momentum are hard to arbitrage away because it's hard to arbitrage away bad behavior.**

Behavioral folks initially reacted negatively to charting, trend following and related concepts, because it was sort of seen as voodoo. But as we build the psychology behind these concepts, they gain greater acceptance.

Michael: You're a relatively young guy, but your work is pretty deep. How did you get your start? What's the backstory?

Daniel: My dad is a financial advisor and investment manager, so I grew up steeped in that world. Started out at college with an eye to following in his footsteps. A couple of years into my college experience, I dropped out to go be a missionary in Southeast Asia. Came back from having lived in the Philippines for a few years with… we'll call it a bleeding heart, so to speak, and wanted to do good in the world. I said, "You know what? I'm going to be a psychologist." Got about two or three years into a PhD in psychology and realized that I didn't want to talk with sad people all the time. But I did enjoy thinking deeply about why people did the things they do. And I found the market to be a natural backdrop against which to measure human behavior.

The amount of data that we receive, the sort of real-time updates you get about human sentiment, are fascinating. This is something that clinical psychologists aren't afforded in the same way. I've been lucky to have two great loves in investment management and human behavior, and to be able to combine those in a satisfying way.

Michael: Tell me the guinea worm story.

Daniel: Everybody either loves or hates the guinea worm story! I grew up in Alabama, I live in Atlanta now. I love the American South, it's such a weird and wonderful place. And so I tried to start the book with an Atlanta story. Atlanta is the center of epidemiological research in the world—we've got the Carter Center, and of course we have the Centers for Disease Control and Prevention (CDC). A project that the Carter Center and the CDC did together was for the first time in history, they eradicated a disease for which there is no cure: guinea worm. Guinea worms were infecting millions of people each year in Africa, decimating economies and the prospects of people who lived in these countries. There were no pills, there was no shot, nothing you could do. And so they said, we're going to take a different path.

When you get guinea worms, they exit through your feet, and the only way you can get relief is to put your feet in water. In these villages, there are communal water sources and so someone runs selfishly down to the water source to get this relief and ends up infecting the rest of the village. So the Carter Center and the CDC came up with behavioral interventions which were teaching the villagers to identify and then to quarantine—to create a social construct whereby if you identify your neighbor, sister, brother, or whoever, has guinea worms, you don't let them go near that water source. You keep them where they are and you make them gut it out. And by doing this, they literally eradicated millions of cases of guinea worms a year and saved the economies of a number of sub-Saharan African countries.

The reason I relate to this story is because by following a few simple rules, they brought about this frankly miraculous effect of something that's never going to go away until we come up with a cure. Investors are likewise saddled with this disease of irrational behavior. We're about as ill-equipped to invest as we are to do anything as a human family. But by following a few simple rules, we can have a similarly powerful effect.

Michael: You quote the economist David Ricardo in your book: "Let your profits run and cut your losses short." He set that foundation down over 200 years ago. That simple rule is trend following foundation number one, but it's extremely difficult to get across because everybody wants to buy more when the price starts to drop.

Daniel: We want to get back to zero and lock in our gains, so we sell our winners short and let our losers run. And that's exactly the opposite of what we should do. The thing about investing is none of it is rocket science. The ideas are so simple, but they're not easy. So you need rules, you need an advisor, and you need whatever else it takes to help constrain your bad behavior.

Michael: When you say easy, you mean easy relative to what one knows at a certain point in time. For certain populations, it won't be easy; perhaps more so for some experienced populations. I had a conversation with Larry Hite and he was telling me it's so easy, because he's been doing it for 40 years and he knows deep in his bones that if he's got a loss, he's taking the loss.

Daniel: The reason these things stick around is because they go against the grain of human behavior. These things are going to persist where these silly little anomalies like calendar effects and days of the week are easy to arbitrage away. It's hard to get the crowd to move against its best impulses. And because that's the case, any sort of investment discipline rooted in psychology has a better chance of sticking around.

Michael: You point out that we must invest in risky assets because if we don't, we're stuck with the interest rate a bank will give us. But on the flip side, your premise is, "Okay, we have to take risky choices, but to take those risky choices you need mentorship." Why don't you explain this paradox from your perspective?

Daniel: The paradox is that God couldn't design a worse investor than the average human being! The rules of investing run contrary to what is simple and easy for us to do in our everyday life. We don't do well with uncertainty. We don't do well with volatility. We live in the present and not in the future. All these things are hard for us to do.

This is why there is a need for a lot of people to get guidance. You talked earlier about Larry Hite saying it was easy, because he's been doing it for so long. But, for example, we lose 13% of our IQ under duress, so even if someone's a regular listener of your podcast, has read all your

Investors are saddled with the disease of irrational behavior.

books, has read my books, has done all these things to educate themselves, that knowledge tends to be out the door when we need it most. There is research around people who work with professionals versus those who don't, and those who work with professionals tend to do much better. It's not because most investment advisors or even most stock pickers know what they're doing. It's because a professional advisor keeps you from making a handful of egregious mistakes over an investment lifetime.

Michael: If you don't have the rules that you're going to stick to—buy, sell, how much you're going to buy or sell, creating a portfolio—then why play?

Daniel: A lot of people engage in investing as an ego exercise. They want to prove how smart they are. They want to be the master of that destiny. And that's an impulse that I understand because elsewhere in life, if you do more, you get more. But in investment management, so often when you try to overcomplicate it, you get less. It's a natural impulse, but not one that leads us to a good place.

Michael: You mentioned ego. In *The Laws of Wealth* you quote a scene from *Fight Club*, which says you're not special, you're not a beautiful or unique snowflake, you're the same decaying organic matter as everything else. What made you think that *Fight Club* was an appropriate reference?

Daniel: So many times we know the rules but think they apply to other people. We are prone to say, "I know bad stuff happens, I just never thought it would happen to me."

There are studies on how we tend to delegate the dangerous and own the advantageous. When you ask, "How likely are you to get divorced or have a car accident or get cancer?" people rate that likelihood as extremely low. When you ask, "How likely are you to win the lottery or pick a great stock?" people rate that as extremely high. The hallmark of a good investor is realizing that the rules do apply to you—this isn't just something that applies to other people. Failure to own that the rules apply to us explains a lot of bad investment behavior. You have to own the fact that you're no better, you're no more special, you're no more gifted than the next person, if you're going to be truly great.

Michael: Even though the wisdom of the stoics and perhaps the Eastern Zen traditions goes back millennia, stoicism and Zen are not something the average American today grew up with. Both of those traditions fit with where you're going.

Daniel: They do. And you're right, these are understudied in the United States. It's consistent, this idea of being a roll-up-your-sleeve, hardworking stock picker. There's something red meat, apple pie, and baseball about doing fundamental research, picking 10 stocks, and living and dying with that. Unfortunately, the research doesn't necessarily back that up. But I agree, there is something American about that way of doing things.

Michael: We also get caught up in the big story. It's kind of crazy that as long as the United States has been around and as many successful investors as there have been, most people only think of Warren Buffett and that's it. He set this up a long time ago, there's first-mover advantage. He has a unique structure. I take nothing away from him. But the idea that Buffett has a half-dozen stocks that he picked a long time ago and held on for dear life and now he's made a fortune—that's not exactly what happened. It's a touch more complicated than that.

Daniel: I love Buffett, but there's a strong element of "Do as I say and not as I do," with him. He's badmouthing derivatives while owning them. And I get it—he's speaking to folks at his meetings who shouldn't be operating at the same level of sophistication that he is. But there's the quotable Warren Buffett and then there's Warren Buffett in practice.

People who have that personal benchmark are much more likely to stay the course, follow their rules, and end with higher closing account balances.

Michael: You have said that as investors we control what matters most and I would argue that what matters most is loss. If we go into the markets, we all have the ability to control how much we are willing to lose, don't we?

Daniel: When you ask most people, "What's the best predictor of your ability to meet your financial goals?" they're going to say, "The economy and the Fed," all these externalities. The research shows that most investors tend to leave about 50% of their gains on the table because of poor behavioral decisions. This is over a long period of time; most investors barely keep up with inflation. This is me trying to say, "Look, you are the best predictor of your success or failure, so own that from the outset and don't blame it on the market."

Michael: Let's talk about passive index funds. It's all the rage. What I don't get is that if we have a, say, 50% drop in the overall equity indices—which we get from time to time—are people going to be comfortable holding that passive index fund?

Daniel: Let me try to dissect it. I refer to this as, excess is never permanent. There are two major streams of research here. One is around developing quantitative measures of investor sentiment, and the other is around developing composite quantitative measures of broad equity market valuation. As we're talking here in 2016, right now in the United States my metric is just out of the 90th percentile for the S&P 500 relative to history. That means it's as expensive as

God couldn't design a worse investor than the average human being.

it's ever been in history, with the exception of maybe 2000. So, we're in 2000 and 1929 territory with respect to valuation. We know for sure how expensive things are. But we don't know how exactly that's going to turn. Trend followers can watch for that turn and catch a 10% dip, maybe, instead of a 50% dip.

But there's no denying that drops in equity markets occur, and with greater or less severity relative to how tightly stretched valuations are. I conceptualize it a bit like a bow and arrow—if you stretch that string tightly, when you let it go, the arrow gets propelled at a higher speed. Similarly, when you stretch valuations to an extreme point, when you let go of that arrow, the momentum starts to flag, and you get a negative reaction. In that respect, people who are passive are going to have a bad time.

I have talked about how three-quarters of what are marketed as active funds are passive. And so unfortunately a lot of the reasons why active management has gotten a bad reputation are well earned. You've got expensive, low-conviction products that aren't following rules, that are making investors susceptible to all the behavioral biases of the managers. All the research shows that active investment managers tend to sell low and buy high and do everything you shouldn't do.

Michael: Whether it's active or passive, so much of Wall Street comes down to fees, and whatever smart guy can slosh the money around from this pile to that pile and get a fee as well. Why do you also speak to the passive guys, though? Because the passive guys are all indoctrinated in the efficient market theory. They aren't behavioral by and large.

Daniel: What I've tried to do with my work is share a little bit of a middle ground. If on one extreme we have buy-and-hold passivity, and on another extreme we have high conviction, active management, trying to pick 10 winning stocks, I try to be somewhere in the middle. I try to show that there are some things that are laudable about the passive management movement, like managing fees, tax alpha, diversification—these things make a tremendous difference over time. But there's a middle ground and I do think you need some sort of protection. And it's getting harder and harder to get that protection through only a simple diversified strategy. The only thing that went up in 2008 and 2009 was correlation—no matter what you were holding, you were in trouble. And so there needs to be a greater element of risk management.

Another thing here is that even with increased information in our age, we're not seeing markets get more efficient—we're seeing them get less efficient. We're seeing more frequent bubbles, panics and crashes. This new normal is going to see more dramatic rises and falls, partly as a result of how closely we're monitoring all this stuff.

Michael: You hinted at the idea of too much information. I look at the trend following world, and it has a focus on price action. Instead of trying to go through all the fundamentals, which I think is impossible, one says,

"You know what, I'm going to trade this price action." It's literally like a video game of trading price movement; it has nothing to do with value.

Daniel: There are four pillars in what I think is a sound active management approach. One of the pillars is clarity. Again, it's an American idea that more is better. A lot of people want to look at every possible variable they can, so I talk about why that doesn't make sense and I share some of the research that shows that, at some point, considering more variables actually gets you a worse return. And I talk about how the Fed releases 45,000 pieces of economic data each month and you can't make sense of it all.

I'm not a strict momentum investor, although I do incorporate it into my strategy. But one of the things that is nice about your approach is that it relies on one signal, more or less. There is cleanliness and clarity in that.

Michael: You write about the 4Cs: consistency, clarity, courageousness, and conviction.

Daniel: Consistency is the world's best approach. That's been well covered at this point. Clarity is how to avoid information overload and focus on a handful of important impactful things. Courageousness is automating the process of buying low and selling high—or, like you talked about, letting your winners run and selling short losers. And then conviction is finding that sweet spot between holding one or two stocks, and being over-concentrated and owning the index.

Michael: What can we learn from Sigmund Freud?

Daniel: Sigmund Freud gets a bad reputation for being all about sex and indeed that underlay a lot of his theories. But Freud is at the base of pretty much any psychology you would care to study and so his work impacts us in a behind-the-scenes way. He introduced notions such as the unconscious mind, cognitive biases, and heuristics. He blazed a trail by introducing ideas that were heretical at the time, but now are part of our daily life and so deeply interwoven into the theories of behavioral economics that you don't even recognize them.

Michael: You say, "Trouble is opportunity." I've seen it said in different ways, but those three words together are nice.

Daniel: This is one of those things that everyone knows and no one does.

If we think about March of 2009, we need a couple of things to take advantage of these kinds of situations. The first is that we need a metric, a way of quantifying where are we relative to history—what kind of opportunity do we have? My sentiment measure was at a 5 out of 100 in March of 2009; the lowest sentiment I've ever seen. I could have told you then, by using that measure, "Hey, this is likely a good time to get going." Whereas if you're relying on your emotions, it feels too dangerous. So, in order to take advantage of trouble being opportunity, we need an objective measure of what sort of opportunity we're looking at.

And the second thing we need is an understanding of how poor our free will is, or our free will act. For example, people think that marital infidelity is highly correlated for something like religiosity or self-professed morals. But the best predictor of marital infidelity is opportunity. The best predictor of whether or not you're going to sleep with someone who is not your spouse is if anyone wants to sleep with you, which is a nice way of saying, we're not as strong as we think.

So we need to set up rules that keep us from making poor decisions. This is another instance where in order for us take advantage of trouble being opportunity, we need have a system in place that makes us do the scary thing that we don't want to do.

Michael: Going back to March 2009, the other side of the coin from the value perspective could have been once it hit its lows—somewhere off the low moving up—a breakout, a moving average, something from a trend following perspective would have got you in. There are different ways to skin the cat, but I don't think anybody picked the exact bottom.

Daniel: Being a behavioral investor means you give up the notion that you're ever going to pick the tops and bottoms. What you can do is use a momentum strategy or a value strategy—I favor some combination of the two, because mean reversion tends to be stronger or weaker depending again on how stretched we are from fundamental value. If you pair a value strategy with a momentum strategy in a March of 2009, and you say, "Look, we're at a depressed valuation. And now the sentimental momentum is starting to turn too," these are two good signals that tell me it may be time. Pairing those two things is awfully powerful.

Michael: I guess what you're saying is that if you take value and you take a momentum time series, it usually gives you more return and less risk on the efficient frontier.

Daniel: It does. As part of my research, I've studied simple momentum strategies. If you look at a simple 200-day moving average strategy, over long periods of time you do well. You beat the benchmark, you manage volatility, you compound off of lower lows and your final sum is higher than it would have been if you just index, but you still get a lot of false positives. What I found is you can get rid of a lot of those false positives if you pair value and momentum. Because when valuations are not excessively high, the market is not perfectly efficient but it's kind of efficient. So people tend to get back in relatively quickly, and the drawdown tends not to be too steep. It hovers right there around fair value. But when we get greatly disconnected—the high valuations—and you also have flagging momentum, that's when I get scared.

Michael: Many people, even smart academics, perceive volatility as risk, but it's not necessarily. Standard deviation as a measure of risk can lead people to perhaps incorrect conclusions.

Daniel: People need to understand why standard deviation got introduced as a proxy for risk. It helped us build elegant, beautiful mathematical models, and people could get Nobel Prizes and build their careers on ideas like this. But it's not a useful thing in practice.

Again, like a lot of these things, risk and volatility are related, but it's far from a perfect relationship, and your ability to exploit that can make you a lot of money.

Michael: If the benchmark is down 50%, then okay you matched the benchmark (it's all relative), but that's not a good outcome. That's how so much of Wall Street runs and makes so much money.

Daniel: It does so much bad for our industry. It's how we get this low-conviction, crummy, expensive, not differentiated, active strategy. The reason that's the case is because Wall Street's benchmarking to the S&P

or whatever, and they have that carrier risk, so they don't want to differ dramatically from the benchmark.

For average everyday retail investors, it leaves us in a poor position. We can think of two groups here: people who benchmark to the S&P versus those who benchmark to the returns they need to live the life they want to live. The people who have that personal benchmark are much more likely to stay the course, follow their rules, and end with higher closing account balances. There is nothing good about indexing to something impersonal.

We need to set up rules that keep us from making poor decisions.

Michael: One of the reasons the benchmark concept sells so well is, again, right into your psychological sweet spot—people have a fear of not being exactly like their neighbor.

Daniel: There is a great Harvard study on this. I'm going to get their actual dollar figures wrong, but they asked students, "Would you rather make $40,000 a year in a neighborhood where the average salary is $25,000, or $200,000 a year in a neighborhood where the average salary is $400,000?" And people will take less money and a better relative position, which is crazy.

Take Sir Isaac Newton. Famous in his day, well respected, wealthy, piles into the South Sea Company, makes a ton of money, gets out early, then sees that his neighbors have stayed in and that they're getting richer than he is, and piles his money back in, loses it all in a bubble and dies penniless because he couldn't keep his eyes on what he needed. He had to benchmark relative to someone else instead of having that personal benchmark.

Michael: What does IQ have to do with investing success? If we use Newton as an example—not much. That's a good place to end this conversation!

PART 2
Irrational Behavior Persists

Michael Covel: I like the basic building block you state: people are the fundamental unit of capital markets.

Daniel Crosby: This is drawn from early work in physics. Folks had fancy ideas about what the fundamental units of matter would look like. They would say, it's a microcosm and it's tiny galaxies all the way down, and each galaxy is made up of tiny atoms.

It was only once we grasped what the fundamental units of matter looked and felt like that we could begin to do important work in physics. It's my assertion that until we accept that humans are the fundamental building blocks of capital markets and work hard to understand humans, we're not going to get far.

Michael: People will get their particular app, their particular piece of software, they'll print out charts, they put candlesticks on everything, they have all this kind of stuff, but what are those charts representative of? Those charts are representative of a price. Once you have that philosophical construct, you see it's people determining whatever it is they want to believe is the price that particular day. It's human behavior embedded in the price.

Daniel: I remember when I was a young college student, my dad, who's a financial advisor, asked me if I would ever want to go into the field. And me saying, ah, I don't like math, I like people. I look back at what a silly misunderstanding that was and how little I knew about how markets worked. It's not math, it's people all the way down.

Michael: But on the flip side, you're comfortable using math as a tool now to represent those people.

Daniel: That's the thing I love about being a psychologist who works in markets. If you're a shrink practicing out in the suburbs somewhere, you don't get a lot of real-time information about the attitudes, values, fear and greed of the people you're working with. If you're a psychologist who's conversant in math and knows a bit about capital markets, you've got minute-by-minute information on how the people of the world are feeling. This is a cool canvas against which to study human behavior.

Michael: We humans are stuck in social terms, and often ignore objective terms. We stay in that social space. That might not necessarily be a good thing or a bad thing, but we have to recognize that we do it.

Daniel: Things that are good for us as a species—things that have led to evolutionary success, have led us to live long and happy lives and pass on our genes—have made us poor investors. This tendency to reason in social terms is perhaps foremost among us. If you think about what differentiates humankind from the rest of the animal kingdom, it's not communication, because dolphins can do that. It's not using tools, because crows can do that. The thing that makes us different **Finance is people all the way down.** is that we're able to believe in these functional fictions. My ideas here were vastly informed by the work of Yuval Harari, who wrote *Sapiens*. He talks about how the thing that sets us apart from the rest of the animals is that we can believe in things that aren't true in any objective sense, but that allow us to build great civilizations.

An economy is something that's not true. Fiat currency is something that's not true in any sort of objective sense, but the fact that we all agree upon it allows us to build a great civilization, the borders of the state of Georgia, or the Constitution of the United States. None of these things exist objectively in reality, but since we create them, we dream them up and then we all shake hands and agree that they're true, they allow us to build great big civilizations and interact with people who we don't know that well.

A monkey can only know and do business with about a hundred other monkeys, because that's all the monkeys it can know, trust, and vet. Well, we can do business with people we've never met. I could drive to Iowa right now and buy a Coca-Cola from someone I've never met. That exchange would go very nicely, because we're all playing by the same rules.

That's good news for building civilizations, but it also means that we reason in social terms. If other people disagree with you about something, it can actually physically alter your perception of the world. Because we reason in social terms, we don't see the world in objective black-and-white truths. That doesn't make you a great investor, even though it makes you perhaps a member of a great civilization.

Another easy example is loss aversion. If scientists look at why Homo sapiens persisted while Neanderthals and Denisovans and a group called the Hobbits who lived in Indonesia and all these other different groups didn't make it, one of the things that they point to is loss aversion. We as a species were more cowardly than the next guys, but because we were more loss averse, we took more calculated risks, we moved to new places if the food supply started to run short. Our tendency to be loss averse led us to spread out. It led us to live and pass on our genes when our other humanoid counterparts were out making decisions that were brave, but perhaps stupid. We're here today because our great, great, great, great grandfather was a coward! That was a good thing for the preservation of his genes, but it's a bad thing for us now trying to navigate capital markets in the 21st century.

People project the past into the future indefinitely.

Michael: You're outlining an anthropological history, a history of human evolution, but the keyword is *history*. And when it comes to past experiences, we're not good at this market history stuff.

I've had so many people write me about market volatility over the years. They say, "Look what's happening in this market right now—what does that mean?" I shake my head, because I've written a lot of stuff about longer-term perspectives and how when you look at a particular trading manager, you might want to examine a track record that goes back decades. How are these, I'm assuming, fairly bright people missing the market history part?

Daniel: There are at least two psychological phenomena at play here. One of them that's so damaging for investors is the tendency for us humans to project the recent past into the future indefinitely. I did a study that asked investors what they were expecting from the U.S. market over the next 10 years. The answers were somewhere about 13.5% annualized. It's as if people look at the last 10 years when we've gotten 15% or 16% annualized in the United States, and they think that will continue to be the reality into the future. Whereas in markets, we know that—at least in the medium term—the future tends to look exactly the opposite of the past.

The truest words in investing are: this too shall pass. If we've had a good 10 years, you can expect a not so great next 10 years—that's the truth of markets.

The other thing is there's a huge difference between an intellectual and a visceral understanding of something. Even if someone has an intellectual understanding of market history and they've read the right books, they're familiar with the studies, that's very, very different than gut-level, visceral, lived understanding of these things.

I give the example of our own mortality. You know you're going to die, but you don't think about it much, it doesn't impact your behavior moment to moment, until maybe you have a close call in a car accident or something. In that moment you go, "Oh my gosh, I'm going to die one day. One day I'm not going to be here."

And so those two things are at work. People project the past into the future indefinitely and even if they have read the right books about market history, it doesn't live with them on any kind of visceral level.

Michael: If people don't have an awareness, if they don't have a plan, they lose track of the bigger picture.

Daniel: It can be tough to get out of. It's why I'm such an advocate for rules-based trading and rules-based investing. Your gut's wrong 100% of the time. The thing that feels right for you to do in the moment is always the wrong thing to do. That's why you have to take those lessons of history, you have to take those truths and those pillars that you understand about

Our loss aversion
led us to live and
pass on our genes—
we're here today
because our great,
great, great, great
grandfather was
a coward!

good trading and investing behavior, and you have to automate them to the greatest extent possible. You have to set rules and lock those things in place because you're nearly always going to want to do the wrong thing at the wrong time if left to your own discretion.

Michael: It's about the rules. It's not about seat of your pants. What are some of the factors that people need to go cold turkey and stop?

Daniel: I've identified four primary behavioral biases. I took the universe of investor misbehavior, which is approaching 200 different biases and ways you can screw up your trading and investing, and I looked at the psychological phenomena that underpinned them. It turned out there's not 200, there's more like a handful, and there's some consistent themes that underlie each of them.

The four that I came up with were ego, which is overconfidence in all its many forms; emotion, which is what it sounds like; attention, which is our tendency to confuse salience with probability; and conservatism, which is this tendency to prefer what we know, to prefer the status quo, and to prefer inaction.

There are lots of ways within each of these four biases that people get sideways. But if you think about what gives traders brain damage, just pick one! Ego is the bias that emboldens all other biases, because this belief that we're better, different, and luckier—all of which are facets of overconfidence—emboldens bad investing behavior.

The fundamental realization that someone can have about themselves as an investor is that they're flawed, mediocre, and prone to all the same stupidity as the next person. Every other thing you will learn about your life is an adjunct to that first realization that you're not that great. It takes that realization to have any subsequent realization about what you should be doing differently.

Michael: Once you admit that you're average and you've got all the same biases and problems that every human has, then you can get right back to the rules mindset and say, how can I create some heuristics to keep myself going on the straight and narrow?

Daniel: The market is full of paradoxes. One is that only by realizing how not great you are can you become truly great. You can have an extraordinary life and generate spectacular returns, but all of those things are strangely predicated on admission of your mediocrity.

Michael: For people to admit that, hey, I'm average and I'm not Superman, but I'm one lucky lottery ticket away from everyone in the world knowing that I'm Superman. How do you get people over that hump? Because if people are unwilling to even acknowledge this, it's going to be hard to get them to see your point of view, isn't it?

Daniel: It is tough. There are a few ways that we can do this. The first thing is to look at the data. The correlation between self-reported investment performance and actual investment performance is indistinguishable from zero. Most people, as a function of this overconfidence, aren't up to speed on their trading record, they just assume that it's good. And so take a long period of time and compare the relevant stats, because the research shows that among people who think they've beaten the market, one-third of them have lost, have underperformed by 5% or more, and another 25% have underperformed by 15% or more.

The second thing is you have to teach. Richard Feynman, the famous physicist and great thinker, had this great technique for figuring out what you don't know, which is teach it to a kid. This is why I write books. I've written a book about every two years, and the reason, candidly, is not because it makes any money, it's to figure out what I believe and to hone my own thinking. If you think you're sharp at something, I would encourage you to try to write a book about it, write a blog post about it, teach others about it. If you can't teach others about the basics of a topic, you don't know it that well.

> **Ego is the bias that emboldens all other biases.**

The third thing I encourage folks to do is to look at base rates. I had a prospective financial advisor come to me who wanted to start their own firm and they thought that they could get to $100m in assets under management in less than six months. I said, "Hey, that seems optimistic to me. Why don't you look at the base rates? Why don't you look at how long it takes most people to get to $100m?" The answer was closer to eight years. So, a third way is to plan your relative to averages—so if it takes most people three years to write a book, it's probably going to take me three years—and then be surprised to the upside if you outperform.

So, those three things. Look at the data, but be dispassionate. Look for ways to teach other people—that's going to help identify gaps in your own knowledge and learning. And finally, look at the averages. We would, as a culture, be so much better off if most people would own that you have a 50/50 shot of getting divorced. You ask people on their wedding day, "Hey, do you think this is going to work out?" and 100% of people will say yes, and yet we have a 50% divorce rate. If we were a little more honest about that from the outset, we'd work a little harder. We might go to premarital counseling. We might do the work we needed to do. It's only when you own those averages and those probabilities that you can do the hard work that you need to do.

Michael: You're right. When it comes to relationships in the modern age, you've got to look at the base rates. You've got to say, what is average, what is the probability? That doesn't mean you go into something looking for the worst, but you also should not be wearing the rose-tinted glasses.

Daniel: I want to be clear here, because if you look at the base rates alone, no one would ever start a small business, no one would ever open a restaurant, because probabilistically speaking these are both low percentage shots. I'm glad people start restaurants and I'm glad people start small businesses, but use the base rates to chasten your thinking a bit, rather than say, "Oh well, 50% of the world gets divorced, so my marriage is doomed." That's not the takeaway. The takeaway is that 50% of people get divorced, so work hard at it. Take a class on communication, go to counseling, look at your own quirks before you try to bring someone else into your life.

The same can be applied to investing. More than half of individual equities have catastrophic losses over their lifetime. The life of an average stock is nasty, brutish, and short. If you think you know something, if you think you want to take a large position, or you think you want to invest in something, be damn sure that you've done your homework, make sure you have an edge, and know the probabilities are not on your side. Don't *never* take the shot—but make sure it's an informed shot.

Michael: If we dig in a little bit further, perhaps we'll find out if those winners did something a lot different than the people that bailed or the people that did not succeed? It becomes a challenge. There's never a sure-fire way. You've got to do the work.

Daniel: One of the surest ways to have a disappointing trading life is to believe you can perfectly manage risk. You have to walk the tightrope and accept there's some risk inherent in any good thing you would ever do. If you try to live in bubble wrap, you're going to be broke and sad. Take risks, but take appropriate risks. Managing overconfidence is one of the primary means by which you can help walk that line.

Michael: We're talking about big populations under the bell curve in the middle. Most Americans that have their typical retirement account are slammed into a passive index fund. Kids are going to do the standard-issue, four-year degree and try to get the standard-issue job—if it still exists. There's a lot of bubble wrap thinking. It does require you to get outside the box to get into the mindset of the behavioral investor.

Daniel: It does. One of the things that's true of life and markets is many people are content to work their mediocre jobs with their mediocre degrees and come home and have a Hungry Man dinner and fall asleep watching their favorite shows, right? For most people under the bell curve, that's always going to be the case, but you've got to remember that therein lies the potential for success, the potential for arbitrage for the behavioral investor, for the person who's willing to stay up a few hours later to do a little extra homework, to endure a little extra discomfort, because if there's no pain, there's no premium.

Michael: If one wants to go down this path of further thinking, rules, and pushing discretion out of the toolbox, there's no particular personality type, is there?

Daniel: There's not. I was interested in this. I go to so many conferences and I hear so much bad information set forth by trading gurus and behavioral coach types that are loosely regulated and experts in their own mind. One of the big ones was this idea of a personality test that's going to tell you if you've got the right chops to be a trader and a good investor—and here's the personality traits that you need. I dug into the research and it's nonsense. I mean, people of all stripes and walks of life can be great investors. It's more about following the rules than a specific personality type. This is good news, because science is telling us now that about 50% of your personality is set genetically. Effectively, what these gurus are saying is, you're born with it or not. I would take strong exception to that. Personality types of all kinds are potentially well positioned to be good investors.

> **People of all stripes and walks of life can be great investors.**

The other thing that I found consistently was misinformation around emotion. These folks were saying you should tap into emotion as a sort of sixth sense of what you should be doing. Long story short, the data does not support the fact that strong emotion is a good trading signal. In fact, it's usually very bad.

Michael: So, you're at a conference and there's an audience of, let's say, 500 people, and there's a guru on the stage saying you need a certain personality. How many people in the audience think, "My gosh, that's absolutely bullshit," versus how many people think, "My gosh, he's going to tell me if I'm in the club or not?"

Daniel: One truth about life is that people want easy answers to hard problems. A personality test that'll tell you if you're on the right path is an easy answer to a complex thing. And so, I imagine there's many, many people who want to pick up what this guru is putting down, but there are certainly people who are informed consumers and understand that in a lot of cases, this is a sales pitch. Again, going back to our person that's eating their TV dinner, there's always going to be people who think, "Oh good, here's a silver bullet and this guy's figured out what it takes." But the ability of some subset of the population to think more critically, take the road less traveled, is where our potential for performance lies.

Michael: I'm looking at a particular quote from Pliny the elder that you cite in your work: "The best plan is to profit by the folly of others." That is hardcore for some people. I assume you meant it for what it is, but of course one can take that emotionally—you could give it a negative connotation or you could take it like you said, which is if you want to be average, you can be average; but if you want to spend a few extra hours a night, you can find out how the game works. And the game does work by channeling money from people with bad plans making bad decisions to people with good plans making good decisions.

Daniel: I don't want that to sound overly aggressive or antagonistic. It's a fact of life. There's always going to be a large percentage of the world who's trying to get rich quick or take shortcuts or not do research or not do anything. Those people who are willing to endure the pain to get the premium and the people who are willing to do the work, it's not like they're tricking other people or they're being mean. They can sit back patiently, knowing that they are systematic and cool, calm and collected, and other people won't be taking that same path.

Michael: From a conceptual perspective, people often don't like to be challenged if they're set in their ways—they don't want to hear it.

Daniel: Probably my favorite psychological bias is something called the Dunning-Kruger effect. Dunning and Kruger's research was prompted by one of the most amazing things I've ever heard, which is someone tried to rob a bank covered in lemon juice! Of course, he gets caught very quickly. But he's flabbergasted to be caught and he goes, "Oh my gosh, how could you see me? I thought I was invisible." And the bank people go, "What?" And he said, "Well, when I was a kid, I'd write on paper with lemon juice and it was invisible ink. So, I thought that the lemon juice would make me invisible too and I'd be able to rob the bank."

Dunning and Kruger did research on how effectively dumb people are too dumb to know how dumb they are. And the same thing can be said of arrogance or overconfidence. If you're listening to this podcast and thinking, "What an idiot, this guy doesn't know what he's talking about, I'm not susceptible to any of this," the fact that you think you're not susceptible is the surest indicator that you are susceptible to it. And paradoxically, if you've been listening to this and going, "Wow, I have some improvements to make, I could do a lot better," you're probably okay.

It's a weird thing that the most overconfident people in the world aren't well positioned to realize their own overconfidence, except if they experience those feelings of defensiveness. A good gut check is if you feel enraged by what someone's trying to teach you—if you feel defensive or angry or whatever—that might be a good prompt to check your ego at the door.

Michael: Here's a line of yours that I love: "Data without theory and theory without data produce spurious results."

Daniel: You need three things: theory, data, and psychology. The reason you need theory is that the Fed produces 45,000 different pieces of economic data. If you put all of these data points in a blender and regress them against the S&P 500 over the last 100 years, you're going to find some correlations and a lot of them are going to be meaningless. This is data without theory and you can get silly results that have no basis in fact. Now the flip side is also problematic. You've got some great macro narrative, you've got some theory about the golden mean or whatever sort of fanciful idea you have, but that needs to be backed up by the data. If there's something there, your theory needs to be sound and you've got to have the data to prove it. But it also needs to be rooted in behavior, because market anomalies that have no pain, that have no behavior associated with them, quickly get arbitraged away.

The only enduring edge is the confluence of these three things. It needs to be grounded in a sensible theory. There needs to be data to back it up. And there also needs to be some sort of behavioral reason why it exists, because irrational behaviors persist. Even if people know about something, it can be hard to arbitrage away because of bad behavior.

I would bet money—if there were a way to do it—on American obesity getting worse over the next 50 years because even as we become more informed about nutrition, even as we have more healthy food available to us, it's still hard to eat the right things, and it's still hard to exercise. I would bet on that bad behavior going forward, even as new information comes online. Similarly, I would bet on things like value and momentum long into the future because they have behavioral underpinnings to them.

Michael: You're laying out a contrarian perspective. It sounds good to all of us entrepreneurs, but it doesn't mean it won't hurt. Once somebody goes down the path that you're outlining—put aside the discretion, get your system, automate, automate, automate—that doesn't mean you're going to make 5% a month every month year after year after year.

Daniel: No, it doesn't. And in fact, any reputable system you could dream up is going to have periods of underperformance. If you've back tested something and it never underperforms, then you've got spurious results. The emotional response to being a value investor is akin to things like being picked last at kickball and social isolation. Being a true contrarian, which is exceedingly rare, hurts like hell. It's socially isolating. You're going to think you're crazy. You're going to think you made the wrong choice. If you're not experiencing those things from time to time, you're not a true contrarian.

> The true way to determine if you are a contrarian is how much it hurts.

Rebels through the ages, such as a gutter punk, have more of a uniform than your average businessperson. People who have mohawks and leather jackets think they're going their own way, but they adhere to tighter social protocols than your average stock broker, in terms of what to say, what to listen to, and what to wear. Contrarianism is one of those things that everyone thinks they are, but not many people genuinely are. The true way to determine if you are, is how much it hurts.

Michael: I see quite a bit these days where people are involved in social media and they put their public face out there and are perhaps associated with people that have radically different views. But because of these social constructs whereby they don't want to upset the apple cart, they stay associated with it all. Even though it might be bad information that's coming into their feed every day, they still do it. Then on the flip side, they might go outside of the social network and complain with other people that have the same view. This social pull to fit in, even if it's against your nature, this desire to be a part of the team and not feel isolated, that's tough to overcome.

Daniel: It is tough. And yet personally, I quit Facebook a few years back, and it was like an immediate 10% boost in productivity and happiness. You think you're using these tools to become socially connected, but all of the research points to social disconnection and fleeting, superficial connections.

I do think social media can be a catalyst for real-life connection that can be very, very powerful, but if all you're doing is arguing politics with other social media users, the damage can be considerable and the upside is limited. Put me in the camp that thinks of Facebook as the new Philip Morris in terms of its contribution to society.

CHAPTER 12
CHARLES FAULKNER

PART 1
Money Metaphors

C HARLES W. FAULKNER is an internationally recognized cognitive-behavioral modeler, speaker, innovator and trainer specialising in situation analysis and decision making under uncertainty and complexity. He is also a program and product developer and a noted author. He consults for individuals and executives of privately held firms and corporations on forms of influence, human decision making, the human factors in risk management, leadership and change management. He was originally featured in *The New Market Wizards* by Jack Schwager.

Michael note

Charles Faulkner has appeared on my podcast at least five times. He's easily one of my most popular guests. He also appeared in my film *Broke: The New American Dream* (still on Vimeo), and was featured in my book, *Trend Following*. Charles has also over the years given me swift kicks in the ass when needed, but he's generally done that in private!

Michael Covel: If you give a Nobel to Eugene Fama and one to Robert Shiller—the standard issue finance on one side and the behavioral world on the other—I can only imagine how the average person must feel trying to walk into this subject of money when the famed Nobel committee is seemingly schizophrenic about how they give out awards.

Charles Faulkner: That's a wonderful place to start because it parallels, if you will, Dickens' novel of *Dombey and Son*. At one point in the novel, the young son, Paul, who's five years old, turns to his father and says, "What is money?" and his father, who's a businessperson and wants to be a more successful one, says, "What is money, Paul?" and his child's going, "Yes?"

Dickens tells us that Mr. Dombey in his mind wants to talk in terms of circulating medium, depreciation of currency, volume and rates of exchange, value of precious metals, and so forth. He looks down at his son and realizes that this is probably not an appropriate way of answering him. So he turns and says, "Gold and silver and copper, guineas, shillings, and half pence." Then he goes on to tell his son that money can make you honored or feared and respected and courted and admired, and that money makes you powerful and glorious in the eyes of men.

> The idea that we can think objectively about money because it has numbers on it is paradoxical to our actual situation.

Then to his amazement, Paul looks up at him and asks, well, if money can do all that, how come money couldn't save his mother's life and why is he himself such a weak and fragile child? And he says, "Money isn't cruel, is it?"

I bring that up because there is this duality complementarity, which you called schizophrenic.

We have system two and system one thinking. System two is our logical, deliberative, thoughtful, and conscious decision process. We're told that money is objective. It's got numbers on it and we're adding, subtracting, multiplying, and dividing it, and that's a conscious abstract idea. That's system two. When we think about things consciously and deliberately and step by step, then we're thinking in terms of system two.

Whereas system one, as behavioral economics has shown, is the unconscious, automatic, and wildly associative part of us. It's the part of us that lets us be able to read people's emotions when they smile or when they look confused or such. It's the part of us that lets us have intuition and ideas, and we develop associations. To this part of us, money is physical. To this part of us, money has many associations, many emotions.

Now, the situation is that system one came first in our species. It's much older. It's what we call our gut feeling, when we go with our heart, all those ideas of utilizing our body to think, which even two decades ago was not considered how it's done. But now the science is in and we know we do it that way, and we do it all the time. Meanwhile, our system two—this thoughtful, deliberate, conscious, putting things together, whether it's the emergence of the Renaissance or the Industrial Age or now smartphones and all the rest—this successful part of us requires deliberate energy and attention and is easily exhausted. The research has found that these two processes are going on all the time and we don't outgrow them. Rather, system two consciously suppresses system one.

In the same way, our earlier images, associations, ideas, impulses, emotions about money—the ones that we had as a child, we grew up with, the ones that are in the background of our society—they're running all the time. Meanwhile, we're told that, of course, money is abstract and logical and objective, but again, that process can be overwhelmed by strong emotion, by stress, by being tired, by being intoxicated in some way, either with chemicals that come from the outside world or generated internally. Isn't that what happens when people are trading or investing— that they get emotional? So we often substitute the thinking of system one for system two, and then afterwards tell ourselves how rational our decision was to get out of that stock when it went down—but now it's back up a bit again, and we didn't get back in.

The idea that we can think objectively about money because it has numbers on it and because there are economic theories like Fama's is paradoxical to our actual situation that we're making these so-called irrational—but I wouldn't say they're irrational, I'd say they're associative— decisions about money that Shiller talks about in his research.

Michael: That's a good point about associative versus irrational, because I think the quick way is to immediately say irrational, but there is a rational process going on with system one.

Charles: The problem with rational-irrational is the same problem with conscious-unconscious. The word order gives precedence to the rational, gives precedence to the conscious. But there are two sets of processes, and the fact of the matter is the so-called unconscious process or the automatic system one process is running much, much more of our lives than the conscious and so-called rational.

It is better to call them associative in contrast to logical, for example, or automatic in contrast to conscious or deliberate, because then they draw people to notice their properties rather than giving preference to one or the other.

Michael: In my travels, I've seen a lot of different cities and a lot of shopping malls that look identical, and in these malls you have your same stores. They stand like monuments influencing the masses as they walk by every day and think, "This is the highest thing you can shoot for." Their unconscious minds are seeing these images of extreme wealth, of extreme materialism and consumerism—I'm not saying those are necessarily bad things, but it's interesting.

Charles: To give a historical perspective to this consumerism or whatever you want to call it, H. G. Wells more than a hundred years ago wrote, "Money means in a thousand minds a thousand subtle different roughly similar systems of images, associations, suggestions, and impulses."

How do they get in there, these images, associations, suggestions, impulses? Well, from our family we grew up with, but also now we grow up so much in public, so much in the media.

People who think they're thinking originally about money or about their life or about the choices they're making, if they step back in their mind's eye—that is to say, if they were to repress those thoughts for a moment and use their system two—they'd find out they're pretty much wanting what everybody else wants, because that's what's out there to want. To become the contrarian investor, the independent thinker, the trader who discovers something new is, in fact, quite a challenge and takes deliberate effort.

Kahneman, decades ago, noticed that the smarter people are, the more they fell for these so-called heuristics and biases, the more they thought that these foibles and problems of decision-making didn't apply to them. They applied to those other dumb people who were falling for it. It turns out that the smarter you are, the more you fall for them.

If you know nothing about trading and investing, in a sense you're better off than somebody who's read a few books, gone to a seminar or two, because then you think you know something, and you're even more dangerous if you're in the middle of the process because at that point you go, "I got a handle on this." At which point, you're no longer self-critical. You're no longer questioning what you're doing. You're going, "I understand technical analysis," or "I understand the amount to put on a position," and so on. That's when you can hurt yourself, so to speak.

Michael: Singaporeans have a term *kiasu*. Essentially, it means being afraid to lose out to others and you must be number one. For example, they'll queue up overnight for new condos. If there's going to be a big shopping launch at the mall, they'll wait all night. They don't want to lose. They must be number one. I guess if you're in the pure consumer world and you're simply looking to buy something, it's not necessarily an incorrect way to think. However, if you were to take that *kiasu*-type concept to the markets, that's dangerous.

Charles: This reinforces the idea that attitudes and emotions, especially when one is experiencing those emotions, run the decision process. When you're in system one—and you're emotional and not prepared to lose— you'll be restricted to the decision processes you have in your automatic unconscious. If your trading strategy or approach requires a longer timeframe, requires more conscious or thoughtful application of a system, well, you'll tell yourself later why you didn't do it, but you won't have done it.

This goes back to Ed Seykota, and his idea that the emotions you're unwilling to feel are your trading system. When you put the behavioral finance stuff

> **To become the contrarian investor is quite a challenge and takes deliberate effort.**

together with Ed's thought there, you understand why. If the person is afraid of losing and can't go, "Okay. Take your loss and go on your next trade," then of course, you stay in the position until it goes to zero or you scramble in and out of it and you try to chase the market and all the other behaviors we know so well come out.

Michael: Part of the reason I mentioned *kiasu* is to consider how this concept has gained traction in a place like Singapore, which is capitalism on fire. The highest percentage of millionaires per capita in the world. How does that idea reinforce when you have such a successful country, a successful population, and they have a concept like that built into the culture? In many ways, it seems like such an incorrect way to think about things. However, they would say, "Look at our success."

Charles: That's right! We're going more into the decision-making side of my work than the ideas about money, but to take up your question, they're claiming a primary cause, and that's a conscious mind, system two thing to do. What's the reason this is happening? In most life experiences and most decision-making, there are multiple causes and multiple effects. Is it their high degree of education? Is it the homogeneity of their people? Is it the fact that they're building their technology infrastructure now? We know that as countries come later to the technology revolution, they have an advantage over countries that have older infrastructures.

Right there, I named three possible causes, and we can add the idea that maybe their fear of losing is getting them to save more or be more diligent. Now, we have four possible sources of success. Are they equal amounts? In what way do they synergize and affect each other? What are sources five, and six, and seven, and so forth?

We do this as humans, and it's almost always retrospective. We look back and go, "We became great because…" but we're often making it up. I love Nassim Taleb's phrase, "The more we think we can explain the past, the more we think we can predict the future."

> It's a mistake to think because the world is complicated, you need a complicated model.

Any model is a simplification of reality, and models, analogies, systems are all ways of making sense of experience, because experience is complex and ambiguous and subject to stochastic processes, which is to say randomness, and it's not determined, in many cases, by what's going to happen. Our system one is very much see and respond. Up close and personal, in both time and space, it works well: "How is Michael feeling this morning? I can hear you're excited going into this podcast," and so forth. We're good at that, but as we get into bigger-scale stuff like the Singapore economy or longer timeframes like what's going to happen in the markets next year, we use the same near-and-dear process with less and less reliability.

We do what we know how to do and we don't often know where the limits are. This is where your own research into trend following was to find the simplicity of that approach, the ease with which one can take a class of information price, in the case that you're studying it, and then make a measured bet about the future. People go, "That's too simple—I like a complicated model because the world is complicated." But it's a mistake to think because the world is complicated, you need a complicated model. Maybe, but also you need to think that one thing could be the answer. You've got to find the fit.

Michael: People often ask me one question and they want one answer and they expect the answer to be one word long, and seemingly, they will then have everything they need to know on the subject.

Charles: That's well-known. I was thinking of the H. L. Mencken quote, to show that this idea goes back generations. I'm going to misquote it, but it was something like: "To any question or problem, there's a solution that's clear and easy to understand and it's wrong."

This reflects the kind of work that I'm drawing on, which is that we now know that the less you know about something, the clearer the image, the more certain you are that it's real and true. So when they come to you and want that one-word answer, they want you to help make their pictures clear so they can feel settled in their decision and feel they did the right thing. Of course, we know there are all sorts of different offers in the marketplace that will do that for you—pick all highs, pick all lows, our foolproof system and so on and so on, appealing to people's need for certainty.

Michael: How extensive is that need for certainty?

Charles: It's basic to our biology. It's fundamental to our thinking processes. In fact, part of my work is to show that there's almost literally a one-to-one correspondence between the number of ideas you can hold in mind and how developed your mind is. We start out with one picture in mind, and then if you can hold two pictures in mind, you move to a different kind of thinking. If you hold three pictures in mind, you might even be able to build a strategy for doing something in life, but that doesn't kick in till 12 or 13 years old, and even after that, most people still go back to one picture.

Michael: Where are you looking to ultimately take people?

Charles: That's a big question. The first part of it, going back to the Fama–Shiller issue, is that it's not schizophrenic. Those are two ways of thinking about things, and both of them are profoundly useful. Whether they meant to or not, the Nobel Prize committee did a good thing. It's two pictures, right? Remember I said about one picture, two pictures, three pictures, like one fish, two fish, three fish? It's actually saying, both of these sets of ideas exist—efficient market theory and behavioral finance, to give them big abstract names. Both are ways in which human beings approach the world, or at least approach the financial aspects of the world. They represent the expression of those system one, automatic, emotional, intuitive, pattern-recognizing skills, and the other side, the deliberate, thoughtful, abstract, step-by-step, logical way of thinking. These are two aspects of us and one does not replace the other. Moreover, system one is pervasive in running all the time and system two takes effort.

Michael: A critical distinction. One is running all the time and two takes effort.

Charles: It takes so much effort that often people slip back into one, and then after the fact will claim they did two because we tend to associate ourselves with system two. We tend to associate ourselves with the conscious mind and not with all these unconscious, automatic processes, which if you look at people's lives are also their habits. When people have a habit they don't like, they say, "I can't stop myself." They have an automatic process going on, which in this case they don't see as serving them. We also have the Freudian idea of the unconscious. It's this adversarial thing that's apart from us, that's somehow bad or needs to be controlled or whatever. Now, these are both processes that have different operating systems, to use a computer metaphor. In my work, I'm pointing out you need to learn how each operating system works and use it accordingly.

In the modern world, the most common, persistent, and prevalent ritual we engage in is the exchange of this substance called money for something.

Michael: If someone was to look at the markets and not have a lot of experience, maybe they turn on CNBC, they get all excited, they hear a guy throw a buy signal out, they run to Schwab, they buy something. It's emotional. It's immediate. Whereas on the other hand, the trend traders say to themselves, "Hold on. We need a way to handcuff our behavior and put rigidity upon our trading world, and that gives us better odds of success."

Charles: I would use another analogy. I don't know if it's still around, but it was called the *Club 3000* years ago. You couldn't be a member until you'd spent $3,000 on trading systems. The idea was that it made people thoughtful about the process. We haven't talked much about money, but this goes back to the duality of money. The paradoxical nature of money is that it's objective, and it's out in the world, and it's got numbers on it, and all that. People feel like it's real and objective, and then there's all the emotional attachments and all the ideas and images and impulses that come with it. Those are so mixed up that, yes, the person's watching TV, they get an idea, they run with it. This is something that I hope they wouldn't do in their professional lives, whether they're a mechanic or a manager or an MD, where they realize it takes time, energy, thoughtfulness, experience, and consultation to develop expertise.

Yet in the trading and investing world, famously, people are impulse buyers of stocks, bonds, commodities, ETFs, and the rest, and that makes sense when you think about the emotions involved and the fact that money is this magical substance that can turn anything into anything else. I've got quotes going back hundreds of years, like the German one that "Money not only makes you more handsome, but you can sing better."

We've been spending time talking about system one and system two for people to embrace the idea that they do have this automatic system, and that it will run away with them if they don't make decisions to do something about it. Then there's how you educate system one, but I don't want to get ahead of myself here.

Michael: Let's talk thought experiments.

Charles: Economists have three definitions of money: (1) money is a medium of exchange; (2) money is a measure of value; and (3) money is a store of value. These are the accepted ideas. They seem intellectual. Money can turn into any other thing. Money has this property of being able to become anything you want.

It's magic that you can turn something into something else. That's out of a fairytale. In terms of our thinking processes, turning something into something else is metaphor. My love is a rose. The markets are a game. Things are looking up. It's time to take the plunge and jump back into the markets. All those are metaphorical at their base.

Money is the most basic metaphor. Money is the most pervasive metaphor we have, and it's not a metaphor only in language. It's real. A child quickly figures out that you can take this paper or these coins and turn them into other objects, or you can take the objects and turn them into money, and back and forth.

If you think money isn't different than other things, here's the thought experiment: when you next go to work or some other place, pull $10 out of your wallet and give it to somebody you know and say, "Here, have this."

If you bought that person a drink in a bar or picked up lunch for them, there wouldn't be a second thought about it, but if you take that magical substance and you give it to them directly, I think you'll find there's a different set of feelings that emerge.

I used to do stuff like this this when I would give a talk. At a certain point, I'd take my jacket off and I had a $50 bill folded in my shirt pocket. People could see it, and you could watch their eyes tracking the $50 bill. They weren't looking at me anymore, even though what I was offering there was of considerably more value to their work than the amount of money in my pocket.

Michael: What is it doing to us at a biological level?

Charles: The research is finding that it's like cocaine in the brain. Money lights up the dopamine areas like nobody's business. It is the reward that goes across all the different types of things in our brain because it is all the different types of things in our brain. Money represents the physical object we talked about. Money represents certain kinds of accesses and opportunities. Money means people will treat you in certain ways. Money means that you could be thought of as a different person than you are.

Current research did not invent this. I've got quotes going back hundreds of years that make these points.

Michael: You're making the case to investors, traders, entrepreneurs, the average person, that before you go down the path of building a business, or even putting a trade on, it is worth your time to take a step back and think about system one and system two.

Charles: How a person thinks about and treats money can be a great motive for them to become a successful trader and entrepreneur, but it can equally be their ruin. You and I both know guys that have gone into the business and made a lot and then lost a lot, and that can be due to the movements of the market, but more often, it's that there are certain ideas, images, impulses, and so forth, that the person has about this substance, which they hadn't noticed, but are running the show.

Michael: I always love the definition of a sunk cost: it's paid for, literally and emotionally, so let it go. I went through a process when I moved to Asia when I gave away a lot of things because you look around and you say, "Well, if I haven't touched this for a year, what am I doing with it still?" I remember one guy in San Diego, I think he got eight suits from me.

Charles: It was similar when I moved house, except we utilized the local charity shops. They got piles of stuff. Again, there are all these associations going on. I bought this stuff with money. If I give it away, aren't I wasting my money? This relates to the behavioral economics idea that if you own something, it's more valuable than if somebody else owns it.

Michael: The understanding of sunk cost lies at the heart of your work, too, because if you can let go of some of that and not hold onto it, you're a step ahead.

Charles: Listen to the metaphor, "Hold on, let go." It's like you've got money. It's a sunk cost, objective, abstract term, system two. Then it's like, well, if you can let go, that's basic, and sensory, and personal, and that's system one. These two thoughts occur in the same moment and people think, "Well, I ought to be able to think this through," and they're trying to do with system two what they need to do with system one.

I'll give the answer right now to the example that we're talking about. You need to have what are called reference experiences. You need to give away stuff, little giveaways. In other words, practice the behavior, because system one, remember, is automatic and unconscious. Put it this way: you do what you do because you've done it before. That's what a habit is. If you want to do something new, then do it in the smallest, simplest way. Once you begin to do it, then you're beginning to do something new. Take something to the secondhand store, the charity shop, the junior league, or whatever. Try doing that with some things. Then you have done that behavior in one area of your life. You get that practice. Then you can do it in another area of your life, such as trading and investing.

Michael: Even though trading and investing might not seem similar to taking used clothing down to the thrift shop, you're making the case that, biologically, it's triggering the same things in us.

Charles: I'm saying that in order to trigger the same aspects in you, you want to first of all get the behavior into your neurology, into your system one. System one is based on experience, whereas system two is based on logic. The secret to running system one is to get yourself the kinds of experiences that will make a difference. Whereas your system two goes, "I want a strategy. Tell me what to do. Yes or no? Bright picture." It's not about a bright picture. It's about doing things.

Michael: So many people want to walk through life imagining because now you have the internet you can be there, you can see it. You and I both know that's not true. There is no experience that I can find in a book, magazine, online, that will give me the same experience of travel to some exotic locale.

Charles: I would put it differently, with the caveat that when people are having experiences through their technology, they're having an experience of their technology. I've looked at places on Google that I might be going to and I can pull up the street map and so forth, but I know that all I'm doing is orienting myself for when I get there, so I have an idea, some landmarks, some still photos along the way, but that's not the experience of being there.

Michael: Do those preparations help? It seems like once you get to that place and you look back on the preparations, it all pales against the experience itself.

Charles: Now you're talking Clausewitz on war, when he says, "You do all this preparation, and then when the war starts, all bets are off," because at that point randomness, ambiguity, and all these things come into play.

Preparation is a ritual for focusing the mind to be prepared for what one is going to do. When you know that, you can engage in that ritual in a useful way and not in a superstitious way. You realize, "I've done my preparation. I'm settled in myself. Now, I can turn my attention outward and be responsive to what is happening."

I go further than that in my work on money. I point out that in the modern world, the most common, persistent, and prevalent ritual we engage in is the exchange of this substance called money for something. It's hard for people to take this in.

For most of human history, most people didn't deal with money. We have what I call the Flintstone factor, which is that we take our current situation and then imagine it backwards. In fact, it is now known that the original uses of money were not to make barter easier, but were for religious and ritual purposes. Money was a way of transferring emotions from one place to another. Money was a way of transferring power from one place to another, and it still is. That's still evident in so-called primitive people's ideas of money and children's ideas of money—the tooth fairy and the quarter under the pillow.

I was in a shop recently and this little girl is there methodically counting out her dollars to buy something. That stuff's still in there. It used to be religions were the rituals we engaged in, or families had their own rituals. The ritual we engage in most often now is with strangers, and it's for the exchange of something, and what is that doing to us?

What I'm trying to get at is the idea that money is both real and practical and magical and alchemical, and therefore paradoxical in our experience.

Michael: Talk about money as a living metaphor.

Charles: First of all, the so-called abstract and economic idea of money is a medium of exchange in the world, in our minds and in our language. That's called metaphor, when one thing can stand in for another. We find that when people talk about money, they talk about bread, lettuce, the lifeblood of the economy, dead presidents, and so on. Every language has lots and lots and lots of words for money often based in the profession the person is in, or related to it somehow. We think of money as having this transformational quality, that we can turn it into the object. Often, the object is used as the name for money, and that's evidence that it's not just in the mind, it's in the world.

Related to that is how we relate to money. We have lots of different metaphors, in words, to describe our relationship with money. On the face of it—and this is the elusive obvious here—if somebody says they have money problems, you think they don't have enough money, or they're spending too much money, or some combination of those. That's the real-world part of it. In the mind, if the person is using a problem frame, a problem thinking process, a way of envisioning in their mind what it is, then they're trying to solve it.

Now, here's the misapplication. When somebody thinks they have money problems, they will try to solve it with a problem framework. Unless you're a professional mathematician, we think that we solve a problem and it's done; you can hear this when people say if they only had enough money, they'd never have to think about it anymore. But the thing is with money, the more you have, the more

Money has this property of being able to become anything you want.

you do need to think about it, or think about who's going to watch it, and then you need to think about them. There's a misapplication of a thinking process here.

People say they're flush. They say they're stone cold broke. They say they're swimming in money. All these different ways we talk about our relationship to money. "Money held me back." How did money do that? What they're trying to say is that the lack of money, actually, somehow prevented them from doing something. That's the objective, if you will, the outer world way; but in our mind's eye, we embody those metaphorical ideas and make them real. People feel money is a person, they're having this argument with money, and money is pushing them around, money is influencing their life in different ways.

If you are looking for money, the assumption is that there's so little of it, it's hidden. It's money as a hidden object and people searching here and there for it, as opposed to, for example, Paul Tudor Jones, who described the economy as this large and incredible system of pipes and liquids and so forth. He would look for a place that he could tap into this plumbing system and draw off some money.

Michael: I love where you're going with this because it forces you to think about what we've done with these terms and the idea of money and how we've allowed it to go in so many different directions. Once you started this process, it opened a can of worms.

Charles: It did. Initially, I had the idea that there was what I called a living metaphor—a personal metaphor that people would have for money. I'd been looking at what I call metaphors of identity. Life is a journey, someone's the hero, and so forth, was the personal metaphor. Then I realized in the background of people's lives, other metaphors were running—the metaphors for their relationships, metaphors for their job, and metaphors for money. As I got along, I realized the metaphors for money were pervasive because of these abstract economic ideas. Money is a medium of exchange, and so we make it a metaphor for so many areas of our life: what it is, our relationship to it, how we use it.

On the other hand, money is a measure of value. We use money to figure out, "Did we spend our time wisely or did we waste years in that relationship?" "Are we living a rich life?" "Did that decision pay off?" "What are the emotional costs of this?" We're using money to measure life, time, decisions, emotions, and relationships.

Once you've used that measure—once you've used money to make sense of that— then you can go, "How much is this relationship worth? How much do I invest in this relationship?" and that measure begins to influence your behavior. It influences your actions. That's the point. The point isn't the language. The point isn't the pictures in your brain. It's the fact that, as John Locke the philosopher said, "The images and ideas in men's minds are the invisible powers that govern them."

Michael: First you have to self-analyze to see how you're treating money, how you're thinking about money, how you're feeling about money, and then start to make some adjustments.

Charles: We can make adjustments because we are so much more creatures of our imagination than we like to think. This goes back to our previous comments about system one and system two. System two: logically understanding cause and effect in the world. System one: images, ideas, associations, suggestions, impulses. This metaphor idea is a window, if you will, into the motives and the means of action that we use. You can influence the metaphor.

Let me give you an example of this that goes deeper into the idea that, first of all, modern money is a social trust or fiat currency. In other words, there's no value in the money. The fact that everybody trusts that the money is worth something is what gives it value. If people stop trusting in money, you get a run on the currency. But some people—gold bugs, as they're known—think that there is an intrinsic value in money and that it's gold and/or silver. This goes back to the images and associations of money as gold—shiny, incorruptible, the color of the sun, and warm to the touch. Those images are young and primitive. In that person's mind's eye, it glows more real, it is brighter, so they think that's real money and the paper stuff isn't.

You can see where the metaphor and the image in the mind's eye are affecting financial decision-making, because that person has reduced the number of choices they have. They're going to say, "Gold is real," and I'm going, well, yes, gold is real, and the stock markets are at an all-time high now as well. That's also real in that outer world sense, but it's the inner world that we're using to respond to that outer world that makes the difference.

Michael: You've outlined all these different ways to think about money and I think all of us can immediately see the benefit, but people are going to be at different points on the scale of how they view money.

Charles: I'm intrigued by that idea because in doing my research I found, initially, I was collecting metaphors from people, and that was cool. You go to a program and get new ones. Then I began to find that there were some themes and, depending on where the person was as an investor or trader, how developed they were in their craft, they would have shifted their metaphors. Then I found that even historically, people will start out with the obvious idea of money as an object. Yes, it is an object, and it's also an object in the mind's eye and the mind's body. What I mean by that is that objects have properties. You acquire them, you value them, you use them, i.e., trade them somehow, and you dispose of them. When I hear somebody saying that they have a money problem or they can't handle money—that's another way people talk about money, with it slipping away from them, that's another metaphor—I say, "No, wait a minute. Let's get a little more detail here."

Michael: These are all excuses.

Charles: I want to be careful here because the typical modern system of intellectual psychology would say, "Those are excuses." Whereas if you analyze it in terms of system one, I'd go, "These are accurate descriptions of the person's inner world. They don't realize they're telling themselves that." Because if they tell me their money's slipping away, I already know it's a physical object and so I go, "Okay. So you can acquire money, you can value money, you can do things with money, you can dispose of money. There's these four skill areas, and you could develop yourself in one skill area." But instead, most people have some reaction like, "I can't hang onto money," and then they stop thinking about it.

> **Preparation is a ritual for focusing the mind to be prepared for what one is going to do.**

The point is the person may have more skills than they realize, but the way they're talking about it is obscuring that fact.

Michael: People that win lotteries. There's been research that people get all the money they think they need and then they blow it all, and they're right back where they started before they won the millions.

Charles: This is a wonderful example of how money in the mind influences money in the world. What they found in the research is that how you get the money and, moreover, how quickly you get it, correlates with how quickly you dispose of it. They call this a mental container, where you're putting your money. The point is that you want to change the container.

Let's say people get a tax rebate. They spend that quickly because the money showed up quickly. What I suggest to clients and people I work with is that you take the money and shift where it is. If you get a tax rebate or you win the lottery or something, put it in the bank or someplace safe and let it sit there a little time, because what'll happen is it'll shift container, and in your mind it'll become different money and then you can utilize it differently.

Michael: How do you direct people to take the next step?

Charles: We're already on the way, in that the first part is to get curious about this and to begin to wonder when words come out of their mouth about money, or how they use money to measure aspects of their life, or when they use a money metaphor. That shift of awareness will lead to the next stage, which is: "Maybe in this area of my life I want to stop using money as the measure." Find out where money does not adequately apply—you sell your car, but you don't sell your daughter—and other instances where you're using money as emotions: "My account is overdrawn." Is that a useful way to think about your emotional life, for example, or would you want to measure emotions in some other way?

On the other side of money as an idea that's actively influencing your life choices and actions is getting curious about the metaphors coming out of your mouth and seeing they're also showing up in your actions, choices, and behavior, and wondering what else they could be. It's getting curious about, "How does that person over there think about money?" You can catch a little of that in everyday conversation by the metaphors and ideas that they use. Early on when I was investigating this and I was presenting to different market wizards, they would say things like, "Money is a liquid. Money is a fuel."

It's about finding out where you are, and then what if you were to try out this other way of thinking about money—that money is something that you are utilizing in the world, and it's always flowing, and there's always more of it somewhere, so it's a matter of tapping into it. That mindset redirects one's thinking even in terms of what kind of trading and investing one does.

Michael: The other thing that we might find, too, is there could be people who get to the top and maybe their views and understandings of money are the same as the average guy. Then you start to bring the factor of luck into play.

Charles: It is, and I agree with you that there aren't magic ways to think about money, and most people could improve theirs. Let me give you an example. We're in the holiday season here. Dickens' *A Christmas Carol* was about Scrooge and the idea of going back to money as an object, and Scrooge was good at acquiring it. He was good at valuing it and putting it to work. Yet, in his disposing of it, he was underdeveloped. In other words, one can be well-developed in one area of money and yet not be developed at all in another area—which is to say, "How can I have that money flow back into the world and enhance my life and the lives of others that I want it to enhance?"

Michael: We all know people—maybe even ourselves—who can consistently bring money home, but those same people can also get into debt and spend too much of it.

Charles: Or they're keeping it and living frugal lives. There's nothing wrong with a frugal life, but are they living the life they wanted? They could choose to live large or magnanimously, or live with great connection into the world, and instead, they're there sitting on their money, metaphorically speaking.

Some people are good at disposing of their money, and I mean that in the sense that they put it back out in the world and it makes a difference— they're getting maximum happiness, maximum fulfillment, from it—but they're not that good at acquiring it. When one begins to look at it as a physical object, as opposed to different skill sets, one can go, "I've got this area knocked over here. It's just I don't have enough money to live the way I want. It's not that money's the problem, it's that I need to look more at my acquiring strategies." It allows a more detailed analysis, if you will.

PART 2
The Five Levels
of Thinking

Michael Covel: Explain the concept of fictional people.

Charles Faulkner: My claim is that famous figures of finance are fictional, and here's why. The way we fundamentally make sense of the world is through stories, metaphors, frames, and so forth. Linguistic devices. We know what they are because we have a deep, rich experience. All of us know what a well-told story is like and we all know when we have a turn of phrase or a way of thinking about things that shows us something in a new light. We can't not use these. Given our limited exposure to Warren Buffett, George Soros, Jim Rogers, or any person that you admire, we only know them through the stories we are told about them.

Those stories are not neutral, starting with the fact they are incomplete. They aren't the person's life. They're selected snippets of their experience. And moreover, what we know now is that they're what people consciously think is important. Whereas the real machinery, the real stuff going on, is often unconscious and outside of the person's awareness.

Even when somebody tries to talk about what they think were the important influences on them, they're going to use the availability bias. They're going to use hindsight bias, blindside bias, and all the rest of the biases from behavioral economics. They, people, us, can't even tell the truth about ourselves even if we wanted to.

Michael: Most people have little or no direct extended contact with famous others, so they only know them through the simplified stories and the idolatry that takes place in the online chatter world these days.

Charles: Absolutely. And even if you do know them, you still know them in limited circumstances. One of the things I get into is how these people who have achieved in one area of their life will then assume they have the same level of insight in another area of their life. When we do this with other people, we call it the halo effect. When we do it with ourselves, other people call it deluding ourselves. We all do this, and we do it through stories.

The idea that the famous figures of finance are fictional is not for the most part a bad thing, but it does mean we need to take things with more than a grain of salt. I suggest that you should get the most down-and-dirty detailed biography of other people, how they live day to day, and of course many people don't want to reveal that, particularly in the finance area.

Michael: The issue is the nitty-gritty details, like you say, because if you can't scientifically break down their process, there's nothing you can learn. You get back to the stories that you're talking about.

Charles: The other part is that it's become popular to say stories bad, data good. My argument is that we are story-generating creatures. We can't stop ourselves. The only choice we have is how we utilize the stories.

Here's where I suggest that people begin to sort out the difference between a story and a strategy. Often people think they have a strategy in the markets when in fact they have a story, and most often they figured out some magic thing and they got rich. To do the nitty-gritty work of figuring out, as you were saying, scientifically what is your system and how it works, takes effort, time, thought, and development of skills and abilities. In the words of Tom Baldwin, everyone wants the money, but who's willing to do the work?

Michael: Let me quote you on something which dovetails with what you're saying: "Most of most people's experience of money markets and market participants is their imagination. And it's not even that imaginative, it's mostly the same conventional ideas, definitions, and experiences that everyone else has about them."

I see that on the internet day in, day out. It's this cacophony of voices that is noise. There's no depth to it. There's no details. There's no learning.

The whole idea of breaking it down, I don't see it. In the big-picture media narratives these days, it's all about fast information.

Charles: Let's slow it down for a second and ask, what was I getting at there? I was getting at the fact that we humans have these ways of processing information. It's called classic style in literature. It means that when we use words, the words have one meaning—they mean what they say. It's like we're looking through a window on the world and the words are accurately representing what we're seeing. That assumption is so deep that people don't notice, so they crank out the 280 characters (on Twitter) or whatever. They think if they have an opinion about something, that opinion must be true, because to them it's clear, simple, and vivid.

One of the key insights from the work of Kahneman and others is that when we get a clear, vivid image in our head and it's repeated a few times, we think that it's real and true. When people get a clear, vivid image of the markets, a market direction, a particular trade, they're going to believe it's true. Unless they've got a deeper idea that moves beyond those conventional categories of what's a **Famous figures of finance are fictional.** stock, what's a bond, what's a moving average, and so forth—unless they begin to dig into what those things are, and more importantly, how they work—then they're going to be using the same kind of information as everyone else.

When you don't think there are different kinds of information, what you will do is try to get it faster, sooner. If you think that's the only reality, then your only edges are more, faster, better. But if you begin to see that all information is complex, ambiguous, has what's called stochastic uncertainty—which means it has noise, false positives, and false negatives—and moreover it's endogenous—meaning the information changes the environment—you'll realize that your view of the information is limited. Your ability to process information is limited. The information you get is limited only by the sources you use.

All those factors mean that you are getting a particular interpretation of the information, not the truth. Then suddenly there are other edges for you to exploit, which is what market wizards do. There are other ways to interpret, understand and take advantage of the markets. But if you think that words are real and true in presenting facts, then you're stuck with faster, more and better.

Michael: I'd like to think about your notion of imagination not being that imaginative.

Charles: People use conventional categories to put things in boxes. We live in a society that assumes everyone is an independent thinker, with their own responsibility for what they think and what they do. When people are thinking within those conventional categories, they see the world the same way everybody else does. Hence, the thinking is not independent. It's herd behavior. It's conventional. It's what everybody else is thinking. In fact, it's not thinking at all.

To think independently, one needs to have thought through and challenged what those categories are. Are they things the person takes on or not? Do they agree with them or not? This means moving beyond authority. It means moving beyond the conventional categories. It means moving beyond herd thinking to where you are thinking what you are thinking because you thought it through and that's what you think—or, to put it in the vernacular of trading, you're a contrarian.

Michael: When you talk about thinking independently, non-conventionally, I would hazard a guess that most people out there that are in mutual funds, long only, have not pondered the idea that at some point in time, to get your profits, everyone's not going to get out at the top. That's an outside-the-box thought—it's not a typical conversation coming up on CNBC or Bloomberg. Everybody's wealthy on paper if they're a buyer and holder of a mutual fund, etc., but everyone can't get out at the high.

Charles: I'm not talking about traders now, I'm talking about mom and pop: how do they handle their retirement? They save money and invest in the markets. I've seen statistics that, depending on when you started saving and when you need to retire, depending on the start date and the end date, the amount left, even though you contributed the same amount in every scenario, could be six times different. In other words, it could be

$500,000 or it could be $3 million, all depending on your start date and your end date.

Michael: The typical conversation is a simple heuristic that for everybody it's the same situation and it's all going to be okay. Trust the little heuristic of buy the mutual fund, go long, and forget about it. I'll give you another example I saw today about the purchasing habits of people on airplanes now that you can buy movies, extra snacks, or whatever. The data shows that if you're sitting next to a guy who buys a bottle of wine, your desire to buy the next goody or the next film goes up something like 30%.

Charles: This is the stuff from behavioral economics. Everybody wants to think, yeah, some other guy will fall for that, but I won't. Almost everybody falls for it.

By developing a much richer appreciation and understanding of your area of expertise, you still may buy the movie on the plane, but at least you won't be buying the next thing because the guy at the next desk or somebody you talked to on the internet bought an investment and then you said, "Well, gee, I should get some action today too."

The idea is that people who realize there are different contexts, different situations, also realize there's a difference between their knowledge of the markets and the choices they make at the grocery store. When people begin to know about these context shifts, as I call them, or situation changes, that's a sign of independent thinking.

Michael: Let's talk about why people, especially those with big egos, demonstrate ignorance around certain issues and at the same time they're oriented to authority and to experts. It's crazy.

Charles: To talk about that I need to start with the idea that there are different kinds of minds—we are not all of one kind of mind. For ease of remembering, I've split them into five kinds. First, there's the experiencing mind, which is what you see is what you get. These are people that reference direct experience. Then there's the imaginative mind, which people think is like fairytales, but no. When you think about the future you want, you are imagining it. When you think about the past, you draw on bits of experience and create a past memory at that moment. It's at least in part,

We are story-generating creatures. The only choice we have is how we utilize the stories.

if not in large part, an act of imagination. People use categories and project those forward: what is the market going to do? Prediction is imagination. The imaginative mind is quite prevalent.

Then there's the reasoning mind, where everybody likes to think they live. This is what we go to school for years and years to develop, because it is so much work and takes so much mental effort to think things through. Even then, we can get clever at what we do, but we won't stop and go, "Is this the best thing to do?" That's the reflective mind. The reflective mind can put the brake on whatever you've got. Is this what I want to respond to? Is this the situation as it is? These are the people who can look at a situation from different angles—they understand the world is ambiguous. And then last is the generative mind.

One of the properties of the imaginative mind is egocentricity. This is from developmental psychology. All the research is in that people will hold to their own point of view. They see the world through their own eyes and yet they're only using whatever imaginative ideas they have. Because of this developmental stage, they are also still looking to authorities.

You've got somebody that is in their own world, but is watching authorities and taking anything that comes along. When they see a resemblance, they go, "Oh, they're the same." It's like Apple is a technology company founded by a young upstart that made a lot of money. Facebook is a technology company founded by a young upstart. I'll bet it'll make a lot of money. That's resemblance. Any kind of resemblance and bang, the imagination kicks in and puts those together. People don't like to hear it but mostly people hang out in this imaginative mind.

Reasoning takes work and most people only develop it in their area of expertise. One of our great illusions is we think that we are our reasoning mind. Why is it that people do that? The point is there are different ways of processing information, and the imaginative mind is image-driven. It sees things and has feelings about them instantly and unconsciously. We know when we look at somebody if they're upset or they're happy. We interpret experience immediately. This is the imaginative mind. To think things through step by step, to use words to put things into sequence, is a different kind of reasoning process. I don't know what it is about the way our brains are built, but we think we are that step-by-step, reasoning, talking-to-themselves person; and we don't think we are that person who sees the guy in the next seat on the plane ordering a wine and so we order something.

Michael: People mostly aren't taking these concepts to heart and mind. Why?

Charles: This has already been described by many professors and popularizers of behavioral economics. If I was to make a connection here, it is that the imaginative mind is system one, and the reasoning, reflective mind—the thoughtful, deliberative, conscious part—is system two. The strategy that I've seen again and again in the literature is you use your conscious, deliberative part to repress system one, to try to hold it in check and not let it run away. These same professors and popularizers admitted that strategy doesn't work. Here it is in a phrase: "Words don't change people, experience does." What do I mean by that? I mean that what one needs to do is to educate one's experience.

> To develop oneself, you need more than a strategy. You need a greater experience base.

Experience changes people. The imaginative mind is educating one's imagination rather than trying to suppress it. This means beginning to think in more unusual ways about the markets—to get outside your comfort zone and seriously take on ideas about how the markets work that you disagree with and see if you can understand how they work in detail.

In other words, have other ways to understand the world and how it works. Since they're both stories anyway, we can't get to the truth. That's the illusion of language—the illusion we have that what you see is what you get and it's all real. No. We're getting an interpretation of a complex, ambiguous, uncertain, limited amount of information world.

Your question was, why does this wash over people? The point is, as long as we talk about it, it does. But when one begins to change one's experience, it begins to change oneself. This is contrary to the usual thinking. Conventional thinking is you need a strategy. I'm not saying you don't need a strategy—it's a good thing to have—but to develop oneself, you need more than a strategy. You need a greater experience base. You need to embrace, for example, that one of the differences between professional traders and amateur traders is, for better or for worse, professional traders often have more exciting lives. They go out and spend their money in ways that one saw in the movie *The Wolf of Wall Street*, or they go and do exotic sports or extreme things. That means they have a wider emotional base than the trader for whom the most exciting experience they have is when the market goes against them.

The professional trader, with the wider range of emotions, goes, "I've been here before. I'm nervous, but I know what being scared is. I did something stupid once and so I know what that experience is like." It offers them a mental context. Whereas for your mom and pop everyday person who's out there trading, unfortunately trading is the most exciting thing they do. Hence they go to the edge of their abilities, except they're actually beyond the edge at that point. They respond emotionally instead of responding to the trade because they don't have as wide a range of emotion.

Michael: I find there's two kinds of market wizards. One kind will tell you exactly what they do. They're so confident and so comfortable they put it all out there and their performance data backs that point of view. But there are others, not necessarily in a nefarious way, whose explanation about what they do doesn't exactly match their performance data. What's so interesting to me are the third parties that will listen to both types of individuals and then not be able to draw a clear conclusion. They get hung up on a word or a phrase that a noteworthy market wizard uses and they don't think that there could be a reason why what they're saying is not 100% true. There's a certain segment that gets confused because they hear mixed messages and they're not comfortable enough in their own skin to make a judgment that perhaps the billion-dollar-plus fund they listened to might have given a little bit of cloak and dagger.

It gets back to the issue of you need the imagination to be able to perceive what's going on versus simply trusting. It's not idolatry. I see that so often in my world—people want to worship. They don't want to understand.

Charles: That's level two. That's the imaginative mind. To add to what you said, given that there are these different kinds of minds, it's clear to me that these market wizards are operating at a higher level. They're operating with a different worldview, a different mindset, a different level of thinking. They're not using words in the same way.

For one thing, they understand words are not reality. You get up to level five, you get up to the generative mind. You start with experience—the concrete every day. You go to the imaginative mind, the reasoning mind, the reflective mind, the generative mind. At the reflective and the generative level, the way they use language is they're aware of its limits. They're aware of what it does, how it influences thinking.

A wonderful example is from Ed Seykota, when years ago he was asked what was making gold go up and he answered, "It has the property of going up." Audience members said, "Oh no, no." And they asked the question again, "What is making it go up? What's the reason why?"

Getting those simple cause-and-effect explanations is a property of the imaginative mind. Ed is up there at reflective and generative and he's not even thinking that way. He's a scientist by training. He already broke free of "why" questions and he started asking how the market works and developed his own trend following approach, and then from there, developed the psychology of that even further. He didn't think in terms of why. He thought it has the property of going up. He wouldn't allow himself to generate a reason that the ordinary person can come up with why gold is going up or down.

Michael: I can think of two market wizards: Warren Buffett and Ray Dalio. I compare those two within the field of trend following traders—I can easily look at their track records and I can see some commonalities in performance. However, when I look at the words of a Warren Buffett or the words of a Ray Dalio, they might be great examples of what you've been saying about using words at a higher level.

Charles: I will differ with that because I think I have a fairly good understanding of both of the gentlemen. I've looked at their writings and their work pretty extensively. In the case of Warren Buffett, he understands the difference between stories and strategies, which is to say imaginative mind thinking versus reflective thinking. When he talks to audiences, he almost always uses stories. But every once in a while, he gets in a situation where people demand strategy from him and the guy digs down immediately. Stories go completely away as he describes it. It's happened at a shareholders' meeting. He can talk for hours without notes explaining how the insurance business was structured through Berkshire Hathaway.

Ray Dalio clearly has a complex and mathematically thought-through strategy, and yet he also produced that video about how the economy works, told in a somewhat story form on the internet so that people could begin to think these things through as well.

You get to that level of thinking and they even know the difference between when they're talking to ordinary folk and when they're talking to another professional and their language will shift a lot. This is the idea that context or situation makes a difference. For most investors and most traders, they want the one strategy that'll work all the time in every situation. That's not how these guys are working.

Michael: Where I was going is those guys are so successful and so original, compared to a more common strategy like trend following where you can see the commonalities quite clearly. They occupy these unique spaces, whereas some other strategies have a little more chance for replication.

Charles: Let's not overlook the fact, at least in Warren's case, he's made most of his money in recent years. It's called compounding. The secret is to get a consistent return over time and let compounding do its work. Time is a huge factor there as well as skill, and people look at these traders and want to replicate that, forgetting how much luck also enters into it.

Being able to run a consistent strategy for a long period of time is a real skill, like trend followers. People shouldn't be getting their excitement from trading, or in the words of Charlie Munger, "Trading should be boring." To be able to grind it out means that you've mastered that craft to the point where you're not seat-of-the-pants every day. Here we enter into the whole motives for why people get into the markets and why they get into money. Money is a substance, a sign, a symbol, a cipher system, a story, a ritual, and an abstraction. Money is in your pocket, but the idea of money is everywhere. We're in this symbol system and it has multiple meanings.

Money is not only comfort. Money is security. Money is power. Money is freedom. All this emotional stuff, all these acts of imagination are taking place around the issue of money. And then people are supposed to calmly and rationally go into the markets and do their thing to create their retirement, except we're human and people are looking for excitement and they're looking for success. They're looking for meaning. It turns into a competition because it has win and lose, and so they begin to apply a competitive frame to their thinking. They'd rather gain a little money than lose any. So they stay in a position, but it doesn't come back, so they lose more money. That's how humans work. Having developed oneself to follow a trend following system through market ups and downs is an accomplishment in itself.

Michael: Absolutely. It's unconventional compared to what you typically learn growing up these days, which is there's still a significant part of the population that thinks markets are efficient.

Charles: It's a skill set to be able to not respond to your emotions. It's a skill set to not have your ideas of being competitive and being successful tied up with the next moment of trading. All around you in the industry, the conventional thinking, they're measuring quarterly results. And yet a true trend follower is not trading for the next day, the next quarter— they have that independent mindset. The development of that worldview, that mindset, those abilities, which are not part of any trading course or investment course that I'm aware of, is key to being able to execute the strategy.

It's an advanced form of thinking to say, "Maybe the world works differently than I thought it did." There's any number of famous people who have said similar things to that. I believe it was Winston Churchill who said that most people would rather die than think and most do. Or Russell who said that when people have a choice between admitting that they are wrong or proving that they're not, most people get right to work on the proof.

Michael, your podcasts give people a chance to broaden their experience. It's an entertaining way to begin to get some vicarious experience to go with real experience and widen their base. That's how you move from one level to another—you've got to increase your experience, increase your imagination, increase your reasoning power. In the trend following area, your books are foundational in this respect. And if people want to find out about Buffett, he publishes a lot. Dalio's publishing a lot. Soros has published a lot. There are people out there who share themselves. If somebody decides they want to be a trader, then go learn your craft, widen your base, learn all the tools.

PART 3
Reasoning by Resemblance

Michael Covel: One of the interesting things that takes place in the mind is we see one set of data and for the things that we don't see, we fill in the blanks in a creative way.

Charles Faulkner: It's well understood now that we see what we've seen before and the language we inherited from our ancestors is identifying aspects of our experience, our so-called reality, saying, "Pay attention to this. This helped us survive. This helped us thrive." We have these words to name things, and processes and ideas that will help us flourish. Since the time of Shakespeare, who coined at least 150 new words himself, by many estimates language has multiplied by a factor of five—that's a 500% increase in the number of words since the time of Shakespeare. That is, more words to identify more bits of our experience that it might be worth paying attention to. What happens with this is a splintering: the young people who are in the cryptocurrency and the blockchain space have all the language for that, while guys of Buffett's generation, who've done well but who don't know those words, cannot identify the things in this new cyber world.

Michael: It's fascinating that two different groups of people that both speak English can't communicate, because they have an entirely different language.

Charles: I'm getting closer to my current interest in this, inasmuch as we use words and assume the other person knows what we mean. In psychology this is part of what's known as naive realism, which is: What I'm seeing in the world is real and what I say about the world is real and words refer to real things in the world. It has been recognized in the field of psychology for a hundred years that this is not the case. We put a name on a process, but in some cases one word actually has multiple related meanings—for example, "coffee" is a word that not only refers to the beans, but could also refer to "Let's get coffee," "Is there any coffee?" and so on. But people don't think of it that way—they think of a word as having a specific meaning. This leap of imagination allows us to get through the world.

We say, "My car is around here somewhere." We use this generic word "car," but we put that little word "my" in front of it and in our mind we know exactly what that car looks like. And I'm thinking, "Oh yeah, I know what that car looks like too, except that you sold your old car and bought a new one since I last saw you. So I don't know what your new car looks like."

What makes humans distinctly different from other creatures is that we have imagination.

Those kind of slippages didn't matter so much when humans lived in the same place most of their life, which is incredible to think about. It was only a few hundred years ago that people who left where they were born were unusual, while people who came from somewhere else were completely untrustworthy. Now it seems normal to us to get on airplanes and fly tens of thousands of miles and meet people we've never met before and so forth, but that's actually fairly new. Our brains didn't evolve in that environment—our brains evolved in environments where everything was pretty much the same. We knew the same people and things were what they were. And so this naming that we do—this understanding of reality as being stable, permanent, and always true— is our default by evolution. Now we're in a world that's changing daily, weekly, yet our brains haven't evolved to deal with that.

Michael: Are we using words we think describe a certain phenomenon to somebody, but it's not accurate and it creates issues?

Charles: It's not the word per se—it's the word, and the concept, and the meaning that it has. It could be a doodle on a page. The point is that the word represents an idea—a concept that we can then use to make meaning of what we're experiencing. When we don't have ways to make sense of that, we develop new language. You say the word coffee and it has these multiple connected meanings. But you use a word like crypto and that also has all these different associations and meanings and people go, "Oh yeah, I understand." Whereas, as I discuss in my TED talk, as we get some little bit of experience, our imagination fills in the rest with what we expect to be there, with what we are familiar with. That's both the wonder of the imagination and the danger as a trader and as an investor, which is that we'll hear something and fill in all sorts of stuff that we ought to have taken a little more time to see whether that's the fill-in that works in that situation or not.

Michael: With all of this complexity in our daily lives with language that means different things to different people, it's a challenge to make good decisions in the face of uncertainty.

Charles: Going way broad brush here, uncertainty historically was something human beings expected to have to deal with; it was dealt with by ritual and by divination. You didn't know what the world had to throw at you, so your religion, stoic philosophy, or whatever, would orient you to certain ways of interacting with the world so that whatever happened you could still be centered in yourself. You'd go, "The world's uncertain, but I'm going to respond in this way," either out of faith or out of reason.

And then the other side of that is, "I want to try to figure out what the world wants, what my God wants, what the spirits want," and try in some way to do something to connect with that so-called randomness. You've got the throwing of bones or the I Ching, all these things where we're trying to say, "If I take some random phenomenon and I toss it into the world, like some coins, those coins are not going to land randomly, they're going to land based on all the elements and everything that's going on around me. And if I know how to read that, then I'll know a little bit more about what subtly is making the world the way it is."

I went down this rabbit hole for a reason, because that's often what forecasting is in markets: it's based on that same deep, imaginative, ancestral desire to try to make sense of the world. It's trying to somehow connect with the complexity of patterns. The danger is that when the coins land or when the number comes up on the VAR or whatever, it's solid and it's particular. So people go, "That must be true, because that one came up at that moment," as opposed to the idea that at that moment that's the way it came up, but that's now in the past and reality has moved on.

Michael: You mention this in your TED talk—the rise of magical thinking.

Charles: First, I'm saying magical thinking never went away. The example I gave, that the divination and prediction in forecasting and the modern era are deeply related to each other, there's whole books on that subject. Back in the 1960s, maybe even the 1940s, a government official pointed out that businesses do forecasts in order to convince everybody to take action. In other words, the idea of forecasting the future economically wasn't that it was in any way accurate, it was like the shaman coming down from the hill and telling the warriors that this was the time to go on the hunt. So they would go on the hunt, although it was dangerous and people were going to die—or in modern terms, people were going to go broke—but if nobody went on the hunt it would be even worse. It was a way of prompting people into action and these methods are still with us. People see a forecast and they go, "I'll act on that," whereas if there wasn't a forecast, if I told people the truth, which is that the system is the best predictor of itself, people would go, "What does that mean?" It means that the system will let you know where the system is going.

Michael: That sounds trend following-esque right there.

Charles: That's where I'm going with this. They say, "What do we do with that, Mr. Wizard?" And I say, "Bogle worked out that what you do with that is you invest in everything in the market. Since the market is the best bridge curve itself, then buy the market." And now we have passive index investing. On the other side, yes, exactly, we have trend following, if the market is the best bridge curve itself. But people go, "That's unsatisfying. I'd prefer to know something specific." And I say, "You want the shaman to come down from the hill, from his meditation or whatever, and give you some definitive thing that's going to …" And they go, "Yes, that's what I'd like." I go, "This is why we still have predictions."

Michael: You rationally map out evolutionary thinking, you talk about imagination, you explain why we have so much trouble dealing with uncertainty, you talk about language, and then people still come back and say, "But Mr. Faulkner, there's a guy on TV and he's telling me sweet nothings and I want the sweet nothings. Why should I believe you? Why can't the magical thinkers possibly be accurate?"

Charles: The thing is—and this goes into the whole probability problem that Nassim Taleb writes so much about in *Incerto*—it's going to be right sometimes. I point out that one of the fundamental reasoning processes human beings have is reasoning by resemblance. I'm not the originator of this idea. We go, "That reminds me, that's like last week." Reasoning by resemblance isn't wrong and it's one of our oldest and deepest strategies for making sense of the world. The problem is that when it is wrong, it's spectacularly wrong.

The point is that in our modern era, science is an assault on common sense. Another way of saying that is that what seems commonsensically right to someone like a Buffett or a Munger and so forth doesn't make sense of the world. There was a point—again, broad brush here—where with technology, we brought a lot of the world under our control, whether it was internal heating or internal plumbing, then we moved on to electricity and different transportation with gasoline engines and so forth, and the world looked controllable.

> Our brains evolved in environments where everything was pretty much the same.

As we were able to connect up more things, more people, more nodes, at faster and faster rates, we recreated a complexity that we thought we'd begun to control about the world. We recreated it in our human world, so that our human world now is complex, which is to say multiple agents, multiple connections, multiple transactions happening at high speeds. Feedbacking was in nature and weather, and people would be trying to divine when to plant the crops and when to harvest them, and when to go hunting. Now that's become our created world, whether it's cryptocurrency or our current politics.

Forecasting
in markets is
based on a deep,
imaginative,
ancestral desire to
try to make sense
of the world.

Michael: Maybe a lot of us think, "With so much complexity, we're getting more perfect. We can predict better. Uncertainty is the dinosaur, it's going away." But obviously it's not. You've made the point that it's a word, it can mean a lot of different things. How would you begin to unpack uncertainty?

Charles: I'm going to back out of the picture and say uncertainty is one quality, one property of complex systems. We live now in complex systems which are interacting multiple agents with intentions, and memory, competing for scarce resources. So much of this is familiar in a somewhat unbounded environment and hence has nonlinear causes and effects.

What does that mean? What we're seeing around the world is what it means. Some little action taken can have huge ramifications. Whether you look at our financial systems or our political systems, you can pull an example of that for yourself. It also means that in other cases, like for example healthcare in the United States or the opioid crisis or the financial system, huge amounts of effort and money will not make a difference.

Another example that one is in a complex situation is when one gets unintended consequences and there's different ways to go. When you break it down, what are the properties of complexity? First, ambiguity—that is, there is no definitive point of view or understanding. There's stochastic uncertainty, there's endogenous effects, there's reflexivity. And there's the perceptual and information processing limits that we as the decision makers have relative to this system that's much larger and moving in many, many ways that we can't track consciously, that we can't even track with our technologies. Going back through those, in a complex system, the ambiguity, the uncertainty, the endogenous effects, the reflexivity are irreducible, meaning that at a certain point you cannot make them less than they are.

By the way, you wouldn't want to make them less than they are. As I've endeavored to explain to some pretty high-level decision makers, when markets are falling they're actually coming out of complexity and coming into order. When you get a price decline, like you get 400 points down in the Dow, that means the markets are coming into order. A complex system needs to be roiling and boiling, it needs volatility. It is a system that is far from equilibrium. The problem is that the economic models we use are equilibrium-based. We talk about the price at the close, the price at the open, and with the language we fail to notice that's an arbitrary point in time. As soon as that point in time has passed, things have moved on, reality has moved on.

What am I trying to say in all this? Are you a dog or a cat person?

Michael: Dog.

Charles: Okay. We'll use a cat.

Michael: I like cats too.

Charles: You've got a cat. If the cat loses its tail, it's still a cat. And if it somehow loses an ear, it's still a cat, right? The point is that the cat can lose certain qualities and still have its catness, but at a certain point it's not a cat anymore, it's dead.

In that way, complex systems are like living systems. A market, for example, needs to have all these participants making exchanges, transacting, and so forth, or it's not a market. And as we know from the credit crisis, when the banks started to not trust each other and wouldn't trade with each other, it suddenly wasn't what it was anymore. The equivalence of that was it was dead. It needs all that activity. It needs that ambiguity, that uncertainty, to be the living system that it is.

Think about markets as an ecosystem. I'm near Lake Michigan, so let's say the markets are like a big lake. There's creatures on the surface of the water and there's creatures in the middle levels, and there's bottom feeders. There's things that are near the shore, and so forth. If you take that system in its totality, it's too big to wrap one's head around. We have an infestation of zebra mussels that were carried in on the boats from China and they came into an ecospace, there wasn't any predator. They multiplied like crazy and the docks and locks are blocked up with these zebra mussels and the lake authorities go, "What can we do about this? Shall we introduce another life form into the lake to try to deal with it?" They're thinking about that, but they don't know what that new life form might do to change the whole system, because in an ecosystem things are not additive—it's not one plus one.

If you add something new into the system, it doesn't just add a new feature, like on your phone, it changes the entire system—that's complexity.

In this situation, in the markets, it isn't that we have the markets plus cryptocurrency, or plus blockchain. Blockchain is beginning to change the way people are thinking of doing transactions in the entire market. Now, you come back to the idea of ambiguity. Warren Buffett sees that lake as a big old fish differently than some small insect that floats on the surface of the water, differently than the bass; so there's different perspectives and points of view and none of them is right—it's only right for that point of view.

Warren's being smart and he's advising people, don't try to be something you're not, but he didn't preface it that way to say, "It's going to end badly, but doesn't mean it doesn't have a great future." There was a washout in cars, televisions, and the internet, and they ended up being huge industries. He was saying, "Know what you're doing."

All of this is shot through with uncertainty—and I use the term stochastic uncertainty, because it's not only that you're uncertain about the future, it's that you also have false positives, like the idea that you could use reasoning by resemblance to say, "I should invest in any internet company that's involved in blockchain that is happening or has the word 'coin' in the name." That might be a short-term stretch of making money, but in the longer term, it's not going to work.

So there are these false positives, where it seems like a good idea and ultimately you were misled—or as Nassim Taleb would say, fooled by randomness. But there's also false negatives, which in medical terms is when you have the disease, but the test says you don't. The false negative that people could take from Warren Buffett is that there's nothing there, when in fact there's very much something there—it's just not something the test was able to detect. The point is the due diligence, the ability to see beyond that, and then how to see beyond that. What I've been making the case for is the more you can understand the nature of complexity, the more you can understand which of the participants—including yourself—in these emerging worlds are going to be the fittest and view that fitness as a sense of success.

Michael: What do we do with all this complexity? Trying to be the person that understands every possible variable, there's only so much time in the day.

Charles: The big question is to know when you're in a complex situation and when you're not. We can say, "Let's get some coffee," and that is sufficiently detailed enough that you and I could go out into the streets of the city we live in and we could get ourselves some coffee. On that local level, it works—that is to say, close up in time and space, which is what our neurology evolved to deal with. We make our way through the world like that, reading other people, in the sense of looking at them and seeing that somebody has a quizzical look or an unhappy look or a happy look on their face. Looking into a café and seeing it's empty and going, "We won't get coffee there. Maybe it's not that good." And then each of us has an area of expertise where we've developed skills, whether it's as a programmer or as an investor or something else, and these are complicated.

A smartphone, for example, is complicated, in that it can have lots and lots and lots of things going on, but it does have predictable causes and effects, and it produces predictable outcomes and people have expertise in the hardware, the software, and so forth.

But when human beings are involved, complexity is trying to get five people in a room to get along with each other in a business or in a family or whatever. We often confuse being **Uncertainty is** in a complex situation with being in a simple **a property of** situation. In other words, we want human **complex systems.** beings to do what they're supposed to do. I see this with young entrepreneurs who understand the controlled world inside the box and the screen they write their code on. And then they want the world into which they're going to introduce their product to have that same predictability, that same regularity, and it doesn't: they're taking one world for the other.

The key to this is that there are those simple strategies, like let's get coffee, and there are those complicated strategies, like here's the way to set up a LAN network. If you apply those to complexity, you are suddenly having the unintended consequences, the out-of-proportion responses, the uncertainty, the unpredictability, because you are not using what is congruent with the situation you're in. That's what happens a lot, if not all the time, with inexperienced traders and investors; they think the markets are complicated and if they only had more software or a smarter guy or another indicator, they could then wrap their head around it and predict what was going to happen—they'd know what to do. The point is that the rules and the actions in the world of complexity are different than they are in the simple or complicated.

Michael: You have seen enough to know that in the 1970s and a good portion of the 1980s, a lot of traders, either for themselves or offering products to clients, would shoot for high volatility-type returns. They'd have no problem shooting for 20% or 50% in a year and they might even take a 50% drawdown on a regular basis.

Charles: It came out after that whole fiasco that they would go into the room and the money guys would say, "You have to promise us that kind of return, or we won't do business with you."

Michael: The crypto generation reminds me of the return-chasing days and being far more comfortable with that extreme volatility than the generation or two before them, because Bitcoin's taken multiple 50% drawdowns so far. It's interesting that people seem to be tolerating this extreme volatility in crypto, whereas they weren't for the last 20 years since the dot-com bubble. You can see these different generations with different information, different language. And perhaps, that market memory is not transferring to a 20-something guy today who's excited about a blockchain in Bitcoin.

Charles: There are certainly guys like that. And then I think there are people that understand this. Let me give you one example from my own work. The words complex, complex system, complex adaptive system— these are terms of art. What people don't realize, outside of the academic world, is that network theory absolutely overlaps with complexity. Self-organization and learning organizations, and Peter Senge in *The Fifth Discipline*, overlap with complexity. Hierarchy theory, which comes out of complex biological thinking, which is what I'm using to design how I think about the markets at this point, comes out of complexity. Take one of those for the moment: network theory holds that networks are not just one-to-one connections—they develop nodes or hubs, superhubs some call them, that are subject to power laws.

Okay, what are power laws? Success, to the successful, is an example of a power law that explains why somebody is famous. He's well-known for his well-knownness. And you get out-of-proportion responses. In other words, it's not, to go back to Nassim Taleb and his work, mediocre stand versus extremist stand. An example of mediocre stand would be the height of human beings—that even the tallest human being is not that much taller than the rest of human beings; it creates that bell-shaped curve. Whereas if you look at wealth, wealth is extremist stand. Wealth is a is a power law, where the people who are wealthiest are multiple, multiple, multiples of everyone else and it's this huge curve that starts way high up with the Waltons and the Koch brothers, and so forth, and then down to 90% of the rest of us. Power laws are operative in complex situations.

And so connectedness is being attached to a large node or hub, like an Amazon, like a Google and so forth. There's mathematics behind this: if you are an early entrant and then you add members to your network at a certain rate 2×, over time you are going to be a major player, whether you want to be or not. I've seen old interviews with Steve Jobs where he describes when he went into Xerox Park and he saw all the Alto graphical user interfaces, computers hooked to each other and hooked to a printer. He could see at that moment that the network of computers and the printer and the graphical user interface were all going to be huge, because he didn't see seven computers hooked up to each other, he saw 7,000 or 700,000. But he started out with one computer hooked up to a printer with a graphical user interface and that was the Mac—desktop printing. That revolutionized that industry and revolutionized Apple. But he also saw the rest of those things happening.

I think that Jeff Bezos knew about network effects and thought, "What company could I build that the underlying software could sell anything?" He started out with something that was non-perishable, that there was a built-in market for, and that had all the characteristics of differentiation that he would want a software to have for any product, and he came up with books. Apparently he took a long time deciding what to sell on the internet, because he knew if he built that platform and he kept adding eyeballs and adding interactive people, the network effects would be on his side. I don't think that Zuckerberg understood network effects when he built Facebook, but as soon as it happened back at Harvard, when he saw all the people that went on the girl comparison thing that he did, he saw that would be the future.

And now we go back to this thing about the difference between our space and cyberspace. We can only make a limited number of connections. I can go out today and meet as many people as possible and it would still be under a hundred. But in cyberspace, vis-à-vis this podcast, for example, I can meet tens of thousands of people. Now we're into network effects, and understanding and leveraging complexity creates a different possibility, like the young guy that created Ether and Ethereum monetary transactions. But it's going to be about medical records, it's going to be about scientific discoveries. Those leaps of imagination in this other space make all these other things possible. People who are operating that way, who understand complexity and how it is structured, are going to have a huge advantage.

Michael: What are some hacks that they can start to think about complexity and what it represents and bring it closer to home?

Charles: Most of our society is based on what we call negative or inhibiting feedback loops, which is to say that we are trying to bring our behavior in line with something. In fact, if you look at a lot of companies, they're trying to make sure that they're doing what they're supposed to be doing—making a profit, which is a positive or amplifying feedback loop. Think about that for a moment. Most of business and most of people's activity is trying to bring their behavior in line with something which is inhibiting to create an amplifying feedback loop. And by the way, an amplifying feedback loop defies perpetual motion machines. Now, perpetual motion means you've got a machine that can run forever, because it never runs out of energy, it doesn't run down. By definition, an inhibiting feedback loop will run things down, but in business we want something that creates more profit than it costs in energy, which means that it's defying the perpetual motion machine.

Power laws are operative in complex situations.

That's the frame. How do we do that as humans? How do we create more value than the energy it took to create it? To me, that's the underlying question you're asking. The way it's done is not the way people think it's done. It's not done by carefully planning one's future: "I'm going to go to this college and I'm going to do this or that." As we're seeing more and more, it's done based on people creating a number of little experiments in their life, trying things. If something works, doing more of that and less of what didn't work.

That sounds so mundane as to be dismissible. But if you think about the number of people who dropped out of Harvard—Bill Gates being one— or Stanford, okay, they tried college and they were also running a Bitcoin mining operation in their dorm room. Ken Griffiths was going to college and also trading out of his dorm room. You can look at that and go, "He was ambitious." And you can also look at it like it was a number of experiments. People don't think of their lives that way and it might be useful for them, as you said, as a heuristic, a shortcut, to begin to think that, as in the old adage, you don't put all your eggs in one basket.

> **In business we want something that creates more profit than it costs in energy.**

Michael: Overall, universities are not looking to the fresh new pups that show each fall and saying, "What you need to do is experiment." What they're saying to them is, "What you need to do is listen and memorize everything." You're painting a different picture.

Charles: I am. And I'm also saying do what they say. If you're going to a university, do what they say as one of the experiments. In other words, that's a possible path.

Michael: That's an expensive experiment.

Charles: That's certainly a conversation people are having these days. "Is that an experiment we're doing?" I'm saying, if you think about it as one path instead of the only path, then maybe people won't want to take those big loans for college and that might be a good decision. I'm not saying it is or isn't, but the mistake people make is they put all the effort into the planning and the execution of the plan and that's magical thinking—that the plan is going to somehow control reality. Whereas that plan is one of the paths into the future and in a complex system with non-linearities and endogenous effects, it's a fancy way of saying that the world isn't what it was last year or two years ago or 10 years ago.

Michael: I'm imagining people thinking, "I'm scared. Charles is talking about complexity. Everything's complex. I feel like I don't know where to turn, where to start. How do I navigate complexity? It's a challenge."

Charles: It's a meta skill. The difficulty here is that it turns out that the ability to identify different contexts, the ability to identify what situation I am in, is a high level of thinking—unfortunately, because that's the skill we all need now. Simple situation: we're going to get coffee—done, it's simple. Complicated situation: how do I program this?

Michael: Every time you start down these paths, it suggests to me trend following, but you give it a different take than I do.

Charles: I take the example of Ray Dalio. He takes the point of view that the markets are essentially a mechanistic system—complicated and mechanistic. He leans into complicated as opposed to complex with that metaphor. Then he has certain strategies which show up in his business, such as the whole idea of radical transparency. What I'm trying to say is that the way people think about the world affects what they do, which affects the way they think about the world. Ray Dalio, to his credit, thinks the world is at the edge, that phase transition between complicated and complex, and that he can pull it back to complicated if he can only get control of his people and get them to be radically transparent and all these other things.

To take another example of that to underline this point, George Soros, on the other hand, thinks of economics as being far from equilibrium. I know I'm using technical terms I'm not taking time to define. But Dalio thinks about economics being closer to equilibrium, that is, that they can come to some balancing point. In other words, when you're doing the numbers, they'll add up at the end. Whereas Soros understands that it's far from equilibrium, which places him in the center of complexity and hence his strategies are different. He understands that how he and other people think about the markets influences the markets.

Michael: I'm biased. Because I've put these books out about trend following, I relate more to Nassim Taleb. I look at Soros and his reflexivity and he's in one camp whereas Dalio's in another camp and it doesn't necessarily mean one's right or wrong, they're just different camps.

Charles: That's my point. The first phase transition is between complicated and complex, the second phase transition is between complex and chaotic, and then that phase transition where the markets are at the edge of chaos—which is not exactly what people think it means—is where we find Bogle, yourself, and Nassim Taleb.

CHAPTER 13

DENISE SHULL

Everyone Has an Achilles Heel

DENISE KAY SHULL is a performance coach who uses neuroeconomics and modern psychoanalysis in her work with hedge funds and professional athletes. She focuses on the positive contribution of feelings and emotion in high-pressure decisions. She is the author of *Market Mind Games: A Radical Psychology of Investing, Trading and Risk*, which explains how Wall Street traders act out Freudian transferences in reaction to market moves and postulates that human perception contains fractal elements in the same manner as the fractal geometry of nature.

Michael note

Denise leverages her training in psychological science to solve the challenges of mental mistakes, confidence crises, and slumps, ranging from Olympic athletes to Wall Street traders. She may also be the inspiration for one of the main characters in the TV show *Billions*.

Michael Covel: How do you start assisting traders?

Denise Shull: I have consulted with a wide variety of traders and portfolio managers. And when I say wide variety, I'm referring to their personalities and their quirks, but also their styles and the amount of money under management. I feel like I have been privileged to realize some common characteristics. At the end of the day, everyone is human.

When I work, it doesn't matter who I'm sitting across from or who I'm on the phone with, I am trying to understand the sequence of feelings the person is experiencing in the decisions they're making and what the patterns are.

We've all been taught to be analytical—I mean analytical in a mathematical, probabilistic, logical way—whereas what we know about the brain is being completely upended, according to research by the World Economic Forum. So, it may be that everything we think about our thinking is wrong from the perspective of how much feeling and emotion is actually in our perception, judgment, and decision-making.

I'm always looking for that dimension of feeling and emotion that the person usually doesn't know they have, doesn't know is repetitive, certainly doesn't know where it comes from or what it means. Then by helping the person to look at their feelings as data, they start to understand the other dimensions influencing their perception and judgment.

Improving rules and following them never completely solves bad technique.

The conventional wisdom is that you solve bad technique through improving your processes, improving your rules, following them. What happens, though, is that it never completely solves them. People make the same kind of mistakes over and over. Everyone that I've worked with has an Achilles heel; this is part of being human, but it's also part of portfolio management training.

Most people attempt to put process and techniques in place, but what happens is people say, "And I did it again." That's when I get them to ask themselves why. Well, why you did it again is this dimension of feeling and emotion that you're trying to set aside, when in fact you need to make it overt, conscious, and analyze it, so that you can not only understand what's driving you to make that same mistake, but also start to be more aware of intuitive feelings that are unconscious pattern recognition.

Technique is the standard answer, but I can tell you this for sure, it doesn't usually solve the problem. It may mitigate it, but inevitably, people will make the same kind of mistake again.

Michael: What's the aha moment people have when you are able to get them to think about that feeling as a piece of data?

Denise: It's sometimes about rationalizing getting bigger in a long-term position. But mostly, it's about proving that they're smarter than the next guy. The aha moment is—I've had this situation in the markets multiple times—I realize I have this set of feelings that drive that. And I realize those feelings are the same as I had when I was a ninth grader and I got cut from the football team. And frankly, what I'm doing has nothing to do with this market decision; it has to do with these feelings related to my self-image and who I am that I can remember from growing up.

The clue, the power, the leverage is in recognizing you have this set of feelings and it's something in your personality development that has nothing to do with the market decision. As you get conscious of the source of those feelings, it's a lot easier to pull that spaghetti bowl apart. It doesn't solve the self-image feelings necessarily at first, but it does start to detach them from the market decision.

Michael: I'm looking at the title of your thesis research, "The Neurobiology of Freud's Repetition Compulsion." Before I let you explain the results of that thesis research, what was the trigger for you as a young person to go down this path?

Denise: I'm impressed. I've been interviewed scores of times and no one's ever asked me about that paper or how that came to be. Honestly, I feel like my whole life has contributed to me being in this position where I seem to have figured out this thing related to feelings, emotions, and performance.

Michael: What's the first age where you knew you were observing the human condition in such a way that you felt like you had something? Is there any early memory where that starts for you?

Denise: There's performance evidence that it started way before I knew it. I was an only child—I was also adopted at four months old. I was unusually mature. My teachers would always say I seemed older than I was. Everyone usually thought I was three years older. When I was 16, I worked at a summer camp and they put me in a senior counselor position even though you were supposed to be in college to do that. They brought the children's home kids out for a week and they called me into the office and said, "Okay, this is going to be kind of weird, but we want to give you the senior high-school girls and some of them are older than you."

I'm an honest person and this was a Christian camp, so definitely ethics was a big deal; but I made the decision that I was going to lie and say I was 19 because I wasn't telling these girls who grew up in a children's home that they were two years older than me.

We had a fabulously successful week. At that point I seemed to have some understanding of human nature that, I think, came from growing up as an only child. I had a lot of time to think and somehow that led me to the position where people considered me more mature.

When I first recognized that there was something to be studied was my mid to late 20s. I started noticing that all my friends would get in these relationships, some were even marriages, and these relationships would break up. And then they would get in another relationship and the people involved would be completely different, but the scenarios would be exactly the same. At the time I was working for IBM and they had a great benefits program, so I thought, "You know what, I'm going to go to therapy as a lark and see what I can learn. IBM will pay for it, what the heck?"

I went to this woman in Cleveland, Ohio. I was dating this guy and one day she says to me, "Well, how do you think he feels about you?" And I say, "Well, blah, blah, blah, blah." Then she says, "Well, how do you think your father feels about you?" And I started to say, "Blah, blah." And I realized the identical words were about to come out of my mouth.

There's a phenomenon where you think your romantic partner is the same as your parent, and the light bulb went on. Lo and behold, I found out that Freud had identified this and called it the repetition compulsion. He has this beautiful paragraph that describes how people get in similar situations while they look completely different. He's actually referring mainly to work situations, but they always end the exact same way for the exact same reasons. I was a biology undergraduate; I'd always been interested in what makes us tick. So, I thought, "If we unconsciously get ourselves in similar situations such that it recreates a certain feeling, then there's got to be a template in our brain."

I was supposed to go to Stanford Business School while I was still at IBM, but I thought to myself, "I don't know if I want to be doing the MBA, rising the corporate ladder thing." I found out that the University of Chicago had this design your own master's program where you only have to take two research-level classes and then get a professor to sponsor you for research. So, that's what I did.

Michael: And that laid the foundation.

Denise: Yeah, totally. At that point, it was called biopsychology. I did what my advisor ended up calling the best literature review she'd ever seen. I went to the library and tried to find articles on child development related to emotions. I was trying to look for the unconscious, because we're not conscious we're getting ourselves into the same situation or marrying the same person or having the same argument with our boss. But there was very, very little written at that time, or even since.

I was sitting in a conference in New York a couple of years ago, one Saturday. The president of the Neuropsychoanalysis Association was giving the keynote. She said, "Let me give you a history of neuropsychoanalysis." And she says, "The first two or three papers ever written in this field," and she has my paper on the list. I almost fell off the chair. I was like, "First of all, I didn't know anyone knew about this paper. And I certainly wasn't expecting anyone to."

Most people have heard of attachment theory, which is how an infant ends up attaching to their caregiver. And it has been qualified as these different styles of organized attachment and disorganized attachment. But my thinking was, "Okay. There's something going on there when a baby is born and how they're starting to recognize that they're separate from their mother or caregiver."

There's also a phenomenon called critical periods. It's most easily understood in birds. Lots of birds, if they don't hear

> **Everyone that I've worked with has an Achilles heel—this is part of being human.**

their characteristic song during a specific point when they're chicks, will never be able to sing it. So I began to realize there's a critical period for attachment and self-image as you ultimately unconsciously assume what your relationship is to other important figures.

And then I started to walk through the biology of child development as to how that could get set up, so that years later, any one of us is acting and reacting in relation to important figures—whether that's spouses, bosses, the police, or the market—and we're reacting out of this template that was built in the first two or three years of our existence.

Michael: That's a tough insight, though, because if some of us had a great two or three years and some of us didn't, then as adults we're all in the pit together, so to speak, debating, arguing, trying to move forward.

Denise: It isn't to say that if someone had a bad early life, they can't mitigate it. People develop coping mechanisms or defense mechanisms that oftentimes serve them. For example, a common one with children is if things are difficult and they feel powerless, one coping mechanism that people develop is blaming themselves, because if you blame yourself for something, it gives you the feeling that you might have some control over it. And this, at least superficially, can be helpful because it can make you work harder, try harder, make you more responsible. So the way people react to suboptimal attachment and self-image doesn't necessarily turn out to be negative.

Having said that, though, at the worst moment when provoked or when challenged extensively by the market, you might see some sort of patterned reaction that could be untangled if you could connect it to the person's feelings about who they are, what their place in the world is, and how they relate to people or situations of authority.

Michael: Let me bring you to the markets. What was the crossover for you?

Denise: I was in Chicago at university and working at the East Bank Club. I played beach volleyball with a group of people, and a couple of them were forward traders at the Chicago Board Options Exchange (CBOE). I was fascinated by trading and I would ask one of my friends questions like, "Wait. You go down there in the morning, and you make $10,000 and you come home at two o'clock? How does this work?" And he teased me, "You should come down there." And I said, "Not a chance!" Then the CBOE introduced a weather futures seat and my friend tried hard to get me to buy. And I say, "What the heck is that? This makes no sense to me."

If we unconsciously get ourselves in similar situations that recreate a certain feeling, there's got to be a template in our brain.

Anyway, when I was finally writing my master's thesis, he was approached in the summer of 1994 to go upstairs in one of the first upstairs trading firms, meaning trading on screen. But of course, you didn't get intraday profit and loss (P&L). And he and his buddy, who was in the same prop firm, said, "Okay, we'll make you a deal. While you're writing that silly thesis of yours and thinking about whether you're going to get your PhD or not, how about you come keep track of our P&L intraday and we'll teach you to trade?" I thought it sounded interesting. Sure enough, within a few months I had joined the firm myself and stopped keeping track of their P&L intraday. I learned to trade from someone named Bob Cantor who had come to Chicago from New York to start this prop firm.

Then I went to Schonfeld for a little bit to learn momentum trading. My PhD obviously went by the wayside. I started reading Mark Douglas, Brett Steenbarger, Alexander Elder, all the trading psychology out there. And *Market Wizards*. I can remember leaving work on Friday night saying, "I don't need to go out and party with you guys. I'd rather go home and read this book and have a glass of wine on my couch." I was totally fascinated by the psychology side of it.

In that first prop firm, we had all sorts of different styles, from short-term momentum to scalping utilities, to relatively long-term illiquid stocks. I was trying to figure out, "What is this like? And how are you successful in this? And how did these guys take these different approaches?" I didn't understand it. It seemed like that interesting, fun master's thesis was never going to be anything more than an expensive diversion.

Michael: I tried for years to have Mark Douglas on this show. He finally had finished his newest work and had committed and then unfortunately passed away. I was so disappointed.

Denise: I sat down with him in 2005. I actually hired him early on when I was trading. I later hired Ari Kiev too, when I came to New York to run a trading desk. But I got back in touch with Mark when people started to ask me to coach after my first few articles—frankly, I was studying in a psychoanalytic institute in the evening when people first started asking me to coach based on these articles. I had the opportunity to see Mark in Las Vegas and hear him talk about the blood, sweat, and tears that he put into those books. If he were alive today, we wouldn't agree on everything, but I had such respect for him because it meant so much to him to get it right. I feel like part of the difference is that I had the advantage of being able to have more insight on neuroscience, which wasn't available when he was first writing.

Michael: Compare and contrast yourself with other trading psychologists or trading coaches, where you see that you have gone in a different way—or perhaps you think it's the better way?

Denise: Well, I do. That's fair. Truthfully, I think first of all, you've got to step back and recognize the mental problem of markets, which is relentless uncertainty and no one knows what's going to happen this afternoon. That's a specific type of problem to the brain where it draws on context to try to fill in the pieces of what's the right decision to make. It definitely draws on feelings, even though an analytical, logically trained person might not realize it. I bring this neuroscience which shows, for example, you need emotion to make a decision.

That master's thesis, by the way, was republished in 2003 in a psychoanalytic journal, and I updated it because it had been originally written in 1994, 1995. In the subsequent years, the role of what an academic would call "affect" had been defined as the difference between before and after you've had a coffee, or before and after you've had a cocktail—a mood of optimism and emotion, which is a specific, intense form of that, which also includes conviction. I've had this conversation with many people in the trading hedge fund space, and I feel perfectly justified in saying conviction is an emotion because it's an intense physical experience.

My work focuses on that dimension and on making it respectable, making it data, understanding it, pulling it apart. Having said that, I couldn't take somebody and make them aware of all their feelings and emotions and not have the training to be a trader or portfolio manager. I'm not saying it's the most important job, but it's the key when you want to seriously improve your performance or fix what is otherwise an unsolvable problem.

Michael: I agree. Talk about conviction as data and how it could be better understood.

Denise: For example, we did an exercise with a hedge fund where we got them to devise a seven-point scale for levels of confidence, which I think is slightly different than conviction, but for all practical purposes we can use them interchangeably. Let's say there's varying levels of fear, uncertainty, and doubt. We asked the analysts and portfolio managers to decide jointly on a scale they're going to use to describe their varying levels of fear, uncertainty, and doubt on their road to confidence and conviction; develop a language around the words of doubt or concern or panic or anxiety; and start to fold the use of those words into their analysis and their conversations. One of the analysts said, "Every time we do risk/reward, we have to also say where we are on our seven-point confidence spectrum because it's like the sum total of everything and we need to check how it changes."

> Conviction is an emotion because it's an intense physical experience.

Let's say you're confident and then you become somewhat concerned. First of all, you need to recognize that your state has changed because somewhere your unconscious pattern recognition is telling you there's something that needs looking at or analyzing. And if you are explicit about it and you can say to your colleagues, "I'm moving from concern to nervous," then you can help each other ask questions about what piece of data or what event changed where you are on that spectrum? What do we need to do to either resolve it or to dig deeper into it in order to resolve it? Or if we dig deeper into it, what does it say about being in the position or position sizing?"

Michael: A volatility measure like average true range? Conviction as a number. Instead of letting conviction be a feeling that's bouncing around between our ears, you want to get it to something you can look at and measure.

Denise: Absolutely. That's exactly it.

Michael: Everyone, whether they're trading or not, could benefit from this idea of taking the feelings inside and taking more control of them—not to try to make them go away, but at least to analyze them in terms of where they are on the spectrum. Are they cold or are they hot?

Denise: Technically in science you can't prove anything, but we're pretty sure the sun rises in the east. The point being, from a brain perception, judgment point of view, what you feel—which can be as simple as heart rate to extreme anxiety or frustration or conviction—and wherever you are on that continuum, there is information in there. None of us have been taught to think about it that way, and we certainly haven't been taught to analyze it in any way. And for those people who do, there's alpha in it, there's market performance in it, and there are fewer bad decisions because you end up being able to mitigate working out your personality in the market, which also opens you up to better instinctive, intuitive feelings.

That reminds me of something I want to say. I would not be sitting here if it wasn't for 2003 or thereabouts, when I first started being invited to write and speak about it, and lots of people in the audience saying, "Oh my gosh, I thought it was just me. I didn't want to tell anybody that my feelings and emotions either got in my way or they helped me in some way. I thought it was my failing. But what you said makes so much sense to me."

I feel like I only ended up here because I was in this crazy situation where I had an interest and some information. And maybe even being an only child who was adopted, I didn't have such a strong family culture that I was able to be a little bit more iconoclastic and a little bit more of a rebel. So, I can say, "Hey, wait a minute guys. The emperor has no clothes. This view on emotion is wrong from a brain point of view and from a practical point of view." And when I talk about it, so many people say it resonates, and it makes sense to them.

Michael: I want to introduce a character some will not know: Benoit Mandelbrot and the fractal emotions.

Denise: When I first started coaching, I didn't realize that my psychoanalytic repetition compulsion background was going to come into direct play. I can remember one client who was so obviously repeating his life story in the problems he had in the market. He was trading on the floor, the Chicago Board of Trade (CBOT). He lost a bunch of money every morning but would always make it back. He was making good money, but he called me up and said, "If I didn't start out the day down 25 grand in the pit, I'd be making twice as much money. Why is this?" It turned out he was born to a mother on welfare; he had this rags-to-riches story. We figured out he was repeating his whole life in every day's trading, and once we unraveled that, he stopped doing it.

By the time it came to write my book and I was trying to think more and more deeply about this and how to describe it, I had come across the concept of fractals, which is patterns repeated on different scales. The easiest way for people to think about that is stalks of broccoli, where one little piece of broccoli looks the same as the whole head of broccoli, but at a different size, or, to use the technical term, scale.

I studied fractals from a market price repetition point of view. Mandelbrot was usually reckoned to be the person who originally identified them and I was reading some of his work when I was writing my book. I realised, "Wait a minute. That's what these repetitive emotions are." You have this pattern like you have a piece of broccoli and it gets reapplied at a different scale in a different situation, but the core pattern is there.

I believe that what Freud called the compulsion to repeat, what I tend to call repetitive emotions, is fractal in the same way broccoli is. In a human being, it's an opportunity to optimize. It happens because you learned it, but the discomfort gives you an opportunity to untangle the pattern.

Michael: I find Mandelbrot fascinating. He was one of the first to say, "The efficient market hypothesis might have some holes in it."

Denise: Clearly the efficient market has some holes in it.

Michael: There's a lot of people at the University of Chicago who might say, "Hold on, Denise. We don't think so."

Denise: There's also a lot of people at the University of Chicago who would agree with me. If you're going to research something, you need some cornerstone to work with, which in a lot of ways is what the efficient market hypothesis is about. But at the end of the day, you've got to say, "Okay. My research sprang from this foundation, but this foundation also cast these questions as to the results. And that has to be reconciled."

Harry Markowitz, who won the Nobel Prize for his theory of portfolio choice, says at the beginning of his paper, "Figuring out what you believe is step one, then figuring out how to apply it is step two. This paper starts at step two and I'm not qualified to speak about step one." Then at the end of the paper, he says, "Remember to go back and try to understand step one, this paper's focused on step two."

CHAPTER 14

JACK CANFIELD

Unlimited Human Potential

J ACK CANFIELD is the founder and former CEO of Chicken Soup for the Soul Enterprises, which encompasses licensing, merchandising, and publishing activities around the globe. As its beloved creator, Jack fostered the emergence of inspirational anthologies as a genre and watched it grow into a billion-dollar market. With well over 500 million books sold to date worldwide, more than 250 titles in print, and translations into more than 43 languages, "Chicken Soup for the Soul" is one of the world's best-known phrases and is regularly referenced in pop culture.

Michael note

Jack Canfield is easily the most successful author to have appeared on my podcast. I am forever honored to have had the chance to talk with achievers like Jack. He is a one-man example of the benefits of a nonstop positive mindset.

Michael: I'm not the first person to tell you this. You have a certain energy and I know that goes into your work and the way you live your life. I know you know you have it.

Jack: A lot of people say I look like I'm in my late 50s, early 60s. I would say four things. Number one, I started eating healthily and taking lots of supplements when I was in my late 20s; I got involved in the whole health food movement. Number two, I exercise regularly, do yoga, meditate. Number three, I've forgiven everyone in my life. Number four, I pursue the things I love.

When you're not living in resentment, frustration, blaming, and complaining, but you're living a life of passion doing what you love to do, that helps quite a lot. I have a great wife and great kids. There's a lot of love in my life. I've chosen to be loving and to be of service rather than to be in fear.

All those things add up. I'd also like to say it's good genes, but my younger brother looks older than I do. And my youngest brother died already. So I don't know.

Michael: You said you've forgiven everyone in your life. That strikes me. I see so many people that get stuck in the past. Forgiving is ultimately about letting go of the past, living in the moment.

Jack: A lot of people think if they forgive somebody, they're somehow condoning what they did. They sexually abused me. They robbed me. They embezzled money from me. They talked behind my back. They had an affair. Whatever it is. The reality is when you're forgiving, you're giving for yourself. You're not condoning their behavior.

It was such an important thing in my life when I realized that everybody is always doing the best they can to meet some basic need with the best knowledge, skills, and tools they have at the time. If somebody embezzled money from me, they were trying to maybe feed their family or whatever. At the time they didn't have the skills to ask, negotiate, or earn the money on their own. A gang member, when they're out there stealing your car, they didn't learn enough in school to be effective at making a living. And so they're out there wanting to be included in the gang. They want to feel like they belong. They want to be able to take their girlfriend to the movie. So this is what they do.

One of the sad things about our prison system is we don't teach people new skills and new concepts, but we punish them. They teach each other how to be better criminals. For me, I realized early on I had a lot of things that I felt resentful for. I'd had a divorce where I felt like I got screwed by the justice system. I had people embezzle money from me. I had a person screw me in a real estate deal. I can go down the list. The point is, every time you think a negative judgmental thought, especially of anger and resentment, you're actually secreting more acid into your body. We know that your body is healthy when it's in an alkaline state, which is why I eat mostly a plant-based diet. Why I do the supplements I do. Why I don't want to have any of those feelings living in my body, creating cortisol, ruining my neurotransmitters and all that good stuff.

For me, forgiving is a gift. One of my friends said, "Nothing ever happens against you. It always happens for you. You think about the things that happened." My first wife screwed me financially, but it forced me to get creative about how to make more money. As a result of that, I did well.

It's when I started doing things like Chicken Soup for the Soul and I had to get creative and thank God all of those things happened. Garth Brooks has a wonderful song called "Thank God for Unanswered Prayers." In the song, he says you go to your high-school reunion 25 years later and that girl you had a crush on who wouldn't go out with you is now this overweight alcoholic. And you go, "Thank God for unanswered prayers."

I think we realize that everything does happen for us. If you at least live your life from that principle, then you don't have to carry around a lot of resentment.

Michael: I want to understand Jack as a young man. What were you doing at 13? What were you thinking?

Jack: I was a typical Midwestern kid at 13. I was probably freaking out how to survive when my parents moved to a new part of town where I didn't know anybody. I was trying to be cool, have everyone like me, ride my bicycle, engage in BB gun fights, and all that crazy stuff you do growing up in West Virginia.

I was in a military school at the time. I was poor, but I had a rich aunt and she had a son named Jack who was killed in an automobile accident. She kind of adopted me, not to live with her, but to give me some advantages that my brothers didn't get. If my name was Bob, I might not be talking to you today.

I got a good education, but I went to a school where all the other kids' parents were doctors, newspaper editors, lawyers, and my dad was selling cash registers. It was a different world. I always felt like I was in that world, but I wasn't of that world. I didn't belong to the country club, but I got to be a lifeguard working at the country club pool. I was in that world, but I was looked down on. I was trying to be included. That's probably what was going on for me.

Michael: Were there inspirations, mentors, influences that ultimately ended up shaping you when you were putting together something like *Chicken Soup for the Soul?*

Jack: By my early 20s, I was going to graduate school at the University of Chicago, learning how to be a high-school teacher. I taught history for a number of years, during the civil rights movement. Someone I met at the laundromat invited me to go to Jesse Jackson's church. I thought, okay, why not? I went that Sunday and I got inspired by someone who had a message of motivation, self-empowerment, and self-responsibility for African Americans in Chicago. It was an integrated church, although it was probably 95% black. That was the beginning of opening up my eyes. Then the same person who I met in the laundromat invited me to go to a lecture series called "Masters of Motivation" or something like that. There was a guy named Herbert Otto, who was the director of the National Center for the Exploration of Human Potential, and he said that we're only using 10% of our brain, our mind power. I said, "Wow, I want to use more than that." I went up after the talk and I said, "Where can I learn to do more?" He said, "Well, there's this growth center called Oasis in Chicago. You could go and take workshops there."

> At some point you have to transcend the ego and get in touch with your true self.

That next year I took 17 weekend workshops. I think I paid for 10 of them and the rest of them I volunteered to hand out Kleenex, workbooks, clean up afterwards, whatever. I ran out of money, but I got exposed to all this human potential which is unlimited. That's where I met someone who introduced me to W. Clement Stone, who was a friend of Napoleon Hill, who wrote *Think and Grow Rich*, and that changed my life.

Michael: What year?

Jack: Around 1968 or 1969.

Michael: 1968 was a volatile year for America.

Jack: Martin Luther King was killed that year. Bobby Kennedy too. There was a lot going on. I was teaching in a black school in 1965 when Martin Luther King was killed. We had riots in our school.

Michael: Why did you feel comfortable doing something that probably to this day, a lot of white Americans would not want to do? What made you go to a completely different church with a completely different group of people?

Jack: When I first got to the University of Chicago, it was a Master of Arts and education degree. We had this orientation where they took us around to a bunch of different schools, to give us a sense of the kind of schools that we could teach in when we got to that level. One of them was called Rich Township, which it was—it was an affluent community. Everyone was wearing nice clothes, the school was well equipped, and the teachers were cool. Then the next school we went to was Dusable High School, which was listed as one of the worst schools in America at that time by *Time* magazine. The teachers weren't that motivated, the kids were not being educated well. There were not a lot of supplies and something in me said I could make a difference here. When it was time to ask for our teaching assignments, I said, "I would like an all-black school." And they gave it to me. I'd had a year of that experience when the guy says, "Do you want to go to Jesse Jackson's church?" At that point it wasn't that difficult, but if I hadn't had that tour, I don't think I would've chosen to go to see a black school. It was totally outside of my experience, but when I went there something in me woke up.

Michael: So far, it doesn't seem to be this great well-laid plan. It's more like you seem to be inspired to follow the best course of action in the moment.

Jack: People often ask me, "What's the secret of your success? You're a multimillionaire, you've sold half a billion books. You've been in *The Secret*," yada, yada, yada. I always say, I followed my heart. I trusted my intuition. I trusted the inner guidance that I got. I was working for a training company and doing well. And all of a sudden something said, "Go start your own company."

That was scary. I had to borrow $10,000 from my mother-in-law to start a company. At a certain point I wanted to change that company, not do the same thing anymore. And when Chicken Soup for the Soul was at the height of its success, something in me said, I'm tired of this. That's when I sold the company and started the Kim Field Training Group. So yeah, I think that's true. I've always liked the next thing that I would be exposed to; or something would inspire me and I had the courage to take the risk.

Michael: A lot of people who have either written a book or thought about it can likely relate to your early experience. Correct me if I'm wrong, but *Chicken Soup for the Soul* was not some big advance with a big publisher roll-out, was it?

Jack: No, but let me take you back even further before I answer that. In 1976, I published my first book. It was called *100 Ways to Enhance Self-Concept in the Classroom*. I had met a man named Harold Wells, who was developing something called the Becoming Curriculum for kids in Detroit. We hit it off as friends and I realized we were never going to get this curriculum out there at that time. But I said, let's write a book together. It sold 400,000 copies, which for an education book is ridiculous. I had a good direct marketing guy who worked for Prentice Hall, the publisher, but it was a lot of work, a lot of interviews. I probably did 300 workshops for teachers, spoke at conferences everywhere. I remember my first paid speaking engagement was for $25. I drove through a blizzard from Massachusetts into Connecticut to do a two-hour workshop, drove back through a blizzard. It's amazing I didn't die.

Chicken Soup came along as the second book, which was in 1993. As you said, we got no advance. We were rejected by 143 publishers before we found one who said, "We'll publish it." We said, "How many books you think we'll sell?" He said, "20,000, if we're lucky." My co-author Mark Victor Hansen, my co-author and I said, "That's not our vision." He said, "What's your vision?" I said, "We want to sell a million and a half books in a year and a half." And he laughed at us. I'm sure people listening to this have shared their dream with someone and had them laugh out loud. He said, "There's no way." I said, "There's a way." He said, "How do you believe you could do this?" I said, "We're entrepreneurial thinkers and we're visionaries. And we know how to make things happen." Which in fact we did. We sold 1.3 million in a year and a half. We missed it by 200,000, but he stopped laughing. A year later he bought a private jet based on our income.

Michael: Maybe when someone laughs it forces you to say, "You're going to laugh? Well, I'm going to double down and get there."

Jack: A lot of people are motivated by that. My drive for success came from trying to prove I was worthy. I remember not too long ago, doing some sessions with some people and getting in touch with how I remember thinking, God, I've done 200 books. Is that enough? Am I worthy now? Part of my motivation has always been to make a difference. It's very pure. But there's also been a big self-esteem issue for me most of my life. For me it was more like proving I'm somebody worth paying attention to. For other people you tell them, "No," and they go, "I'll show you." We all have different things that motivate us, and at some point we have to decommission the neurotic drive from the pure drive.

Our ego drives us in the beginning—that's pretty natural, it's part of our evolution. But at some point you have to transcend the ego and get in touch with your true self. I was talking to a guy the other day, who's written a book, I forget the title exactly, but I think it was called *The Book of You* or something like that. He reminded me of a story that I put in the first *Chicken Soup for the Soul* book. He said, "You're the reason I wrote this book." And I said, "Tell me more."

There's a story in that book called "The Golden Buddha Story," about when I went to Thailand with my wife. We were doing some workshops for the government over there, then we had a few days to be tourists. If you go to Bangkok, one of the tourist things you do is you visit three Buddhist temples. One of them is called the Temple of the Golden Buddha. There's a solid gold Buddha, about 10.5 ft tall, worth about 196 million dollars if you were to melt down the gold. There was a little information box right next to it on the wall, where there was a piece of clay. It said in 1954, they

Everybody is always doing the best they can to meet some basic need with the best knowledge, skills, and tools they have at the time.

did not know there was such a thing as a golden Buddha. They were moving this clay Buddha from one side of Bangkok to the other, to make way for a road they were going to put through the site of the temple. As they were lifting it up, it was surprisingly heavy and the crane wasn't ready for that much weight, and it fell back down on the earth and cracked. It started to rain and they put a tarp over it to keep it dry. That night, the head monk came out and he shined a light under the tarp to see if it was staying dry. And something gleamed back from inside the crack. He knew that clay does not reflect light, so in the back where it wouldn't show if he was wrong, he chipped away at it and discovered this golden Buddha inside. Their best guess is that 300 years earlier, the Burmese were attacking Thailand and they were killing everyone along the way and stealing all their valuable things. The message had gotten down to Bangkok, so they covered this golden Buddha with clay and painted it so no one would think it was valuable. And here it was for hundreds of years while nobody knew that the golden Buddha was inside.

The metaphor that my wife and I talked about at dinner that night was inside of each of us there is a golden Buddha, a golden essence. There's a Christ consciousness, whatever you want to call it. It's covered up with the clay of our conditioning—our cultural conditioning that makes some people racist and makes some people not. That makes some people Christians and some people Buddhists and some people Muslims, because it's the conditioning you got growing up.

At some point we're responsible for removing the clay and getting back to the original essence of who we are.

Michael: I remember seeing some of those Bangkok temples and some of those golden Buddhas for the first time. It changes you, broadens you, opens you up. I still don't have my finger on it exactly, but I'm so happy to have had the initial experience and to have it change me.

Jack: One of the sad things I've learned recently is how few Americans even have a passport. The reality is when you travel, your beliefs get challenged. You wake up to other possibilities. The first time I went to the Taj Mahal in India, the first time I saw the golden Buddhas or the reclining Buddha in Bangkok, the first time I saw some of the temples in other Asian countries, the Great Wall of China, etc., it shakes you at some level because you're not familiar with the magnitude, the reverence, the inspiration that is created when you climb a mountain or you go to Machu Pichu or whatever.

Every time I travel, I meet different people. For example, the first time I was in Singapore, I had recently seen the movie *Gandhi*. My grandparents were British and German and when I saw what the British had done to India in the movie, I felt kind of embarrassed about it. I was saying it to this general in the Air Force, whom I was having dinner with in Singapore in his home. He said, "Oh no, thank God for the British." I said, "What? Why?" He said, "We'd have no postal system. We'd have no railroad. We'd have no communication." When you travel, you keep getting opened up to new possibilities.

First time I meditated in a temple in India, I got stoned. Not stoned like from marijuana, but stoned at a level where I didn't know you could feel that happy so quickly with another group of people chanting some words that I never heard before. I've had that same thing in Christian meditation centers and doing Sufi dancing with the Sikhs and with the Sufis, which is a Muslim tradition of spiritual growth. Each of those opens us up to new possibilities and seeing the world through new eyes.

Michael: The great thing about your work is that it's about hope. If somebody's at the bottom, or at a transition, or feeling terrible, if they can find their way into the work that you've put together, they have a chance to rebuild. Even though you've sold all those books, there's a ton of people that have never gone down the path of understanding the messages that you've put together.

Jack: *Chicken Soup for the Soul* sold half a billion books, but you've got eight billion people on the planet. The good news is that there's more and more people out there doing this work. There are more podcasts, more blogs, more people talking. There are more television shows like Oprah's. There are YouTube channels with all the TEDx talks and so forth. Sometimes it takes people to hit bottom to realize there's a better place to be.

One of the things that I learned early on is when a recession hits, when a depression hits, when a pandemic hits, there's no less food on the planet than there's ever been. There's no fewer dollars floating around. They're still there. There's no less toilet paper unless people have hoarded it, but there'll be plenty of toilet paper. Everything still exists. It existed the day before the market crashed. The issue is, are we willing to keep interacting with each other and finding creative ways to support each other? Can I trade for food? Can I do something for you and you do something for me? If I'm a landlord, can I say, "Hey, how about you don't pay my rent for the next three months. I'm not going to evict you." That kind of thing could always be done. But we have to say, let's be humane, let's be loving, let's be kind and let's help each other get through this.

Michael: The statement that you should take 100% responsibility for your life might cause some people to say, "I'm not listening. Forget it. That's the wrong message."

Jack: To understand that statement, you have to understand a little formula I put in the first chapter of my *Success Principles* book. It says E + R = O, which stands for Event plus your Response equals the Outcome.

In an event like a worldwide pandemic, you are 100% responsible for your response to that and the outcome you experience. In other words, there's three things you can control: your responses, your images, and your behavior. So, what you think, what you picture, and what you do or say, you're responsible for.

If you start thinking, I'm going to lose my job, I'm going to lose my house, I'm not going to be able to pay the rent, I'm going to get sick, my mother's going to die, you're going to feel crappy. On the other hand, you can say, I can get through this, I have the skills, the knowledge, the friendship circles, the ability to ask for what I want, the ability to negotiate, the ability to be creative, to start thinking about how I can do business from my home.

There's lots of different ways to become useful and to be able to make a living. If you've lost your job as a waiter there are other things you can do, but you have to get creative because the minute you go into fear—which is a choice—you start scaring yourself by imagining terrible things. You're now in the amygdala, which is in the back of your brain, which hijacks the prefrontal cortex, which is where rational thought and creative thinking come from. When you're in the amygdala, you're going to make decisions that are based on fear. When you're in your prefrontal cortex, you can think rational thoughts about how can we get through this together? Where can I reach out to? How can I get what I need? etc.

I'm responsible for my thoughts, and I can think thoughts that make me feel miserable or I can think thoughts that make me feel positive.

In a calmer time I would use the example, if your husband forgets your birthday, you can think the thought, "My husband doesn't love me. If he loved me, he'd remember my birthday." How does that leave you feeling? Lonely, pissed off, and not that good. If you think the thought, "Somebody who loves me forgot my birthday," you have some concern, but you're not feeling bad. Your self-esteem didn't go down. You're not feeling resentful. Your thoughts are one of the first things that you have control over. And we can think positive thoughts. That's why all these self-help books, podcasts, blogs, and so forth are valuable.

Listen to uplifting messages, listen to the people that can keep you calm. Another thing you can do is visualize three, four, five, six, seven months out that your business survived, that you still have a job, you didn't lose your house, you didn't die, your kids are all well, your mom survived, etc., because all fear comes from imagining something in the future that hasn't happened yet.

Even if there was a rattlesnake or a cobra in your room for you to feel afraid, you'd have to go into the future and imagine that snake coming around you and strangling you or biting you, which hasn't happened yet. It would be much better to be in the rational mind and look for exits, look for a stick, whatever. But sometimes we get so afraid we get into fight or flight. We're not rational anymore.

It's your responsibility to control your thoughts, control your images, and control your behavior in ways that will get you to where you want to go.

Michael: Have you always believed it's possible, whatever it might be, or did you learn how to believe it's possible?

Jack: I learned. I grew up in a negative family. My father was an alcoholic. My mother was an alcoholic. They blamed everything on the government, the rich capitalists, whatever it was. I didn't learn all this until I met W. Clement Stone. I was probably 24, something like that. It was a matter of hanging out with him and the people he hung out with. Reading the books, listening to the audios and the videos, attending seminars and so forth.

Michael: That phrase, "Believe it's possible," seems to be the one part of your work that many people can't believe. You can direct them to some books, but it always strikes me how many people don't believe it's possible.

Jack: I interviewed 75 people when I wrote the first *Success Principles* book. I interviewed generals in the Army, top salespeople, Olympic and professional athletes, movie stars, Steve Jobs, and people like that. And what happened is every one of them believed it was possible. I thought, if you want to be successful and be one of those top 3%, you've got to think like they do. What thoughts are they thinking? What magazines are they reading? What books are they reading? Who are they listening to? Who are the influencers in their life? I want to get myself into that.

I was in India recently. I went to an Ayurvedic healing center in Mumbai. There was a doctor who invited me to come to this clinic, who was amazing. He was in the lineage of doctors from Buddha's physician. So for 2,500 years they'd been passing down these traditions of ancient healing. We often talk about alternative medicine. It's allopathic Western medicine that's alternative. For 2,000 years they've been testing all these herbs and acupuncture points and so forth that we know work. One of the things he told me, when he went to work with his teacher, he said, "I'll teach you, but you have to devote a thousand days to being my student.

It's your responsibility to control your thoughts, control your images, and control your behavior.

Meaning for three years you have to do everything I do, drink what I drink, eat what I eat, think what I think, read what I read, meditate when I meditate, etc. If you'll do that for three years, I'll teach you."

Today we all want to learn something by reading one book, listening to two podcasts, or watching 10 TED talks. The reality is it takes time to get that clay off the golden Buddha that we talked about earlier. Someone once said, "Success is a marathon, not a sprint." That 26 miles, as opposed to a 100-yard dash, takes a little time, a little commitment, but I think we all can learn to believe that it's possible.

I wrote forewords to two books. One was called *From Homeless to Billionaire*, by a guy who arrived in Thailand when he was 19, and now he's 35 and a billionaire three times over. He went from living on the beach in Phuket to being a billionaire. And then I wrote the foreword to another book called *The Billionaire's Secret*, written by Rafael Badziag from Poland. He interviewed 21 billionaires and every one of them from the time they were a kid chose to believe it was possible. A lot of people talked about it being a choice: "I knew that if I was going to be successful, I had to believe it was possible." Because we won't do what's not possible. If I said to you, I'm going to do a seminar tonight, 10 o'clock, it's going to be online, I will teach everyone within one hour how to levitate at least one foot off the ground for 20 minutes, no one signs up. Why? Because they've never heard of anyone that could do it. They don't believe it's possible and I wouldn't blame them. The point is that you have to believe it's possible or you won't invest the time, money, and effort to achieve what it is you want to achieve.

Michael: Of the 75 people that you spoke with for the book, who stands out?

Jack: I'll share a story that jumped out at me that was not my story. It's one from *The Billionaire's Secret* book. When I was reading that to write the foreword, it blew me away. There was a kid in China who was not good in school. In fact, he hated it so much he managed to get himself thrown out. As a teenager, the only thing he could do was tend the cows in his little rural community. At one point he realized he was never going to be anything if he didn't change his ways. He said, "I need to study and I need to learn to read." They wouldn't let him back in school, so he would take his brother's textbook and he would have his brother teach him some words. Finally, he realized he needed to get a dictionary. He went down to the river and with a sickle, he would cut grass in the morning and then sell it to the farmers to feed to their cows like hay. It took him a year and a half to earn enough to buy a dictionary. He memorized every word in that dictionary. Then he realized he needed an encyclopedia if he was going to become educated; it took him three and a half years to make enough money to buy an encyclopedia.

Little by little he educated himself to where eventually—I believe I have the story right—he is now one of the major manufacturers of auto windshields in the world and a billionaire. I thought about what kind of courage, what kind of belief, it takes to know at that young age, if I'm going to be successful, I have to change my ways. I have to believe it's possible. That kind of story inspires me.

The fact is most people want to raise their kids. They want to have a job.

They want to do well. They want to do what they love to do. They want to grow themselves. They want to not get sick and die. They want their children to be healthy, etc. It's our governments that get in the way. And then the media fans all that because whenever there's fear or panic, that's what makes people watch.

They used to say in the media, "Blood sells." I think most people are humane, caring, nice people. There are some crazies out there for sure, but we know who they are. We can feel it when we get close to them.

Michael: I would hazard a guess that right now there could be no greater opportunity. If people let go of their prior scripts that they had planned, the possibilities that have opened because of this trying time are endless.

Jack: To give you an example of creativity, I was on a podcast this morning with a guy in Canada, who is an entrepreneur and works with entrepreneurs, and he was giving some examples of what people are doing. One guy owns a gym. He has a ton of treadmills, bicycles, spinning bicycles, and all that stuff. Of course, you're not allowed to go out and you can't congregate in gymnasiums because of the pandemic. He quickly decontaminated everything, went online to all of his customers and says, "If you'd like to rent a bike or a treadmill or some weights or whatever, I would be glad to deliver them to your home. You'll pay a rental fee. That'll allow me to keep my doors open. I'll be able to pay my rent and so forth. When it's all done, I'll take them back and we can continue on as usual."

That kind of creativity is what's required. When the financial crash happened in 2008, a lot of people went on eBay to sell stuff so they could survive. And this one woman realized most people had never used UPS and they'd never shipped anything bigger than a box like you can carry. Now they're selling dressers and they're selling stereo systems and all that. She put an ad in the local paper and then started taking Facebook ads and Google ads. If you sell something, I'll come pick it up and I'll ship it for you and you'll pay me a small fee for that. She made out like a bandit during that period by being creative.

We're being asked to think outside the box. How can I partner up with people and do things? We're being asked to think in terms of how do we relate to people in general? Can we do something where we're selling from our heart and not from fear? A lot of the selling that goes on is fear-based: there's only three left and if you don't buy by midnight, you're not going to be able to get the discount.

Michael: As you were relating that story about the guy in Canada, I thought to myself, I've got to give Jack one that he can pass on to the next person. Vietnam exports a lot of dragon fruit to China, but in the middle of this, the exporting of dragon fruit has stopped. There's a lot of rotting dragon fruit in Vietnam. The enterprising bakers in Saigon have figured out that if they use dragon fruit pulp instead of water when they're making banh mi bread, they end up with loaves that have a pink hue with a kind of aromatic fruit taste, very light and delicious. I'm sure in the not-too-distant future, Vietnam will become famous for its pink banh mi.

Jack: There you go. A lot of that that will happen. Another thing, too: this is a time when people are sequestered in their home. I teach something in the morning called "The Hour of Power," for example, which is 20 minutes of meditation, 20 minutes of reading, and 20 minutes of exercise. Now you don't have that hour-long commute in the morning and evening, why not read those books you've been putting off? Why not engage in some self-reflection? Why not engage in meditation? There are so many things right now that you can do to get fitter, to develop your brain, to get some more information, to clean up some messes, spend time with your family, spend time with your kids, develop your website, write that book you've been thinking about.

The key thing is to look at the opportunities that exist. I often teach this concept called turning a have-to into a get-to. I used to have to drive on the 405 Freeway in LA. And if you know anything about that, it's 12 lanes wide. It looks like a parking lot at five o'clock, but I created some games I could play as I was driving home. One game was called "Don't touch the Brake." It was like golf. The low score wins, and I'm always trying to break my score. If I drive really, really, really slow and leave enough space between me and the car in front, I'll never have to hit the brake. But if I drive too slow, a car's going to come in from the right side or the left side into the lane that's now got an open space in front of me and I have to hit the brake. It's a fun game to play. This commute that used to be a pain in the butt became a fun time.

CHAPTER 15

CHARLES POLIQUIN

Strength Sensei

C HARLES POLIQUIN was a Canadian strength coach. He earned a master's degree in Exercise Physiology. He began working as a strength coach while he was in graduate school in Canada. He helped popularize German Volume Training. In the late 1990s, he founded Poliquin Performance, opening the first Poliquin Performance Center in Phoenix, Arizona in 2001, and the Poliquin Strength Institute in East Greenwich, Rhode Island in 2009. He trained numerous Olympic and professional athletes.

Michael note

Olympic athletes, pro athletes—you name them, Charles trained them. For those of you out there that want to get in better shape, or any kind of shape, Charles's insights into the physical and mental connect directly with good investing, even if that was not Charles's original intention.

Michael Covel: How did you and (famed trend following trader) Ed Seykota connect?

Charles Poliquin: We're producing together a seminar for executives who want to improve their (trading) performance. Obviously within the training communities, I'm highly respected, but I've worked with a lot of executives by default. My background's working with elite athletes and they tend to associate with elite people in the business world and some of them used to come to my center.

I saw the need for developing (trading) educational programs, because if you look at the successful executive, their mindset is the same as that of an Olympic athlete, but they have different goals. They also have the same problems like concentration, sleep, memory, and so on.

Michael: Even though your disciplines are different, I assume you instantly saw the commonality in the way you and Ed think.

Charles: Correct. Success leaves clues. There's a lot of things successful people do that are common, whether it's Schwarzenegger, Ed, the world champion of alpine skiing, or the Olympic medalist in shot put. For example, the growth mindset, the ability to take calculated risk, and so on.

Michael: I want to read something from your website: "There is no such thing as discipline. There is only love. Love is the most powerful creative force in the universe. You are the result of what you love most. You either love finely etched, muscular abs more than donuts, or you love donuts more than washboard abs you could do your laundry on. It is simple as that. Don't beat yourself up that you have no discipline or further drown yourself in a sea of refined carbs out of guilt. Admit that you like crappy food more than you love strength." That sums it up.

Charles: True, because you have two ways you can make choices in life. You can make choices out of fear. You can make choices out of love. If you make all your choices out of love, you're going to be successful and happy. If all your choices are fear-based, you're not going to go anywhere in life.

Michael: It's simple but there's so much depth behind that, because a significant part of the population, including myself at some points in time, resort to the fear motivation.

Charles: It's human nature. Especially if you grew up Catholic, as I did. Shame and blame are the two motivating forces, right? You were taught to fear and feel shame, and your parents would blame you, and that fosters a lot of negative output in your life. If you say to yourself, "Okay, everything I'm going to do from now on is based on love. I prefer to have a healthy life image and live for my grandchildren," then you'll make the right choices. But if you prefer to stuff yourself with Krispy Kremes, then you prefer to stuff yourself with Krispy Kremes.

Success leaves clues.

At the end, there's no discipline. Discipline is a myth. That article you quoted from is the most popular article on my website and the one that's most translated. I figured that out a long time ago. People who were successful, they didn't experience the economy of discipline, they just loved doing this more than anything else.

Michael: You mentioned your religious background and now I see words like sensei are part of your vocabulary. Clearly you've made a transition and I'm gathering that the Eastern traditions have drowned out your initial religious upbringing.

Charles: I was the second-youngest black belt at the age of 14, and I've done six different martial arts. With the Eastern philosophies, the vision of what you do and the consequences are different than those I grew up with as a Catholic. I'm more into karma and Buddhist trends, having done both and seeing what it did to my life and what it does on a daily basis.

Michael: You mentioned being a 14-year-old black belt. For those of us that did some sports, we know it takes dedication as well as athletic prowess. What was driving you to that early athletic achievement?

Charles: When people asked me what I wanted to do when I grew up, I wanted to be Tarzan. You have the ideal lifestyle: don't have to wear clothes, good exercise every day, save the world. Early on, I thought Tarzan was the man. And then, a man tried to molest me when I was 10 years old, and luckily I survived. My father said, "You need to do something to protect yourself." I said, "Can I do karate?" I started to do karate, and as soon as I put on my gear the first day I fell in love with the activity. I love it because you have to be concentrated. The power of focus, breaking my first board, and so on.

Back then, you had to listen to the news to know what the weather was going to be. They forecasted a snowstorm, that was a Friday night. The buses wouldn't run as usual because there'd be too much snow. I woke up extra early, had breakfast, and walked to the dojo through snow up to my knees. Once I got to the dojo, I was the only kid who showed up, not because I had discipline but because I loved karate more than staying at home and watching cartoons. My sensei said to me, "I'll drive you home, but since I'm already here, I'm going to work out." I said, "What do you mean you're going work out?" And he said, "I'm going to lift weights."

In 1975, people who lifted weights were actual weirdos. They were a subculture. They used to hang around together. The weightlifters, the body builders—there was no such a thing as separate gyms. There was just the iron that was a common friend.

I said, "What can I do?" There's such a thing in my field called the iron bug and I got bit by the iron bug that same morning. I loved it. I said, "Okay, I'm going to lift." I asked my older brother, "Can I get some weights?" He officially gave me those cement blocks wrapped in plastic, cheap weights, and a rusted bar, and then every time I had some spare money, I would buy little plates and more weight.

At the age of 17, after working as a waiter in Japanese restaurants, I was able to afford a Swedish Olympic barbell—they're still the best in the world. I started bringing athletes out to my house. One guy at the gym who was in a national volleyball team said, **You are the result of what you love most.** "Hey, man, you're pretty strong. Can you write me a program?" I was already in first year in university, and that was my first national team athlete I started to train. That's how it started—it was me showing up because I wanted do karate. There's no karate because of the snowstorm and I lifted weights, fell in love with it. Even my sensei, who I see on a regular basis, was proud that I chose to name myself as strength sensei, because in my first book, I acknowledged that he's the man who first showed me how to lift weights.

Michael: You mentioned this traumatic event that happened in your youth, and then shifting to the martial arts and weightlifting. What age were you when you knew pretty much you could defend yourself against all comers?

Charles: By age 12, I was already a blue belt. Not a black belt yet, but enough skills to realize I could do it. Once I started to lift weights, of course, that went exponentially. Over the years I've done a lot of different martial arts because there's not a perfect martial art. I would say age 12 was the start of the inflection point in the curve and another point at age 14, when I started to lift weights; there was no looking back after that.

Michael: That feeling of at one point being, "Okay, I don't have complete control," to "I know I can take care of myself." That's a special transition.

Charles: But you know what? I always tell my classes, once you're the alpha wolf, then you don't have to prove anything. One of my favorite authors is Robert Sapolsky, who wrote *Why Zebras Don't Get Ulcers*. One of his best books is *A Primate's Memoir*, where he describes how monkeys' social hierarchy is built around confidence.

Michael: Predators avoid confidence.

Charles: Correct. That's why they pick on kids. The thing that saved my life is seeing a Hercules movie in which a bad guy was chasing Hercules and he threw sand in his face. I was smaller than the predator, of course. I was playing with cars on the gravel and I knew I was in danger. I grabbed the gravel, threw it in his face, ran to my neighbor's backyard, jumped over the fence, which I did every day, and then got back to my parents' house and alerted my brother, who chased the guy. It's funny that I got the trick to get out of that situation by watching a Hercules movie.

Michael: Most men, regardless of age, including guys in their late teens and early 20s, would be envious or perhaps inspired by you physically.

Charles: I'm 54.

Michael: In my world, I see all different types of physical prowess. I see young programmers at 22 whose bodies look atrocious. Perhaps speak to those people that either have an excuse, or they've given up, or they don't realize that the body is malleable and it will recover if you give it a little work.

Charles: There are studies done in Florida with 90-year-old males. If they lift weights three days a week for 40 minutes, after 12 weeks their biological age reverts to age 55. That means a 90-year-old man is progressively fitter than a 75-year-old man, 65-year-old man, back down to 55 after only a few months of strength training.

Michael: What's going on there physically?

Charles: There's a phenomenon called sarcopenia; the etymology of the word means muscle death. As you age, some of your muscle cells die because of inactive use. You also get what we call fat marbling, where the spine muscles are marbled with inflammatory fat. In the spine muscles of these 90-year-olds, what you see is that if you start training on those muscles, the fibers atrophy, but the fat marbling is gone. The most important thing to remember is the concept of progression, not perfection. What discourages people is that they want perfection and they want it three weeks ago.

The most important thing I tell people is that there's a huge mathematical difference between training four days a week and training three days a week. I ask people, "Can you commit four hours a week to training? Let's say Monday, Tuesday, Thursday, Friday, split the body in half. In four months, people won't recognize you." It's not that much work and the most important thing is to avoid cardio, because cardio further stresses adrenaline glands. It makes you insulin-resistant. Even top cardiologists like Bijan Pourat will tell you that the best way to avoid cardiovascular disease is strength training.

Michael: I've heard you use the expression, "skinny fat."

Charles: Skinny fat is low muscle mass but a high percentage of body fat. A person may look thin, but the quality of the body is horrendous. People think that marathon runners are lean. They have lean limbs, but when they take their shirt off, they don't look so lean.

There are six major problems with cardiovascular work—I'm talking about slow long-distance work, not interval training. A lot people go for, let's say, a 20-minute run, or a 20-minute bike ride, or a 20-minute row, but at an even pace the biggest problem is brain aging. We know now that the more cardiovascular long-distance-type exercise someone has done, the faster their brain has aged. At the Olympic level, the athletes with the worst brain functions are cross-country skiers, rowers and so on, and all the anaerobic sports, the short-term, explosive sports, those guys still have their heads.

Michael: That's fascinating.

Charles: When you do aerobic work, the slow long-distance stuff, you make this stress hormone called cortisol. This oxidizes your brain, the same way metal turns to rust. When you do a lot of work, your brain gets older. Everybody that I know in my age group wants to have a younger brain. They realize they've only got one and they've got to take good care of it. That's my number one pet peeve with aerobic work.

Second thing is that Dr. Schwartz Spine, who is probably the best endocrinologist in relation to diabetes, is against aerobic work, because she says that fat people who do aerobic work worsen their health at the adrenal level, but also the insulin sensitivity issue. And Alzheimer's is now considered to be related to type three diabetes and late-age diabetes. When you become more insulin-resistant from cardio, you accelerate brain aging.

The fourth reason why I don't like cardiovascular work is that you will need amino acids from your body to repair the damage, which is normal, but the body has only so much of an amino acid pool, and you have to make choices. The amino acids that go towards cardiovascular recovery are not going towards muscle recovery. Tufts University in 1982 demonstrated that the best predictor of lifespan is muscle mass and the number two predictor is strength; so those beat things like blood pressure, cholesterol profile, inflammation profile, and so on. We know from a physiological standpoint that cardiovascular work interferes with muscle strength and muscle mass.

Discipline is a myth.

Michael: I've tried to keep up a fairly regular sprinting practice. I'll go out to the track with some friends and we might be there for 20 to 30 minutes, but after that I'm done, I don't have anything left. I give it all that I got and I'm not trying to do any big distance. Am I crazy?

Charles: You're exactly on the right track. Look at it this way. We're designed to run and throw a rock at a rabbit; we're not designed to run after the rabbit. When we do sprints, we're mimicking how we used to feed ourselves. Let's say you want to kill a bison—you do a 100-meter sprint to throw a spear, that makes sense. Sprints are great for you because the hormonal response of a sprint versus long-distance cardio is completely different. One of the things that happens when you do sprints is you produce more growth hormone, which is what repairs connective tissue in your body and burns fat. It's the hormone that prevents you from losing muscle mass with age. The more growth hormone you produce, the better off you are, but the best way to do that is either strength training or sprinting.

Michael: One of the myths that people have about weight training is that, "Okay, these young guys are going to increase their muscle mass, but when they get old, they're going to be fat." That thought gets connected to something like one of the fittest men ever in terms of weights, Arnold Schwarzenegger, at the age of 68 goes for a walk along the beach and people go, "Oh, that confirms my view, Arnold Schwarzenegger did all this weight work and now look at him!" Those are the wrong conclusions.

Charles: Correct. Let's say if this is a case where his body fat is up and it used to be shredded, you've got to recognise the contrast. There's a difference between 2% body fat when you're 35 years old and you weigh 110 kilos of muscle mass, versus being 68 years old and his priorities have obviously changed in life. I saw him at the VIP lecture group when I was teaching at the Arnold Classic sports festival in Melbourne, and even wearing jeans and a shirt I wouldn't call him fat.

Michael: The bigger issue I want you to address is the idea that if you do weights and increase muscle mass and then you stop exercising, it doesn't

The most important thing to remember is the concept of progression, not perfection.

make a difference whether you did weights or not. If you stop exercising and eat bad, you're going to look bad. It's not connected to the weights.

Charles: That's right. The other thing we know from years of experience is that when you stop weight training, you tend to return to the genotype you have. If you are an ectomorph, you go back to being skinny. If you had a tendency to be obese, you'll go back to obesity. It certainly doesn't turn to fat because they're two different chemical reactions. Let's say you live for four decades and you stop lifting. If you are fat now it's because of the wrong choices you've made. But you're 100% right, it's not muscle turning into fat. It's because when you stop, you're going to lose that muscle mass. You see actors getting in shape for an action hero movie like Superman and then they stop. If they go back and eat pretzels, drink beer, and sit on their butts watching TV, they're going to get fat like anybody else. It's not magic.

Michael: One of your great expressions is, "Train like it's your last workout." That requires a certain toughness mentally. What are some of the ways that one can go about it? Do you come back to the love concept?

Charles: The best way to train like it's the last workout is to have two training partners. I've found from experience that there's always one out of the three that's up, one out of the three that's down, and one that's in the middle. And that role varies, right?

> Once you're the alpha wolf, you don't have to prove anything.

One thing that I love to do still is betting. I'll say, "I'll bet you this I can do that." When you've trained with the same guys for a long time, each with their strength and weaknesses, you make fair bets—in other words, "Okay, if I do 200 kilos on this, you've got to do 250 kilos because you're bigger." You keep pushing each other and keep up the competitive spirit.

The other thing that I find important is to have goals within the expiry date. For example, I spent a month with Dmitry Klokov, who used to be world champion at weightlifting, and silver medalist in weightlifting at the Olympics. When he retired from competition, the students asked him, "How do you keep that physique?" He says, "I take a lift." He wants to do a snatch with a two-second pause at 200 kilos. There are no competitions for that. It's an odd lift. He says, "That's my goal this year." Mentally he can't compare it to what he's done at the Olympics, but he's going to do something pretty impressive.

I've found that the guys who stay in shape are still into goal setting, because if it doesn't have an expiry date, it doesn't mean anything. There's no pressure. One of my good friends is Ed Coan, world champion 12 years in power lifting. He's also in his 50s, and even though he's out of competition, he picks whatever lift to do for his age. There's a guy called Brooks Kubik who wrote a good book about aging and weight training. He shows you what's normal to lift at what age and he's got all the mathematical data. Once I read that book, I said, "Okay, well, I'm not doing too bad for 54 because on some list I'm still 35 years old." That's how I motivate myself to do it.

Michael: Let's talk about sleep—sleep in your life, what you know about sleep, what lessons you can pass along.

Charles: Most of my life, I worked 20 hours a day. That's including everything, workouts, whatever. If you were to ask me, "If you relived your life, what would you do different?" I would say probably sleep more. People said, "You're a lucky man." Yeah. I was a lucky man because I worked hard and I didn't sleep. I did the work of three people per week, right? But I would've reorganized my life and picked up on priorities. When people ask me what was the turning point, it was becoming a father. If you want to be a real father and take care of your child, you have to have quality time. That's when I started to cut back on work.

I would say sleep is the most underrated factor among the elite. Elite people are so driven that they say, "You can sleep in a cemetery." I would disagree now. If there's a lesson I want to pass on to the younger generation it's to go for quality sleep. Because in the end, the amount of quality work you can do when you sleep is enormous. A friend of mine who's an MD quoted me something a few years ago: "The general who sleeps the most wins the war." Alexander the Great, Napoleon, Churchill, all big military leaders were known to nap. If you're not going to sleep eight hours in a row, at least nap—I'm a big believer in power napping. There's quite a bit of evidence now that fragmented sleep is good for you. Apparently, our ancestors did not sleep eight hours in a row; they spread their sleep around.

But quality sleep is what I call an unfair advantage and few people know how important it is to repair tissue. Look at babies—they spend their time sleeping because they're in growth mode. If you want to grow, you need to sleep. And if you want to grow your empire financially, you want to grow your strength, you want to grow your relationships, be able to make the right decisions, sleeping well is ultra-important.

Michael: You've trained Olympic athletes, pro athletes, some of the highest achievers, world record holders. Give me a few names of your most impressive athletes.

Charles: They are probably not household names by any means. The first one is Adam Nelson, who has won the most medals in history in shot put. What's unique is he's short, only a meter 80. The guys who would beat him beforehand would be at least two meters tall, two meters 10. But he compensated for his lack of height through maximal power. That guy was devoted to training. He's inspiring, dominating, tough. He's one of those guys with charisma. He won a silver medal in Athens and then eight years later, they found the guy who beat him positive for the Athens urine sample, so they gave him his gold medal eight years too late. He's not been financed by a lot of people; he got there through hard work.

The second name is a Canadian skier, Karen Percy, who won two bronze medals at the Olympics and silver at the world championships in skiing. She is my favorite athlete I ever worked with because she exuded concentration. I've never seen anybody who could joke around between sets and when it was her turn to train, she was literally on another planet. I wish I could see what was inside her brain, but the dedication she put into that set was inspiring. She started skiing way later than anybody else on the national team. She had done pretty much every sport known to man beforehand. She was a latecomer and despite that she was an Olympic medalist. For me, the attitude and the inspiration the athlete provides is more important than the celebrity status.

Michael: What is your view on yoga?

Charles: Yoga is good. Again, if I could replicate my life, I would probably have done yoga much younger. It's underestimated as a practice in the sports world, because everything we do, those of us who are dopamine dominant, tends to be yang. We're the fire, but the intensity of your flame is a function of the oil reserve, which is a yin reserve, and the more oil you have in your lamp, the more the flame can burn. Yoga is yin to the yang of weight training. If Richard Branson says to me tomorrow, "I want England to dominate the world and I give you eight years and unlimited funds," I would probably search out the best yoga instructors and they would be responsible for 25% of the total training load. The advantage of yoga is that it's not depleting, it's repeating.

Michael: I was a baseball catcher from the age of 10 to 21 and I think that the squatting motion helped me with heavy squats. The thing that I notice in Asia is the Asian squat. I can't get as deep as most, but I can get a few centimeters away. It's a fascinating, simple flexibility, strength exercise.

Charles: It's also an osteoarthritis preventer. There's a good Australian study where they measured knee and hip degeneration at the cartilage of a ligament level, but also at the bone level. What they found is that age-matched Indians who were born in India and live in India have far less hip degeneration that Indians born in Australia, because as soon as they adopt Australian culture, they don't full squat anymore. Full squatting is one of the best ways to prevent degeneration of the lower extremity and the spine. There's a good set of data from the Swedish Olympic Committee that shows that the further your knees can travel over your toes, the least likely you're going to suffer all types of sports injury, whether it's meniscus tears, hamstring tears, growing tears, and so on. That study was further supported by a study on 40,000 Swiss soccer players. The deeper a kid could go on a squat, the least likely he was going to get injured playing soccer.

> Sleep is the most underrated factor among the elite.

Michael: I'm not about to brag about athletic prowess, but I'm quite proud I can do the full splits. I know that's something that's difficult for guys to do and the only reason I can do that is because I tore my hamstring at age 15, playing baseball. After that, I started stretching my hamstrings all the time. It was almost like your story of the traumatic incident turning you into sports. My flexibility is a direct result of an injury.

Charles: Everybody gets an epiphany about why they start something, right? Usually the more severe the trauma, the more you will change. But to do the full splits at 47, that's pretty impressive, because it does require quite a bit of commitment. But anything worth achieving requires effort. They make selection for Navy SEALs hard, which is why there's not a lot of Navy SEALs, but that's why those guys are the ones we rely on when we need special operations. Anything that's high status does require commitment.

Michael: I had a friend in San Diego who was a SEAL. He was 5 foot 8, but probably over 200 pounds. The quiet confidence that man carried was something unique to see up close and personal.

Charles: He's the alpha lion and he doesn't have to prove himself. If you could kill people with your bare hands, you don't have to show it off. If you look at research, it is men with the lowest testosterone who are the most violent. For example, Iran and Iraq have

Anything worth achieving requires effort.

the lowest testosterone levels we know around the world, and the main reason is because the soil does not have any zinc. Zinc is what's responsible for testosterone production, hydrochloric acid production, and so on. On top of that, if you have a low meat intake, it's going to be hard to have a lot of testosterone and that leads to violent behavior. Testosterone decreases aggressiveness because you can kill all the other animals, so you don't need to prove your point.

Charles: When I teach lectures, I always tell people, if you look at average blood values, what you have to picture is Homer Simpson. Being average, you're Homer Simpson. You're not Conan the Barbarian. Our physiology dictates our behavior. Men with low testosterone, because they have low zinc and eat a vegan diet, will be violent. It's a drama that people don't associate physiology with behavior. If you give a lion a diet of what you give the fish in your aquarium, he's not going to behave so well. If I throw a ribeye in the aquarium, the fish's not going to rush for it. We have to eat according to our genes.

Michael: When you talk about this connection between testosterone and violence, do you face criticism?

Charles: No, because I've always given the references. There are thousands of studies on testosterone and violence. You can also find connections between zinc and violence, because the best sources of zinc, as far as biological absorption, are things like oysters and red meat. If you're vegan, that's never part of your diet. Look throughout world history who's been at war the longest. I'm not making this up. How long has Iran been in conflict with Iraq? Forever, right? And it's been low testosterone forever. How many times have you heard that Brazil's at war with somebody? Never, right? Because Brazilians have the highest testosterone levels. When you have a population that has high testosterone, they tend to be quite peaceful.

Michael: "Empty your mind, be formless, shapeless, like water. Now you put water into a cup, it becomes the cup, you put water into a bottle, it becomes the bottle, you put it in a teapot, it becomes the teapot. Now water can flow or it can crash. Be water, my friend." For me, that Bruce Lee line is the most fabulous expression of Eastern philosophy, reduced to one paragraph.

Charles: Bruce Lee shaped a lot of my thinking. One of the things he said a long time ago is, "Use what is useful; reject what is not." When he created Jeet Kune Do, he took the best of every martial art and blended it all. The parts that he thought were stupid he left out. When people ask me who influenced my strength training philosophy the most, I say Bruce Lee. He said, "There's a difference between martial arts in movies and martial arts for fighting in real life. It makes as much sense to kick someone in the face as to punch them." In other words, it looks great in the movie. But if you know somebody knows how to fight, when you kick them in the face, it gives a lot of warning. A punch in the face is more effective than a kick in the face. You kick the guy in the face when he's already been knocked out.

Michael: There's a great clip of Bruce Lee. It's a casting call, video clip. I think he's 24 or 25 years of age, somewhere in Hollywood. He's got a suit on and you can see the magnetic personality and they're asking him some questions and they say, "Can you give us a little demonstration of some of your kicks or punches or something?" They bring out some older white guy to stand there. To watch the speed at which Bruce throws a punch and to not hit this man in the face—amazing. Bruce says, "No, don't worry. I won't touch you."

Charles: I love what he did. No need for discipline. Put the hours in. In the sporting world, he was one of the earliest proponents of strength training. My karate sensei lifted weights because Bruce Lee did. He said, "If that guy is that fast and he lifts weights, weight training made him fast." He dispelled the myth of being muscle-bound. He said, "You want to get fast? You got to lift weights."

Michael note

Charles passed away before we could have our second conversation. One of my great regrets.

ABOUT
MICHAEL COVEL

Michael Covel searches. He digs. He goes behind the curtain to reveal a state of mind the system doesn't want you in. Characterized as essential and required reading, Michael teaches beginners to seasoned pros how to generate profits with straightforward and repeatable rules. He is best known for popularizing the counterintuitive and controversial trading strategy, trend following.

An avowed entrepreneur, Michael is the author of six books including the international bestseller, *Trend Following*, and his investigative narrative, *Turtle Trader*. Fascinated by secretive traders that have quietly generated spectacular returns for seven decades, those going against the investment orthodoxy of buy and hope, he has uncovered astonishing insights about the right way to think, develop, and execute trend following systems.

Michael's perspectives have garnered international acclaim and have earned him invitations with a host of organizations: China Asset Management, GIC Private Limited (a Singapore sovereign wealth fund), BM&F Bovespa, the Managed Funds Association, Bank of China Investment Management, the Market Technicians Association, and multiple hedge funds and mutual funds.

He also has the distinction of having interviewed seven Nobel Prize winners, including Daniel Kahneman and Harry Markowitz, and he has been featured in major media outlets, including *The Wall Street Journal*, Bloomberg, CCTV, *The Straits Times*, and Fox Business.

Michael posts on Twitter, publishes a blog, and records his podcast weekly. His consulting clients are across hedge funds, sovereign wealth funds, institutional investors, and individual traders in more than 70 countries. He splits his time between the United States and Asia.

Author's Note

If you would like to reach me directly, I can be found here:
www.trendfollowing.com/contact

My podcast can be found here:
www.trendfollowing.com/podcast

All of my books and foreign translations can be found here:
www.trendfollowing.com/translations

My training courses and trend following systems can be found here:
www.trendfollowing.com/products

To receive my free interactive trend following presentation, send a picture of your book receipt to:
receipt@trendfollowing.com.

A big thank you to my assistant Joanne Umali. She put in many long hours to help me pull all of this great content together.